On Faith and Free Government

On Faith and Free Government

EDITED BY
DANIEL C. PALM

FOREWORD BY DAN QUAYLE

ROWMAN & LITTLEFIELD PUBLISHERS, INC.
Lanham • Boulder • New York • Oxford

ROWMAN & LITTLEFIELD PUBLISHERS, INC.

Published in the United States of America
by Rowman & Littlefield Publishers, Inc.
4720 Boston Way, Lanham, Maryland 20706

12 Hid's Copse Road
Cummor Hill, Oxford OX2 9JJ, England

Copyright © 1997 by Rowman & Littlefield Publishers, Inc.
Chapter 4, "The Christian and Rebellion against Authority," © 1997 by Glen E. Thurow.

British Library Cataloguing in Publication Information Available

Library of Congress Cataloging-in-Publication Data

On faith and free government / edited by Daniel C. Palm.
    p. cm.
    Includes index.
    ISBN 0-8476-8602-7 (cloth : alk. paper).—ISBN 0-8476-8603-5 (paper : alk. paper)
    1. Christianity and politics—United States. 2. Freedom of religion—United States.
3. Church and state—United States. 4. Christianity and politics—United States—
History—18th century—Sources. 5. Freedom of religion—United States—
History—18th century—Sources. 6. Church and state—United States—History—
18th century—Sources. I. Palm, Daniel C., 1957–
BR115.P7053 1997
261.7'0973—dc21   97-18641
                                                                                         CIP

ISBN 0-8476-8602-7 (cloth : alk. paper)
ISBN 0-8476-8603-5 (pbk. : alk. paper)

Printed in the United States of America

⊖™ The paper used in this publication meets the minimum requirements of American
National Standard for Information Sciences—Permanence of Paper for Printed Library
Materials, ANSI Z39.48–1984.

Contents

Contents

Foreword

With all the recent twists and turns in American politics, more than a few Christians are wondering, "Where exactly do we fit in?" While a few find cause for optimism in the 1995 Religious Freedom and Restoration Act, others are discouraged and demoralized by an activist judiciary, federal and state court decisions, and general downward trends in the American academy and popular culture. Some have recently gone so far as to suggest that American values may have deteriorated beyond repair and that, ominously, Christians may have to rethink their role in our nation altogether. With dire predictions about the future coming from several corners, it's high time that Christians—and all Americans— pause to take a look back at the manner in which our nation's founders addressed the questions that surround faith and politics, church and state, in our country.

This book does that for us, bringing together original documents and sermons from the founding era with new essays, reminding us that the founders' generation did indeed confront many of the very same questions that concern us now. And looking back, after giving them fair consideration, we find that the founders answered these questions quite wisely. We are reminded that the founding fathers understood from the outset that this nation would differ from others. Not founded simply on a specific piece of territory or restricted to one ethnic group, it was to be built on an idea, or, to be more precise, a political principle. They began by pointing out that there are certain political truths that any reasonable person can understand and that these "self-evident truths" should serve as the foundation for government. Chief among these was the idea that "all men are created equal," five simple words that laid down the principle of equality before law. And, one can't help but note, words that would remind all who might later forget that the framers had no doubt that we human beings owe our existence to a Creator.

Certainly the founders did not anticipate how things would turn out for us these many years later. But clearly they depended on us, their inheritors, to maintain a strong religious faith. In fact, they did not expect that our free system of government, and our cherished individual liberties, would survive if we abandoned our religious heritage. As John Adams wrote, "Our Constitution was made only for a moral and religious people. It is wholly inadequate for the government of any other." That does not mean Americans must line up behind one denomination or one faith. It does mean, however, that we must always be mindful of our nation's religious heritage—and, when discussing issues respecting faith and free government, return to the wellspring of the founding generation.

Dan Quayle

Preface

Few points about American politics in the past decade are more clear than the increasing prominence of Christians in electoral politics. The "Christian Right," as it is routinely characterized in the press, has been credited more than any other class with recent tides in American politics. No longer simply an adjunct to other interest groups—or even an interest group simply—Christian voters support issues and policies of interest to decent citizens because they represent the conditions for decent family life, itself a precondition for free government.

And yet, for many Christians—including many Christian leaders—their role in the political arena is unclear. How far ought Christians go in their political activity? What exactly does God command respecting our participation in political life? Many Christians are troubled by their interpretation of biblical passages (Rom. 13, in particular) that appear to place limits on Christian political activity. Some read these passages as precluding Christians from any political activity that might be interpreted as rebellion against authority. And this raises some interesting questions. For example, were the American colonists who rebelled against their established government—King George III and the British Parliament—wrong to do so?

To this is added a more general confusion about the role of religion in American politics. The typical American college student has heard something about "separation of church and state" and reckons that the words appear somewhere or other in the Constitution or Bill of Rights. Beyond that catch phrase (in fact a line by Jefferson in a letter written in January 1802 to the Danbury, Connecticut, Baptist Association), he or she knows little about the subject. Most Americans seem unaware that religious faith and morality were once thought to provide the very foundation for free government. These problems point to a fundamental confusion about politics and religion in the United States, both on the part of the faithful and on the part of their less devout fellow citizens. And in this our generation differs greatly from those that have gone before, calling into question the prospects for continued free government in the United States.

What can be done to remind Americans of the rightful place of faith with respect to politics? Our nation's founders, whom Americans still admire greatly, understood the relationship between the two and addressed the matter at every stage of the founding era. Because of that fact, our best strategy is to dust off what they wrote two centuries and more ago and give it our attention. Several recent scholarly publications have collected sermons and tracts of the founders' generation, and they make the point well. This work, in contrast, is directed not only to the community of scholars but to the larger community of students and citizens as well. My intention is to bring together the best and most important statements by the founding generation, demonstrating their understanding of the Christian's role in political life. These few statements—in my view, the best yet written on the subject—deserve to be returned to the common mind of the public. They should be familiar to every American, regardless of religious persuasion.

Alongside these documents and sermons, this book offers the reader five essays by scholars who have considered in some depth various aspects of these larger questions. In our first essay, Thomas G. West takes a comprehensive look at the founders' understanding of religious faith and freedom and their role in the new republic. The question of religious toleration, and how it differs from religious freedom, is considered in the second essay. The modern tendency to confuse the two notwithstanding, the founders' generation appears to have understood the two as altogether different and they regarded religious freedom as one of the base elements of the regime they were engaged in creating. Harry V. Jaffa addresses what Thomas Jefferson, in the Declaration of Independence, described as certain "self-evident" truths, first among which are "that all men are created equal, and that they are endowed by their Creator with certain unalienable rights, that among these are life, liberty, and the pursuit of happiness." But are these truths really self-evident? Have they ever been? Much of modern scholarship has been engaged in the task of proving that they are not, nor are they even "truths," because truths do not exist, only perceptions. Were the founders of our country merely products of their age, an age that had not yet learned the awful "truth" that nothing is right or wrong, true or false?

Glen E. Thurow attends in his essay to the question posed above about George III and British rule: How should Christians regard rebellion against authority? Is rebellion against a bad regime permissible? Various arguments have been put forward by Christians contending that rebellion against authority is either inappropriate or unwise, and yet the founders did indeed rebel against civil authority—an authority that was, in several respects, a liberal and good regime. What led them to reject these arguments? Finally, how did the founders think about civil rights and civil liberties, and how should Christians understand them? The answer to this question, argues James Rogers, depends largely on how we understand the idea of happiness. Needless to say, the modern narrow understanding has little in common with that held by the founders.

As all of the authors represented here would agree, the best avenue to understanding the founders' views on faith and free government is a careful reading of their own writings. Accordingly, I have devoted half of this book to original documents and sermons. Much more than what I present here is readily available, and readers interested in giving their attention to additional material from the American founding are directed to three fine collections: Charles S. Hyneman and Donald S. Lutz, eds., *American Political Writing during the Founding Era, 1760-1805* (Indianapolis: Liberty Press, 1983); Ellis Sandoz, ed., *Political Sermons of the American Founding Era, 1730-1805* (Indianapolis:

Liberty Fund, 1990); and John Wingate Thornton, *The Pulpit of the American Revolution, or The Political Sermons of the Period of 1776* (1860; reprint, New York: Da Capo, 1970). These books served as sources for the documents, in addition to their full text imprints in the microform collection, *Early American Imprints, 1639-1800,* published by the American Antiquarian Society.

Acknowledgments

This book would not have been possible without the generous lead support of the Anschutz Foundation. Subsequent generous support for this endeavor came from W. Robert Stover, Ransom Linkletter, Olive Sue Linkletter, Crawford Linkletter, and Denise Mermet Lilette.

I owe much to the assistance of Thomas G. West, who offered helpful advice in the selection and reproduction of the original documents included in the second half of this book. Harry V. Jaffa offered helpful comments as the project took shape. The government documents staff at the Claremont Colleges' Honnold Library and the librarians at Azusa Pacific University were, as always, generous with their time and assistance. Brian Holmes diligently and capably proofed documentary text, and my ever-patient wife Tobey lent a hand with the index. Special thanks are due to all my colleagues at the Claremont Institute, especially Vice President Michael Warder and David DesRosiers, for organizing the financial support that made the book possible, and Institute President Larry P. Arnn and Executive Vice President Chuck Heatherly, who offered thoughtful comments and encouragement from the project's beginnings to its completion.

Part I: Essays

1

Religious Liberty: The View from the Founding

Thomas G. West

In December 1944 American soldiers were fighting desperately against the last great German offensive of World War II, the Battle of the Bulge. Men were dying in large numbers. The counterattack had bogged down in mud and rain. Planes could not fly because of low clouds. General George Patton, commander of the Third Army, called his chaplain into his headquarters and said:

> Chaplain, I want you to publish a prayer for good weather. I'm tired of these soldiers having to fight mud and floods as well as Germans. See if we can't get God to work on our side. . . .
>
> Chaplain James O'Neill: May I say, General, that it usually isn't a customary thing among men of my profession to pray for clear weather to kill fellow men.
>
> Patton: Chaplain, are you teaching me theology or are you the Chaplain of the Third Army? I want a prayer.
>
> O'Neill: Yes, sir.

The prayer was printed on a card and distributed to every soldier of the Third Army. It read:

> Almighty and most merciful God, we humbly beseech thee, of thy great goodness, to restrain these immoderate rains with which we have had to contend. Grant us fair weather for battle. Graciously hearken to us as soldiers who call upon thee that, armed with thy power, we may advance from victory to victory, and crush the oppression and wickedness of our enemies, and establish thy justice among men and nations. Amen.

An editor's footnote in Patton's memoirs tells what happened next: "The day after the prayer was issued, the weather cleared and remained perfect for about six days. Enough to allow the Allies to break the backbone of the German offensive and turn a temporary setback for the Allies into a crushing defeat for the enemy."[1]

Patton's request for a weather prayer perhaps sounds flippant or even impious. But at bottom, Patton was completely serious. He was convinced that God was on the side of America, justice, and liberty against Hitler's regime of tyranny, slavery, and mass murder. The cause of America was the cause of liberty and God. Therefore, it was perfectly reasonable to order the chaplain, a

3

paid official of the government, to ask for God's aid in the great war against Hitler.

Or was it?

Many Americans would agree with Chaplain O'Neill that religion has no business supporting a political cause, especially not a war. Christianity in particular seems to call for peace, not war; love of enemies, not their death; and care for all mankind, not just one's own people. God does not take sides, it seems, in quarrels among nations.

In today's view, not only should religion should keep its distance from government, but above all, government should keep its distance from religion. In 1947, the Supreme Court ruled, for the first time, that it is unconstitutional for government "to support any religious activities or institutions, whatever they may be called, or whatever form they may adopt to teach or practice religion."[2] Although the Court has not always applied that dictum consistently—military chaplains are still permitted—it has largely guided government policy ever since.

Today's view is the opposite of that of America's founders. Like General Patton, they believed that God was pro-liberty. They also believed that there are many occasions when government should "teach or practice religion."

Until the Vietnam War in the 1960s, Americans never hesitated to issue official prayers for victory. During the Revolutionary War, Congress prayed for God "to smile upon us in the prosecution of a just and necessary war for the defense and establishment of our inalienable rights and liberties"—including the right to religious liberty. As we will see, the founders' understanding of liberty was consistent with, and in fact called for, weather prayers and their equivalents.[3]

Liberty, License, and Reason

The victory of relativism has made the founders' understanding of religious liberty alien to us. Liberty today is taken to mean "the right to choose," the right to do whatever one pleases.

Surprisingly, both liberals and conservatives agree on this definition. Their disagreement is over the extent to which government should impose limits on abuses of liberty. A sign of our shared view of liberty is that we often speak of balancing liberty with order, with responsibility, or with community. If we define liberty as the unlimited right of the irresponsible will, we do have to look to a source outside of liberty for some restraint on it. But if liberty is *inherently* responsible liberty, as the founders thought, it does not need to be balanced by anything. It contains within itself its own balance.

For the founders, the irresponsible, irrational will is not free. It is enslaved. James Madison said that "the tyranny of their own passions" led the Athenians to condemn Socrates to death. What Madison meant by this phrase was spelled out by the Reverend Samuel West of Massachusetts in a 1776 sermon: "The most perfect freedom consists in obeying the dictates of *right reason*, and submitting to *natural law*. When a man goes beyond or contrary to the law of nature and reason, he becomes the slave of base passions and vile lusts. . . . Hence we conclude that where licentiousness begins, liberty ends."[4]

Intellectuals today no longer believe in "right reason" and "natural law." For them, freedom is not obeying the law of reason and nature, but having the right to break that law, or any law. That is one reason that serious religious conviction is so much feared and disliked by elites in our time: if God exists, his law limits our freedom. He, not we, defines the meaning of existence. In contrast to the founders' view, three justices of the Supreme Court wrote in 1992, "At the heart of liberty is the right to define one's own concept of existence, of meaning, of the universe, and of the mystery of human life."[5]

Since we no longer distinguish between liberty and license, we no longer understand the founders' conception of liberty, including religious liberty. For them, the freedom to follow one's religion should be protected, in George Washington's words, as an "inherent natural right." No one may be harmed or punished for his mode of worship. But religious liberty is not religious license. Government may therefore *prohibit* religious practices that are criminal or immoral. And government may and should *promote* religious practices and convictions that accord with reason, which favors individual responsibility and political liberty.

Jefferson's "Wall of Separation" Letter and the Declaration of Independence as Violations of Religious Liberty?

In his famous letter to the Baptists of Danbury, Connecticut, Thomas Jefferson, quoting the First Amendment to the U.S. Constitution, wrote: "I contemplate with solemn reverence that act of the whole American people which declared that their legislature should 'make no law respecting an establishment of religion, or prohibiting the free exercise thereof,' thus building a wall of separation between Church and State."

Liberals and libertarians are fond of this passage. They take it to mean that government should avoid practicing, teaching, or supporting religious views of any kind. The Supreme Court has declared that the "wall of separation" forbids government officials, such as school teachers, from engaging in or sponsoring public prayer. Yet Jefferson closes this very same letter, written in his official capacity as president, with a prayer: "I reciprocate your kind prayers for the protection and blessing of the common Father and Creator of man." If today's liberals were right, Jefferson would be breaking down the wall of separation at the very moment he proclaims it.[6]

I propose to show that although most of the founders wanted a "separation between church and state"—call it a "wall of separation" if you like—they emphatically rejected a wall of separation between religion and public life, between God and politics. The founders opposed an official state-sponsored church, but they favored government support of religion through public laws, in official speeches and proclamations, on ceremonial occasions, and especially in public schools.

The strangeness of today's approach, from the point of view of the founders, can be seen most vividly in this fact: by the logic of today's view of religious liberty, it is unconstitutional to teach the Declaration of Independence in public schools. The Declaration contains four distinct references to God: he is the author of the "laws of . . . God"; the "Creator" who "endowed" us with our inalienable rights; "the Supreme Judge of the world"; and "Divine Providence." The Supreme Court has ruled that government may not "teach or practice religion." It may not exert "subtle coercive pressure" on students by prayers or religious instruction. If the Declaration were taught in a public school *as the truth*, the teacher would "teach religion." She would be exercising the kind of "subtle coercive pressure" on students forbidden by the Court. She would be teaching them that God is our lawgiver, creator, judge, and providential protector. She would be promoting an establishment of religion in violation of the First Amendment.[7]

But this is absurd. A nation whose principles are the God-given equal rights of mankind cannot be obliged by its very principles to forbid public officials to "teach religion"—to teach children the theology of the Declaration, that their rights are given to them by God.

Of course, teaching the Declaration has not been declared unconstitutional, but that is only because the Court has been unwilling to admit the full consequences of its view of "establishment." To avoid the public outrage that would follow if the Declaration were banned from the classroom, the Court falsely asserts that that document is not really religious. The Court pretends that reciting "official documents such as the Declaration of Independence which contain references to the Deity" bears "no true resemblance" to school prayer. Such exercises, Justice William Brennan asserts, *"no longer* have a religious purpose or meaning. The reference to divinity in the revised pledge of allegiance, for example, may merely recognize *the historical fact* that our nation was *believed* to have been founded 'under God.'"

In other words, the Supreme Court will allow the theology of the Declaration to be taught in the classroom as long as it is understood that it belongs to "a world that is dead and gone," that it has nothing to do with the world that we live in here and now, that it is not a living faith that holds God to be the source of our rights, the author of the laws of nature, and the protector and Supreme Judge of America. Brennan's claim that the words "under God" in the revised pledge have no "religious purpose or meaning" is flatly contradicted by the House Committee on the Judiciary, which explained in its 1954 report that the words were added to affirm "the dependence of our people and our Government upon the moral directions of the Creator."[8]

Conservative Confusion on Religious Liberty

Conservatives today are unable to provide any coherent defense of government support of religion. They argue that liberals have distorted the views of the founders and of the earlier tradition, but their argument has been weakened by its inability to square the historical record with the idea of religious liberty.

The American tradition is full of examples of government-sponsored prayers (daily in public schools and on all kinds of ceremonial occasions), religious music (in school Christmas programs), religious devotion (in Thanksgiving and Prayer Day proclamations of presidents), and much more. Liberals explain these traditions as relics of an earlier era of religious bigotry, when the separation of religion from politics was neither understood nor practiced. Conservatives are not quite sure how to explain them.

Many say that government may promote religion as long as it does so *nonpreferentially*. In this argument, government sees religious *diversity* or *pluralism* as a good thing, and it is free to promote religion as long as it promotes all religions, and not any particular belief. Law professor Michael McConnell gives the ablest scholarly defense of the view that government may promote "religion in general," but "must not favor one form of religious belief over another."[9]

Sometimes conservatives are even tempted to make use of the liberal view that government must be completely neutral between religion and "irreligion." In the *Rosenberger* case, the University of Virginia funded a variety of student publications, but it refused to fund a Christian journal. Michael McConnell argued to the Supreme Court on behalf of the Christian students that "the state should be completely indifferent to whether students use those benefits to participate in religious activity." The Constitution requires "neutrality between religion and its various competitors in the marketplace of ideas." The Court agreed. Unfortunately, McConnell's victory for the Christians was also a victory for Satanic, sadomasochistic, pedophile, and Nazi publications. They too are "competitors in the marketplace of ideas." They too have a right to government funding on an evenhanded basis.[10]

Supreme Court liberals have easily shown that the American tradition of government involvement with religion cannot be justified in neutralist, nonpreferential, or pluralist terms. Take the example of legislative chaplains. Historically, taxes have supported chaplains to offer daily prayers at legislative sessions. Conservatives on the Supreme Court won a small victory when that practice was upheld in a 1983 case. But the Court could offer no principled argument in its favor. The majority admitted that the prayers in question were *not* neutral with respect to all religions, but were "in the Judeo-Christian tradition." Clearly the government was not just promoting but funding a noninclusive religious exercise.

Chaplains' prayers are usually offered to God, that is, God the Father, thereby excluding such deities as the "three goddesses (Cali, Quani, and Enna) from Hindu, Buddhist, and Philippine religions." These three were prayed to at the 1993 Re-Imaging Conference cosponsored by the Episcopal Church of the United States, along with "Our Sweet Sophia," to whom these words were addressed: "We are women in your image. With the nectar of our thighs, we invited a lover. . . . With our warm body fluids we remind the world of its pleasures and sensations." If chaplaincies were truly nonpreferential, these goddesses, and even the bloodthirsty gods of the Aztecs, would have to be invoked at least occasionally. All the Court could say in the 1983 case was that legislative chaplaincies are "deeply embedded in the history and tradition of this country." That is true. But the dissenters responded, quite rightly, that long practice does not make something constitutional.[11]

Some conservatives have tried to resolve the seeming contradiction between *individual liberty* and the *tradition of government support* of monotheistic and biblical religion either by embracing liberty and rejecting the tradition of support (libertarians such as the Cato Institute), or by embracing the tradition and rejecting the Declaration of Independence (traditionalists such as Russell Kirk).

American public life *was* far more religious before the 1960s, when Americans thought their pro-religious policies were consistent with their principles. As we will see, they believed that what they did was not only compatible with religious liberty but also a necessary foundation of that liberty.

Free Exercise of Religion as Part of the Right to Liberty

The Declaration of Independence calls liberty an "unalienable" right, meaning that we are born with it ("endowed by our Creator") and can never rightly surrender it to any person or government. As we are born free in all respects, we are also born free to worship God. That freedom is absolute.

The New Hampshire Constitution of 1784 explains: "When men enter into a state of society, they surrender up some of their natural rights to that society, in order to insure the protection of others." For example, in a state of nature, we have the right to punish those who injure us. In a state of society, we give up that right to the government. We do so on condition that it protects us better than we can on our own in a state without government. However, continues New Hampshire, "Among the natural rights, some are in their very nature unalienable, because no equivalent can be given or received for them. Of this kind are the rights of conscience. Every individual has a natural and unalienable right to worship God according to the dictates of his own conscience, and reason."[12]

Every early state constitution except Connecticut's contained a guarantee of free exercise of religion.[13]

The founders advanced three further reasons in defense of religious liberty, in addition to its foundation in the natural right to liberty.

First, politically empowered religion is dangerous.

Second, religious freedom is good because under it religion will thrive. That is good because it enables men to perform their duty to God, the highest obligation in life.

Third, religion is a foundation of morality.

Fourth, religion is a foundation of liberty.

Let us briefly consider these claims.

Freedom of Religion as a Means to Prevent Majority Tyranny

James Madison wrote in his *Memorial and Remonstrance against Religious Assessments* (1785), "Torrents of blood have been spilt in the old world by vain attempts of the secular arm to extinguish religious discord by proscribing all difference in religious opinion." Madison deplored the imprisonment of Baptists in Virginia as late as 1774: "There are at this time in the adjacent county not less than 5 or 6 well-meaning men in close jail for publishing their religious sentiments, which in the main are very orthodox."[14]

Madison also made the antityranny argument for religious freedom in *The Federalist*. "A zeal for different opinions concerning religion," he wrote, ". . . have in turn divided mankind into parties, inflamed them with mutual animosity, and rendered them much more disposed to vex and oppress each other, than to cooperate for their common good." The solution: "In a free government, the security for civil government must be the same as for religious rights. It consists in the one case in the multiplicity of interests, and in the other, in the multiplicity of sects."[15]

New York's constitution of 1777 explained its guarantee of free exercise in similar terms:

> And whereas we are required, by the benevolent principles of rational liberty, not only to expel civil tyranny, but also to guard against that spiritual oppression and intolerance wherewith the bigotry and ambition of weak and wicked priests and princes have scourged mankind, . . . the free exercise and enjoyment of religious profession and worship, without discrimination or preference, shall forever hereafter be allowed.

Many of the most ardent supporters of religious liberty in early America were Baptists, Methodists, Catholics, Jews, and other minority denominations. They feared with some justice persecution by the majority Congregationalists (in New England) or by Episcopalians (in the South).

The Transcendent Purpose of Religious Liberty

The language of the Virginia Declaration of Rights shows that religious liberty had not only a secular but also a religious purpose:

> That religion, or the duty which we owe to our Creator, and the manner of discharging it, can be directed only by reason and conviction, not by force or violence; and, therefore, all men are equally entitled to the free exercise of religion, according to the dictates of conscience.[16]

Virginia is saying that it protects free exercise of religion not because it is *indifferent* to religion, not because religion is a *threat*, but because religion, uncoerced "by force or violence," is "the duty which we owe to our Creator." We need liberty to discharge our duty to God.

Madison's *Memorial and Remonstrance*, commenting on the Virginia provision just quoted, explains that the free exercise of religion is an unalienable right . . . because what is here a right towards men, is a duty towards the Creator. . . . Before any man can be considered as a member of civil society, he must be considered as a subject of the Governor of the universe. And . . . every man who becomes a member of any particular civil society [must] do it with a saving of his allegiance to the Universal Sovereign.[17]

In the name of James Madison, Philip Denenfield of the American Civil Liberties Union objected to the Catholic view (in the Second Vatican Council, 1966) that religious freedom enables men to "fulfill their duty to worship God" and acknowledges that men's obligations to God "transcend by their very nature the order of terrestrial and temporal affairs." Denenfield said this understanding violated the spirit of the founders' understanding of religious liberty.[18] But as we just saw, what Denenfield calls the "Catholic view" is identical to the view held by Madison, who would have been astounded to see his authority used to contradict the very arguments he made on behalf of religious liberty in his most famous writing on the subject. Denenfield, and others like him, simply do not understand that the religious freedom fought for in the American Revolution is not freedom *from* religion, as he would like, but freedom *to be religious*, to fulfill one's highest purpose.

If "allegiance to the Universal Sovereign" is as important as Madison says, then why, a believer might ask, should government *not* prescribe man's religious obligations to God? Is not government turning its back on God if it fails to bring men to the salvation of their immortal souls? Some conservatives are asking that very question today, implying that America would be better off if it returned to the coercive approach of pre-eighteenth-century Europe. For example, Kenneth Craycraft writes, "From a Christian point of view, it simply makes no sense to say that we have a fundamental human right to religious freedom, which necessarily entails a right to reject God's love and grace."[19]

The founders gave two answers to Craycraft's challenge. First, human beings are fallible. Their selfish passions, and their all-too-human prejudices and ignorance, make governments bad judges of religious orthodoxy. Governments too often gravitate to theological doctrines that justify, says Madison's *Memorial*, "superstition, bigotry, and persecution." In Madison's argument, the right to religious freedom is not "a right to reject *God's* love and grace," as Craycraft thinks; it is a right to reject the forcible imposition, by fallible *men*, of *their views* of "God's love and grace." Madison never asserts, as do today's Supreme Court liberals, that there is a human right "to define one's own concept of existence." Religious freedom is the right to follow God's concept of our existence, rather than to be compelled to submit to some man's concept of it. This is so far from a rejection of God that most Christians during the founding era, and throughout American history, believed, as founder Tench Coxe maintained, that the denial of religious liberty is "impious" and "a trespass on the Majesty of Heaven."[20]

Second, from a Christian standpoint, we have a right to religious freedom because the nature of faith itself is contradicted by compulsion. This is Locke's argument in his *Letter Concerning Toleration*. The Virginia Declaration of

Rights says worship "can be directed only by *reason* and *conviction*, not by force or violence." Faith, to be genuine, must be freely given; if it is compelled, it is no longer faith. As Jefferson wrote in his draft of the Virginia Bill for Religious Freedom, "the opinions and belief of men depend not on their own will, but follow involuntarily the evidence proposed to their minds" because "Almighty God hath created the mind free."

Harry V. Jaffa has written that "the tragedy of Western civilization has been the unfettered attempt, by political means, to vindicate claims whose very nature excludes the possibility that they can be vindicated by political means." Medieval governments sometimes used force to compel people to be Christians or Moslems. Marxist governments use force to compel people to give up their religious faith and accept the authority of science and reason alone. But force vindicates neither revelation nor reason. "The unprecedented character of the American founding," writes Jaffa, "is that it provided for the coexistence of the claims of reason and of revelation in all their forms, without requiring or permitting any political decisions concerning them." Religious liberty is the bow of the political to the dignity of the Transcendent.[21]

The Worldly Purpose of Religion: God and Morality

The noblest purpose of liberty is to enable man to do his highest duty to God, but religion also has a crucial secular purpose in America: securing the moral conditions of freedom. In the founders' view, without morality, there can be no freedom; and, as founder Benjamin Rush put it, "where there is no religion, there will be no morals."[22]

This argument is not well understood today. As I said earlier, we tend to equate freedom with individuality, the right to choose, the right to do anything one pleases. The founders rejected this view, for two reasons.

First, they thought a person is not really free if he is a slave to his irrational passions. We quoted earlier Madison's statement that the Athenian people were in the grip of "the tyranny of their passions" when they condemned Socrates to death.

Second, the founders believed that a people enslaved to their passions would be unable to restrain themselves from injuring each other. That would mean that government would have to enslave the slavish people politically as well—for their own survival. Madison explains: without sufficient self-control, "nothing less than the chains of despotism can restrain them from destroying and devouring one another" (*Federalist* 55).

I do not want to misstate the founders' position. They were hard-headed enough not to rely on citizen virtue alone. As *The Federalist* explains, the Constitution therefore makes prudent use of governing structures and self-interested motives to prevent the people's passions from breaking out into injustice. "Ambition must be made to counteract ambition," wrote Madison. The Constitution's framers placed much of their trust in checks, balances, and separated powers. But they also knew that although constitutional devices can compensate for to some extent the absence of better motives, there is still some need for virtue. When Madison wrote, in *Federalist* 10 that "neither moral nor religious motives can be relied on as an *adequate* control," he implied that these motives do have *some* beneficial effect on conduct. In fact, he believed that "religious motives" were indispensable. In a private letter, he wrote, "The belief in a God all powerful, wise, and good, is . . . essential to the moral order of the world." Religious faith, then, proves to be an important ingredient in the moral formation of the people.[23]

To sum up the Founders' consensus, I quote George Washington's Farewell Address: "Of all the dispositions and habits which lead to political prosperity, religion and morality are indispensable supports. . . . And let us with caution indulge the supposition that morality can be maintained without religion."[24]

The Worldly Purpose of Religion: God and Liberty

Jefferson—the founder most often singled out for his supposed indifference to religion—thought that the American belief that God is the author of liberty was not just beneficial but essential to the survival of freedom. In his *Notes on Virginia*, he asked, "And can the liberties of a nation be thought secure when we have removed *their only firm basis*, a conviction in the minds of the people that these liberties are of the gift of God? That they are not to be violated but with his wrath?"[25]

That God gives all men the right to life and liberty, and that he therefore favors the American cause, was widely believed during the founding era. In *Federalist* 37, Madison wrote that "the man of pious reflection" could not fail to perceive in the work of the Constitutional Convention "a finger of that Almighty hand which has been so frequently and signally extended to our relief in the critical stages of the revolution." In his First Inaugural Address, Washington said, "Every step by which they [the American people] have advanced to the character of an independent nation seems to have been distinguished by some token of providential agency."[26]

Most American Christians in 1776 endorsed the doctrines of the Declaration of Independence. On the occasion of the commencement of the Massachusetts Constitution of 1780, before an audience including the governor, Senate, and House of Representatives, The Reverend Samuel Cooper said:

> We want not, indeed, a special revelation from heaven to teach us that men are born equal and free. . . . These are the plain dictates of that reason and common sense with which the common parent of men has informed the human bosom. It is, however, a satisfaction to observe such everlasting maxims of equity confirmed . . . by the instructions, precepts, and examples given us in the sacred oracles [i.e., the Bible]; . . . that they come from him "who hath made of one blood all nations to dwell upon the face of the earth."[27]

Reason and faith both teach the same lesson: all men are created equal.

Would the founders have supported Christianity if Americans had adhered to the doctrines of the era called by Washington the "gloomy age of ignorance and superstition"? Jefferson believed that "monkish ignorance and superstition" had once taught that the mass of mankind are "born with saddles on their backs," while "a favored few" are born "booted and spurred, ready to ride them legitimately, by the grace of God." In that era, said Jefferson, "the human mind ha[d] been held in vassalage by kings, priests, and nobles."[28]

Obviously, the American picture of earlier Catholicism was exaggerated. Still, it is doubtful that religion and liberty would have been allies if, for example, the orthodoxy of seventeenth-century French Canada have prevailed in the United States in 1776. The goal of the French religious education, reports historian Francis Parkman, was "to make obedient servants of the church and king." In practice, that meant unquestioning submission to "a body of men clothed with arbitrary and ill-defined powers, ruling with absolute sway an unfortunate people who had no voice in their own destinies, and unanswerable only to an apathetic master three thousand miles away."[29]

Before the Revolution, Christianity as Americans understood it had broken with "monkish ignorance and superstition" in three stages that made it compatible with the principles of liberty.

First was the Protestant rebellion from the authority of Rome. David Ramsay, a founder and early historian of the American Revolution, explains:

> all protestantism is founded on a strong claim to natural liberty, and the right of private judgment. . . . Their tenets . . . are hostile to all interference of authority, in matters of opinion, and predispose to a jealousy for civil liberty.[30]

Second was the American revival of the teaching that Christians have a duty to cultivate the virtues of responsible citizenship, especially those that enable them to fight and kill the enemies of their country. (This had been an important element in the Catholic theology of Thomas Aquinas.) When the cause of liberty is threatened, said the Reverend Samuel Davies of Virginia, "then the sword is, as it were, consecrated to God; and the art of war becomes a part of our religion. . . . Blessed is the brave soldier; blessed is the defender of his country and the destroyer of his enemies."[31] The religion of French Canada was at odds with the teaching of "the laws of nature and of nature's God."

How, one might ask, can this be compatible with Christ's "turn the other cheek"? The Reverend Simeon Howard of Massachusetts answers, in a 1773 sermon:

> When our Saviour forbids us to resist evil, he seems to have had in view only small injuries, for such are those he mentions in the following words, as an illustration of the precept; smiting on the cheek, taking away one's coat, or compelling him to go a mile. . . . But it does not follow, that because we are forbidden to resist such slight attacks, we may not defend ourselves when the assault is of a capital kind. . . . Should a person, for instance, whose ability and circumstances enable him to do good in the world, . . . tamely yield up all his interest and become an absolute slave to some unjust and wicked oppressor, when he might by a manly resistance have secured his liberty? [W]ould he not be guilty of great unfaithfulness to God, and justly liable to his condemnation?[32]

The third feature of American-style Christianity was the conviction that the Bible condemns despotism and favors political liberty. This argument was stated in sermon after sermon during the founding era and throughout our tradition. We gave a brief example earlier in this section.

The belief that liberty is a sacred cause was by no means limited to Protestants. John Carroll, the first Catholic bishop of the United States, appealed to the natural rights of all men—"the luminous principles on which the rights of conscience and liberty of religion depend"—in his pleas for full citizen rights for Catholics. The Jewish congregation in Newport, Rhode Island, addressing President Washington during his visit in 1790, said that the government of America, protecting "liberty of conscience" and securing "the blessings of civil and religious liberty," is "the work of the great God."[33]

When Alexis de Tocqueville visited America in the 1820s, he heard the following Catholic prayer on behalf of the Polish struggle for liberty. It shows how far American Catholicism was from the earlier French Canadian teaching of passive obedience to aristocracy and kingship:

> Lord, who hast created all men in the same image, do not allow despotism to deform thy work and maintain inequality upon the earth. Almighty God! Watch over the destiny of the Poles and make them worthy to be free; may thy wisdom prevail in their councils and Thy strength in their arms; spread terror among their enemies. . . . We beseech Thee in the name of thy beloved son, our Lord Jesus Christ.[34]

The Limits of Free Exercise: Injury to Individuals or Society

In his justly celebrated 1790 letter to the Hebrew Congregation at Newport, President Washington summed up the American understanding of the right to free exercise of religion. Washington's generous letter marked the first occasion that any nation had welcomed Jews as equal citizens since biblical days. It also makes clear that there are definite limits to the right.

> The citizens of the United State of America have a right to applaud themselves for having given to mankind examples of an enlarged and liberal policy—a policy worthy of imitation. All possess alike liberty of conscience and immunities of citizenship.
>
> It is now no more that toleration is spoken of, as if it were by the indulgence of one class of people that another enjoyed the exercise of their inherent natural rights, for, happily, the government of the United States, which gives to bigotry no sanction, to persecution no assistance, requires only that those who live under its protection should demean themselves as good citizens in giving it on all occasions their effectual support.[35]

The guarantee of free exercise of religion is absolute, but that does not mean that everything that anyone calls an "exercise of religion" is permitted. Those who refuse to "demean themselves as good citizens" are not exercising but abusing their "inherent natural rights." Consider the extreme case of the Aztec religion, in which human beings were sacrificed in supposed obedience to a divine command. If such a religion had existed in America, the founders would have treated it as a criminal organization to promote the crime of murder. They would not have hesitated to forbid its free exercise. Religion could not be used as an excuse to violate the rights of others or to engage in conduct that would undermine the moral foundations of society. Jefferson once wrote to Madison, "The declaration, that religious faith shall be unpunished, does not give impunity to criminal acts dictated by religious error."[36]

This reservation against religious practices that threaten life, liberty, property, or public morality was made explicit in several of the early state constitutions. New York's of 1777, for example, provided "that the liberty of conscience, hereby granted, shall not be construed as to excuse acts of licentiousness, or justify practices inconsistent with the peace or safety of the state."

The decision on whether to allow a free-exercise exemption from obeying an otherwise valid public law turned on the nature of the religious practice in question. Was it on balance harmful? We can see two opposite reactions to free exercise claims in the cases of nineteenth-century Catholicism and Mormonism.

An 1813 New York case confronted a Catholic practice that directly violated a state law. Does a Catholic priest have to divulge secrets learned in sacramental confession? Father Anthony Kohlmann, a Jesuit priest, was called before the court and asked to reveal the name of a thief who had confessed his crime to him. He replied: "It would be my duty to prefer instantaneous death or any temporal misfortune, rather than disclose the name of the penitent in question. For, were I to act otherwise, I should become a traitor to my church, to my sacred ministry, and to God. In fine, I should render myself guilty of eternal damnation." The court ruled in favor of Father Kohlmann, saying:

> If a religious sect would rise up and violate the decencies of life, by practicing their religious rites, in a state of nakedness, by following incest, and a community of wives; if the Hindoo should attempt to introduce the burning of widows on the funeral piles of their deceased husbands, or the Mahometan his plurality of wives, or the pagan his bacchanalian orgies or human sacrifices;
> . . . then the licentious acts and dangerous practices contemplated by the [New York] constitution would exist, and the hand of the magistrate would be rightfully raised to chastise the guilty agents. But until men under pretense of religion act counter to *the fundamental principles of morality*, and endanger the well being of the state, they are to be protected in the free exercise of their religion.

The case turned in large part, as James Stoner writes, on the fact that Catholics had a "reputation for law-abidingness," and that "on the whole confession does much more good than harm," in spite of the fact that the seal of confidentiality impedes the normal course of criminal investigations.[37]

Quite opposite was the federal government's treatment of the Mormons in Utah Territory in the late 1800s, at a time when their church believed that the practice of polygamy was directly enjoined upon the male members thereof by the Almighty God . . . ; that the failing or refusing to practice polygamy by such male members of said Church, *when circumstances would admit*, would be punished, and that the penalty for such failure and refusal would be damnation in the life to come.

In spite of this sincere religious belief, the Supreme Court ruled that Mormons were not exempt from the law forbidding multiple wives. Polygamy was made a crime in Utah "because of the evil consequences that were supposed to flow from plural marriages." The Court wrote that a "free, self-governing commonwealth" presupposes monogamy, upon which

society may be said to be built. . . . In fact, according as monogamous or polygamous marriages are allowed, do we find the principles on which the government of the people, to a greater or lesser extent, rests. . . . [P]olygamy leads to the patriarchal principle, and which, when applied to large communities, fetters the people in stationary despotism, while that principle cannot long exist in connection with monogamy.

The Republican Party platform of 1856 had condemned "those twin relics of barbarism—Polygamy, and Slavery." Both were viewed as enemies of liberty. Polygamy was thought the antithesis of the proper equality between man and wife. The moral message of polygamy is that one woman is not good enough for a real man. The Supreme Court pointed out, correctly, that polygamy was practiced elsewhere only under despotic governments in Asia and Africa.[38]

Mormons were permitted to become full members of the American community only after they repudiated the practice. The U.S. government viewed the Mormon Church in effect as an organization that promoted the crime of polygamy. In 1890 the Supreme Court upheld the government's right to seize church property. Threatened with the loss of all that it owned, the church accepted the authority of the laws forbidding plural marriages. It had become clear that under the U.S. Constitution, which Mormons believed to be divinely inspired, "circumstances would [not] admit" polygamy. In 1896 Congress admitted Utah as a state. We should note that even before that date most Mormons led otherwise exemplary lives; afterward, they became a mainstay of moral decency and civilized conduct in America.[39]

Political scientist Richard Sherlock believes that this nineteenth-century American intolerance of Mormonism was based on "hostility to serious communal religion," which he traces to James Madison and the American founding. Sherlock sees no significant difference between the early American treatment of Mormons and of Catholics. Yet Catholics quickly overcame the legal disabilities inherited from colonial days, while Mormons were accepted only after they embraced the moral law approved by the rest of American society. Sherlock fails to see that the treatment of Mormons did not arise from hostility to "serious communal religion," but from hostility to immorality. The U.S. Constitution guarantees free exercise of religion, but not for religious practices that, in the words of the Supreme Court in 1890, are "repugnant to our laws and the principles of our civilization."[40]

The Early American Consensus in Favor of Government Support of Religion

We have mentioned three of the founders' reasons for regarding religion as a good thing: because through it men do their duty to God; because it is a foundation of morality; and because it supports liberty. The question naturally arises whether government should limit itself merely to allowing religious liberty, or whether it should actively foster religion by its encouragement and support.

Today's prevailing opinion, expressed frequently by the Supreme Court, is clear: the purpose of the First Amendment "was to create a complete and permanent separation of the spheres of religious activity and civil authority by comprehensively forbidding every form of public aid or support for religion."[41]

No one in the founders' generation would have agreed. There was, however, considerable disagreement among the founders about how far government should go to support religion.

At one end of American opinion was the Massachusetts Constitution of 1780. The people of each town were required "to make suitable provision, at their own expense, for the institution of the public worship of God, and for the support and maintenance of public Protestant teachers of piety, religion and morality."

Pennsylvania's 1776 constitution was closer to the mainstream. It forbad a religious establishment, but contained this provision:

Laws for the encouragement of virtue, and prevention of vice and immorality, shall be made and constantly kept in force, and provision shall be made for their due execution: And all religious societies or bodies of men heretofore united or incorporated for the advancement of religion and learning, or for other pious and charitable purposes, shall be encouraged and protected.

Probably the most obnoxious means by which religion was supported, from the point of view of many of the founders (and of Americans today), was a requirement that some or all state office holders be Protestant (New Hampshire, New Jersey, North Carolina, South Carolina, Georgia) or Christian (Massachusetts, Pennsylvania, Delaware, Maryland). This was done by means of a required oath. For example, Pennsylvania required members of the state legislature to swear, "I do believe in one God, the creator and governor of the universe, the rewarder of the good and punisher of the wicked, and I do acknowledge the scriptures of the Old and New Testament to be given by Divine Inspiration."

However, these tests were soon abandoned. By 1798, only seven of the then fifteen states still required religious tests for holding public office. The remaining state tests were dropped or fell into disuse early in the nineteenth century. The U.S. Constitution outlaws all religious tests for federal office.

Congress was forbidden by the First Amendment "to make any law regarding an establishment of religion." This amendment was supported both by those who, like Madison, totally opposed government establishments of religion, and by those who favored them. It had no effect whatever on existing state policies. It kept the federal government out of the business of either establishing a national religion, or disestablishing a state religion.[42]

To see how far we have departed from the founders' understanding, consider some of the many ways in which the federal government promoted religion before the 1960s. For example:

- Congress and the president have frequently called for national days of prayer and thanksgiving. The House of Representatives voted to issue the first such call on September 24, 1789, the same day that it passed the First Amendment, stating that "Congress shall make no law respecting an establishment of religion."[43]

- Every president has invoked God's name or the equivalent in a prayerful manner in his inaugural address. Lincoln's Second Inaugural was an interpretation of the Civil War as a divine punishment of the whole nation for the sin of slavery. It is the most beautiful, and the most theological, of all the presidential inaugurals ever delivered.[44]

- From 1789 to today, Congress has authorized chaplains, paid by public funds, to offer prayers in Congress and in the armed services.

- With Madison's agreement, Congress required in 1787 that a lot in each township in the Northwest Territories "be given perpetually for the purposes of religion."[45]

- Jefferson signed a treaty into law in 1803 that provided to the Kaskaskia Indians a government-funded Catholic missionary, "who will engage to perform for said tribe the duties of his office, and also to instruct as many of their children as possible in the rudiments of literature." An 1819 law authorized the president to employ "capable persons of good moral character" to instruct the Indians. A Protestant missionary, Samuel Worcester, used his appointment to preach the Gospel. The Supreme Court upheld this law, and the appointment of Worcester, as a "humane policy."[46]

- In 1832 Congress approved a land grant to Columbian College (later George Washington University), a Baptist institution in the District of Columbia. In 1833 it approved a similar grant to Georgetown University, a Jesuit school for the education of Catholic boys.[47]

- Inscribed on the wall of the Supreme Court are the Ten Commandments, yet the Court ruled in 1980 that posting the Ten Commandments in public schools is a forbidden establishment of religion. The Court begins each session with the prayer: "God save the United States and this Honorable Court"—written by an official on the public payroll.[48]

- Congress placed the Declaration of Independence, with its account of God's relation to America, at the front of the U.S. Code, as the first of the organic laws of the United States.

From these examples of federal "sponsorship, financial support, and active involvement . . . in religious activity," we conclude that the founders understood the words "establishment of religion" (forbidden by the First Amendment) quite narrowly. An establishment was a designation of a particular sect or sects as the official religion of the state or nation, or government funding of the regular worship activities or buildings of a particular sect.

State governments long engaged in many similar religious activities, most importantly in the public schools. States have outlawed blasphemy against Christianity and required store closings on Sundays. They have given churches exemptions from property tax and allowed them other privileges. Yet almost every state has a provision in its constitution prohibiting an establishment of religion.

Is Government Support of Religion Compatible with Religious Liberty?

We assume today that there is a conflict—or at least a tension—between *free exercise* and *government support* of religion. But millions of American statesmen and voters supported the policies just listed. Is it not presumptuous on our part to assume so easily that for almost two centuries all these Americans were totally ignorant of the meaning of religious liberty, and that suddenly, around 1960, our eyes were opened and we saw the matter in its true light? Is it not more likely that earlier Americans had good reasons to believe that there is no necessary conflict between religious liberty and government support?

We will leave aside the case of state establishments of particular religious sects, which were controversial even in the founding era. No state has funded religious worship or named an official state church since Massachusetts abandoned its requirement that towns fund "public Protestant teachers of piety, religion and morality" in the 1830s.

The Northwest Ordinance of 1787 is one of the organic laws of the United States, printed at the beginning of the U.S. Code along with the Declaration of Independence and Constitution. The same Congress of 1789 that passed the First Amendment voted to reconfirm the Ordinance, which laid out standards for the government of the territories north of the Ohio River—the future states of Ohio, Indiana, Michigan, Illinois, and Wisconsin. The Ordinance required "the fundamental principles of civil and religious liberty [to be] the basis of all laws, constitutions, and governments, which forever hereafter shall be formed in the said territory." Article I of the Ordinance therefore reads: "No person, demeaning himself in a peaceable and orderly manner, shall ever be molested on account of his mode of worship, or religious sentiments, in the said territory."

However, Article VI says: "Religion, morality, and knowledge, being necessary to good government and the happiness of mankind, schools and the means of education shall forever be encouraged." To execute this article, Congress specified that plots of land be reserved throughout the territory for public schools, within which, of course, religion and morality would be taught.

Why did Congress see no conflict between its call for public schools to teach religion and its guarantee of religious liberty in the Ordinance, not to mention its First Amendment guarantee of free exercise and prohibition of a federal "establishment of religion"? The answer lies in the meaning of free exercise of religion, which is much misunderstood today. Consider the language of the Northwest Ordinance: "No person . . . shall ever be molested on account of his mode of worship, or religious sentiments." (The Massachusetts

Constitution said, "No subject shall be hurt, molested, or restrained, in his person, liberty, or estate" for his mode of worship.) Religious freedom is freedom from injury because of one's religion. No one is "molested" or injured when taxed to support a religious teaching he does not agree with, any more than he is injured when taxed to support any other government activity he does not like. Of course, the founders considered taxation legitimate only when it serves the common good, in this as in any other activity of government. That is why the Ordinance justifies its policy of support by saying that "religion [is] necessary to good government and the happiness of mankind" (just as Massachusetts said that towns were required to support religion to "promote their happiness and to secure the good order and preservation of civil government"). Government support of religious content in public education is not molestation. *There is no conflict between "free exercise" and "government support," as long as the support in question does not penalize individuals for adopting, or failing to adopt, a particular mode of worship.*

Or course, when government support benefits a particular religious sect, it unavoidably disappoints or angers those not funded. It also treats them unequally, as Madison argued in the *Memorial*. When public officials offer prayers, the more sectarian the prayer, the more those who are not of the same sect are offended.

These considerations have led most presidents and other leading public officials to speak in as nonsectarian a manner as possible in their prayers and proclamations, while avoiding the opposite defect of indifference or absence of content. Washington set the tone in his First Inaugural Address, where God was addressed as "that Almighty Being who rules over the universe," the "Great Author" of every public and private good," and the "benign Parent of the human race." Washington concluded his letter to the Hebrew Congregation at Newport with this ecumenical prayer: "May the Father of all mercies scatter light and not darkness in our paths, and make us all in our several vocations useful here and, in His own due time and way, everlastingly happy."

Government Should Teach Religious Doctrines that Promote Morality and Freedom

We have already shown that the right to free exercise of religion did not excuse, in Jefferson's words, "criminal acts dictated by religious error." How did Jefferson know that criminal acts are dictated by religious error? Could they not be dictated by religious truth? Behind Jefferson's remark lies this argument: Our reason teaches us the difference between morality and immorality. For example, we know that murder, stealing, and slavery are wrong because they violate the self-evident truth that all men possess the natural rights to life, liberty, and property. We know that adultery is wrong because it undermines the core institution of civilized society, the monogamous family. A religion whose teaching violates these moral truths must therefore be wrong.

Samuel West, the Boston preacher quoted earlier, agreed: "A revelation, pretending to be from God, that contradicts any part of the natural law, ought immediately to be rejected as an imposture."[49]

This was an understanding that both believers and unbelievers shared. Believers held that God gives men access to the truth in two ways: through reason and through revelation. Unbelievers placed no particular trust in Scripture, but they too respected the discoveries of reason. The ground common to both reason and revelation was called the natural law.

This common ground made it possible for government not only to reject false religious doctrine (such as polygamy) but also to endorse, without fear of giving offense, theological doctrines that conform to the "law of nature and of nature's God." In his official capacity as president, Jefferson praised America's

> benign religion, professed, indeed, and practiced in various forms, yet all of them inculcating honesty, truth, temperance, gratitude, and the love of man; acknowledging and adoring an overruling Providence, which by all its dispensations proves that it delights in the happiness of man here and his greater happiness hereafter.

In today's America, this consensus has broken down. Many believers now view capitalism as a violation of the "preferential option for the poor" supposedly commanded by the Bible, while others hold that socialism violates the commandment "Thou shalt not steal." Some even believe that the traditional moral law, because it forbids illicit sex and supports the integrity of the family, is evil. Episcopal Bishop Joseph Spong calls the Ten Commandments "immoral" because, he says, they "define women as property."[50] More traditional Christians and Jews see the Ten Commandments as the solution, not the problem. We can no longer speak as Jefferson did of a single "benign religion" that teaches a common moral code. If we look at religion from the founders' point of view, we cannot speak of the goodness of "religion in general" when in the name of religion property rights and marriage are condemned as evil. Therefore, we must state without hesitation that government support of religion is and ought to be preferential.

For the founders, government had no right to compel people to believe, or say they believe, in the religious truth as it sees it. But government also had no obligation to be neutral between religious doctrines favoring despotism or immorality and those favoring freedom or morality. Moreover, government should teach and support the theology of freedom, the theology of the Declaration. That is exactly what was done by leaders such as Washington, Jefferson, and John Adams during the founding era, and by Abraham Lincoln in his great Civil War speeches.

The Theology of the Great Seal of the United States

The founders' conception of God's relation to America was pictured in the Great Seal of the United States, devised in 1782 and printed today on the dollar bill. The reverse side of the seal—the pyramid—represents the theological teaching of the Declaration of Independence.

Much nonsense has been written on the seal's supposed Masonic symbolism. The definitive 1976 history of the seal finds no evidence to support the claim of Masonic inspiration or meaning. The reading of the seal offered here is based on what was approved by Congress in 1782, and on what is obvious to the eye and clearly implied in the words.[51]

The reverse of the seal consists of two parts: a heavenly eye and an earthly pyramid. Each part is labeled with a Latin motto.

In the earthly part, a pyramid rises toward the heavens. Congress adopted codesigner Charles Thomson's 1782 report as part of its law approving the seal. It explains that "the pyramid signifies strength and duration." On the base of the pyramid is the Roman numeral MDCCLXXVI (1776), the date, as Thomson remarks, of the Declaration of Independence. The pyramid has thirteen rows of bricks, signifying the thirteen original states. (The number of rows is not specified in the law, but there are thirteen in codesigner William Barton's original drawing and on the 1778 fifty-dollar bill from which the pyramid idea was originally taken.)[52] The pyramid is the United States, a solid structure of freedom, built on the foundation of the Declaration, in a world hostile to civil and religious liberty. It is unfinished because America is a work in progress. More states will be added later.

"In the zenith" above the unfinished pyramid, the 1782 law calls for "an eye in a triangle, surrounded with a glory." This design and placement of God's eye suggests that America is connected to the divine in three ways.

First, the eye keeps watch over America, protecting her from her enemies. Thomson's report explains: "The eye over it and the motto allude to the many signal interventions of providence in favor of the American cause." The Declaration of Independence had expressed "a firm reliance on the protection of divine providence."

Second, the complete triangle enclosing God's eye is a model for the incomplete or imperfect triangular shape of the pyramid below. The perfect divine shape symbolizes God's perfection, which we know through his laws, which in turn guide and govern the construction of the earthly pyramid. The Declaration says that America, grounded on "the laws of nature and of nature's God," seeks to secure the rights with which the Creator endowed all men. America is a work in progress in a deeper sense than its number of states. No matter how many rows of bricks (new states) are added to the pyramid, America must always look to the Supreme Being as, and at, her "zenith," to be true to what she is and aspires to be. In the spirit of the seal, Lincoln once said:

> It is said in one of the admonitions of the Lord, "As your Father in Heaven is perfect, be ye also perfect." The Savior, I suppose, did not expect that any human creature could be perfect as the Father in Heaven. . . . He set that up as a standard, and he who did most towards reaching that standard, attained the highest degree of moral perfection. So I say that in relation to the principle that all men are created equal, let it be as nearly reached as we can.[53]

Third, the all-seeing eye is not only America's protector and ruling guide; God is also her judge. This theme is not as obvious as the first two, but it is implied by the motto *annuit coeptis*, "He approves of what has been started." These words imply that God will no longer approve if America strays too far from the right path—if the shape of the pyramid departs too far from the divine model. In the Declaration, America "appeal[ed] to the Supreme Judge of the world for the rectitude of our intentions." Facing the injustice of slavery, Jefferson therefore trembled for his country when he reflected "that God is just, that his justice cannot sleep forever."

In sum, America is a nation "under God" in three ways. God protects America; God perfects and rules America; and God judges America.

The seal has two Latin mottoes, one for the heavenly and one for the earthly part. The mottoes are taken from the great Roman poet Vergil.

The pyramid is labeled *novus ordo seclorum*, "a new order of the ages" (or "New World Order"). Thomson's report explains, "The words under it signify the beginning of the New American Era, which commences from that date [1776]." The phrase is a variant of a line in Virgil's fourth *Eclogue*: "a great order of the ages is born anew." This *Eclogue* describes the return of the golden age, an age of peace and plenty. The change of words is significant. America is a "new order," not just a "great order." Virgil's golden age has come before and will come again, but nothing like the American founding has ever happened. No nation has ever grounded itself on a universal principle, discovered by reason, confirmed by revelation, and shared by all human beings everywhere: "all men are created equal."

"Over the eye," says the 1782 law, "these words, *annuit coeptis*." Literally translated, they mean: "he has nodded [or nods] in assent to the things that have been started"—namely, to the pyramid under construction, the "new order of the ages." In Virgil's *Aeneid*, Aeneas leads a remnant of men from conquered Troy over the sea to a land far to the west. After they arrive in Italy, the natives mount a ferocious attack against them. In the midst of the battle, Aeneas's son Ascanius prays to "all-powerful Jupiter" to "nod in assent to the daring things that have been started." Jupiter hears the prayer; Ascanius shoots, and his arrow pierces the enemy's head. That small band of Trojan warriors will eventually become Rome, the greatest empire in world history.[54]

The two mottoes point to the founding of Rome (the *Aeneid*) and the golden age (*Eclogue* 4). Taken together they suggest that America, with divine approval and support, will become a New Rome, combining the glory of the old Rome with the freedom, prosperity, and peace of the golden age. America's foundation, like Rome's, had to be laid in violence. The enemies of liberty had to be killed, and they will always have to be killed. But unlike Rome, the new order will not grow to greatness through warfare and conquest, but through the arts of peace. (On the front of the seal, the eagle's head is pointed toward the olive branch in its right talon, not the arrows of war in its left.) As Washington wrote to the Newport Jews, in America "everyone shall sit in safety under his own vine and fig tree and there shall be none to make him afraid."

We can now see that General Patton's demand for a weather prayer was well grounded in what we may call America's nonestablished civil religion, as taught in the Declaration of Independence, the Great Seal, and in the last stanza of the national anthem, "The Star-Spangled Banner":

Oh! thus be it ever, when freemen shall stand
Between their loved home and the war's desolation,
Blest with vict'ry and peace, may the Heav'n-rescued land
Praise the Pow'r that hath made and preserved us a nation.
Then conquer we must, when our cause it is just,
And this be our motto—"In God is our trust."
And the Star-Spangled Banner in triumph shall wave,
O'er the land of the free, and the home of the brave.

Why the Founders' Understanding of Religious Liberty Matters

Today, large numbers of conservatives and liberals alike believe that the principle of religious liberty requires the state to be neutral or even hostile toward religion.

The view of liberty, which is grounded in moral relativism, leads people on the left to demand the expulsion from American public life of the few remaining remnants of traditional morality and religious expression. The limitation of marriage to a man and a woman, the lingering presence of Christmas holidays and songs in public schools, taxpayer support of legislative and military chaplains—all these holdovers of the repressive traditions of the past must go.

People on the right, holding the same view of religious liberty, too often conclude that they should despise or deny their country's principles. What other course remains for Christians or Jews who believe that America's principles are indifferent to, or at war with, their deepest religious convictions? What other course remains for one who aspires to the classical ideal of virtue and nobility?

But this is a false dilemma. The prevailing interpretation of religious liberty is wrong.

Liberals need to learn that although the right to free exercise of religion is indeed sacred, it is both appropriate and necessary for government to limit abuses of religious liberty, and to support sound religious convictions, in a nation that means to remain free.

Conservatives need to recover the Founders' understanding that a "naked public square"—a public life that allows no place for the expression of the deepest foundation and purpose of liberty—is not fit for human habitation. They need not be shy about their desire for public acknowledgment of the importance of God in our lives—as long as every individual is protected in his "natural and unalienable right to worship God according to the dictates of his own conscience, and reason."

NOTES

[1] George S. Patton, Jr., *War As I Knew It* (1947; reprint, New York: Bantam, 1980), 175-76.

[2] *Everson v. Board of Education*, 330 U.S. 1 (1947).

[3] See George Washington, Thanksgiving Proclamation, Nov. 1, 1777, authored by Samuel Adams, in *Writings*, ed. Harry A. Cushing (New York: Putnam's, 1904), 3: 414-6.

[4] James Madison, *Federalist* 63. Samuel West, "On the Right to Rebel against Governors" (1776), infra, 126 (my emphasis).

[5] *Planned Parenthood v. Casey*, 112 S.Ct. 2791. These relativistic words were written by Justices Sandra Day O'Connor, Anthony Kennedy, and David Souter—all Republicans.

[6] Letter of January 1, 1802, in *Thomas Jefferson: Writings,* ed. Merrill D. Peterson (New York: Library of America, 1984), 510.

[7] *Everson v. Board of Education*, 330 U.S. 1 (1947). *Lee v. Weisman*, 112 S.Ct. 2649 (1992).

[8] *Engel v. Vitale*, 370 U.S. 421 (1962). Brennan, concurring opinion, *Abington School District v. Schempp*, 374 U.S. 203 (1963), emphasis added. Charles E. Rice, *The Supreme Court and Public Prayer* (New York: Fordham University Press, 1964), 19, 112-13. "A world that is dead and gone" is from Brennan's Georgetown speech, October 12, 1985, in *The Great Debate,* Edwin Meese et al. (Washington: Federalist Society, 1986), 17, 23-25.

[9] Michael W. McConnell, "Accommodation of Religion," in *The Supreme Court Review: 1985,* ed. Philip B. Kurland et al. (Chicago: University of Chicago Press, 1986), 21, 39. McConnell, "The Origins and Historical Understanding of Free Exercise of Religion," *Harvard Law Review*, 103 (May 1990): 1409-517.

[10] Linda Greenhouse, "Justices Hear Campus Religion Case: University Challenged for Refusal to Subsidize Christian Magazine," *New York Times*, March 2, 1995, A11. James R. Stoner, "Religious Liberty and Common Law: Free Exercise Exemptions and American Courts," *Polity*, 26 (Fall 1993), criticizes McConnell on pp. 9-14.

[11] *Lee v. Weisman*, 112 S. Ct. 2649 (1992) (Souter's concurring opinion shows that public prayer is necessarily "preferentialist"). *Marsh v. Chambers*, 463 U.S. 783 (1983) (permitting chaplains). The Re-Imaging conference: *A Catalog of Concerns: The Episcopal Church in the U.S. under Edmond Lee Browning* (Mobile, Ala.: AWAKE, 1995), 14.

[12] Francis N. Thorpe, ed., *The Federal and State Constitutions* (Washington: Government Printing Office, 1909), 2453-54.

[13] South Carolina's free exercise guarantee did not come until 1790.

[14] Madison, *Memorial and Remonstrance*, in *American Political Writing during the Founding Era*, eds. Charles S. Hyneman and Donald S. Lutz, 636. Madison, letter to Bradford, January 24, 1774, in *James Madison on Religious Liberty,* ed. Robert S. Alley (Buffalo, N.Y.: Prometheus Books, 1985), 48.

[15] *Federalist* 10 and 51.

[16] Virginia Declaration of Rights (1776), in *The Founders' Constitution: Major Themes,* ed. Philip B. Kurland and Ralph Lerner (Chicago: University of Chicago Press, 1987), 7.

[17] Charles S. Hyneman and Donald S. Lutz, eds., *American Political Writing during the Founding Era* (Indianapolis: Liberty Press, 1983), 632. Cf. Eva Brann, "Madison's

'Memorial and Remonstrance,'" in *Rhetoric and American Statesmanship,* ed. Glen Thurow and Jeffrey D. Wallin (Durham: Carolina Academic Press and The Claremont Institute, 1984), 9-46; and Peter A. Lawler, "James Madison and the Metaphysics of Modern Politics," *Review of Politics,* 48 (1986): 92-115.

[18] Philip S. Denenfield, "The Conciliar Declaration and the American Declaration," in *Religious Liberty,* ed. John Courtnay Murray (New York: Macmillan, 1966), 120, quoted by Tim Burns, "The Declaration on Religious Liberty: Synthesizing Traditions" (xerox).

[19] Kenneth Craycraft, "Virtue among the Ruins," *The Intercollegiate Review* (Fall 1991): 34.

[20] Madison, *Memorial and Remonstrance,* 634-35. Tench Coxe, "An American Citizen IV," October 21, 1787, in *Commentaries on the Constitution,* ed. John P. Kaminski et al. (Madison: State Historical Society of Wisconsin, 1981-), 1: 432.

[21] Madison, *Memorial and Remonstrance,* 634-35. Jaffa, *The American Founding as the Best Regime: The Bonding of Civil and Religious Liberty* (Claremont, Calif.: Claremont Institute, 1990), 15.

[22] Rush, speech in Pennsylvania ratifying convention, December 12, 1787. Merrill Jensen, ed., *Documentary History of the Ratification of the Constitution,* vol. 2, *Ratification of the Constitution by States: Pennsylvania* (Madison: State Historical Society of Wisconsin, 1976), 595.

[23] *Federalist* 51. Letter to Beasley, November 20, 1825, in Alley, *James Madison,* 85.

[24] W. B. Allen, ed., *George Washington: A Collection* (Indianapolis: Liberty Classics, 1988), 469, 521; infra, 190.

[25] Jefferson, *Notes on the State of Virginia,* Query 18, in *Writings,* 289 (my emphasis).

[26] Madison, *Federalist* 37. Allen, *Washington: A Collection,* 461; infra, 180.

[27] Samuel Cooper, *A Sermon* (1780), in *Political Sermons of the Founding Era, 1730-1805* ed. Ellis Sandoz (Indianapolis: Liberty Press, 1991), 637, quoting Acts 17:26.

[28] Washington, "Circular to the States" (1783), in Allen, *Washington: A Collection,* 240. Jefferson to Weightman, June 24, 1826, in *Writings,* 1517. Jefferson to Madison, December 16, 1787, in James M. Smith, ed., *The Republic of Letters* (New York: Norton, 1995), vol. 1, 458.

[29] Francis Parkman, *France and England in North America* (New York: Library of America, 1983), vol. 1, 1354; vol. 2, 1216.

[30] David Ramsay, *The History of the American Revolution,* 2 vols. (1789; reprint Indianapolis: Liberty Classics, 1990), vol. 1, 28. Ramsay is paraphrasing Edmund Burke, "Speech on Conciliation with the Colonies" (1775).

[31] Samuel Davies, *The Curse of Cowardice* (1758), in *The Annals of America* (Chicago: Encyclopedia Britannica, 1968), vol. 2, 23-24; infra, 94.

[32] Simeon Howard, *A Sermon Preached to the Ancient and Honorable Artillery Company in Boston* (1773), in Hyneman and Lutz, *American Political Writing,* 193-94, 201; infra, 105.

[33] John Carroll, "To John Fenno of the Gazette of the U.S.," June 10, 1789, in *The John Carroll Papers,* ed. Thomas O. Hanley (Notre Dame: University of Notre Dame, 1976), vol. 1, 365. Anson P. Stokes, *Church and State in the United States* (New York: Harper, 1950), 862.

[34] George Lawrence trans., *Democracy in America* (Garden City, N.J.: Doubleday Anchor, 1969), 289-90.

[35] Washington, letter to the Hebrew Congregation of Newport, in Stokes, *Church and State in the United States*, 862; infra, 184.

[36] Letter of July 31, 1788, in Adrienne Koch et al., *The Life and Selected Writings of Thomas Jefferson* (New York: Modern Library, 1944), 451.

[37] Stokes, *Church and State in the United States*, 848-49 (emphasis added). Stoner, "Religious Liberty and Common Law," 23. Gerard V. Bradley, "Beguiled: Free Exercise Exemptions and the Siren Song of Liberalism," *Hofstra Law Review*, 20 (Winter 1991): 245-319, shows that this municipal court case had no force as precedent; as in other states, the confidentiality of the confessional was secured by a law passed by the state legislature.

[38] *Reynolds v. U.S.*, 998 U.S. 244 (1879) (emphasis added). Arthur S. Schlesinger, Jr., ed., *History of U.S. Political Parties* (New York: Chelsea House, 1973), vol. 2, 1204.

[39] The relevant documents are in John T. Noonan, ed., *The Believer and the Powers That Are: Cases, History, and Other Data Bearing on the Relation of Religion and Government* (New York: Macmillan, 1987), 194-207. The quotation is from *Late Corporation of the Church of Jesus Christ of Latter Day Saints v. U.S.*, 136 U.S. 1 (1890).

[40] Richard Sherlock, "Liberalism at a Dead End," *Crisis* (April 1995): 19. *Davis v. Beason*, 133 U.S. 333 (1890).

[41] Dissent of Justice Wiley Rutledge in *Everson v. Board*, 330 U.S. 1 (1947), cited with approval in *Abington School District v. Schempp*, 374 U.S. 203 (1963).

[42] Gary D. Glenn, "Forgotten Purposes of the First Amendment Religion Clause," *Review of Politics*, 49 (Summer 1987): 340-67.

[43] Noonan, *Believer*, 127-28.

[44] Rice, *The Supreme Court*, 177-93, quotes the relevant passages from the addresses from 1789-1961.

[45] Noonan, *Believer*, 138. Rice, *Supreme Court*, 65.

[46] Rice, *Supreme Court*, 64. Noonan, *Believer*, 138.

[47] Noonan, *Believer*, 138.

[48] Rice, *Supreme Court*, 4. Justice Douglas cites other examples in his concurring opinion in *Engel v. Vitale*, 370 U.S. 421 (1962), all of which he says should be ruled unconstitutional. *Stone v. Graham*, 449 U.S. 39 (1980) (Ten Commandments case).

[49] West, *On the Right to Rebel against Governors* (1776), 414.

[50] Spong made this statement at a homosexuality symposium at President Clinton's Foundry United Methodist Church in Washington, according to Mark Tooley, "St. Jack's Gospel," *Foundations* (Newsletter of the Episcopal Synod of America), January 1996, 8.

[51] Richard S. Patterson and Richardson Dougall, *The Eagle and the Shield: A History of the Great Seal of the United States* (Washington: Government Printing Office, 1976), 83-91, 529-32.

[52] Patterson, *Eagle and Shield*, 66-68.

[53] Lincoln, speech at Chicago, July 10, 1858, in *Collected Works of Abraham Lincoln*, ed. Roy P. Basler (New Brunswick, N.J.: Rutgers University Press, 1953), vol. 2, 501.

[54] *Eclogues* 4.5; *Aeneid* 9.625. The line reads *Juppiter omnipotens, audacibus adnue coeptis* (literally, "All-powerful Jupiter, nod to the daring things that have been started"). The same phrase also occurs in Virgil's *Georgics*, 1.40, in a prayer to Caesar; I can think of no plausible connection to the teaching of the Great Seal of the United States.

2

"Where Locke stopped short we may go on": Religious Toleration and Religious Liberty at the Founding

Daniel C. Palm

What motivated the founders to take up arms against the greatest power in the world in the American War of Independence? Typically, one thinks of tea taxes, the Stamp Act, "No taxation without representation!" or the long list of complaints against King George III that comprise the second half of the Declaration of Independence. But to what extent was religious freedom at issue? George Washington apparently thought it a prime factor, going so far as to write in the autumn of 1783, shortly after the final articles of peace marking an end to the war had been signed in Paris, that,

> The establishment of Civil *and Religious* Liberty was the Motive which induced me to the Field; the object is attained, and it now remains to be my earnest wish and prayer, that the citizens of the United States would make a wise and virtuous use of the blessings placed before them; . . .[1]

More than a few prominent American historians have drawn a connection between the political liberty of the American founding and religious liberty—some even resting the former entirely upon the latter. Harold Laski, for instance, has written that "the political liberty of the seventeenth and eighteenth centuries was the outcome of the protest against religious intolerance."[2] Clinton Rossiter concurs, arguing that "the free state rests squarely, both logically and historically, on freedom of religion."[3]

Americans in the late twentieth century are long accustomed to religious freedom and to the multiplicity of religious faiths that thrive in our country, and consequently, we are apt to forget the extent to which we are outside the ordinary. To much of the world, our religious freedom, and the fact that countless varieties of the major faiths exist side by side, remains something remarkable. For some it is nothing less than astounding. Indeed, if America is known for anything, it is the freedom to worship as one pleases, and that freedom serves as much as one of the nation's chief "draws" now as it did in the eighteenth and nineteenth centuries. But if we no longer appreciate our religious freedom, do we even understand it?

One indication that many Americans may no longer understand what "religious freedom" means is the extent to which we use those words interchangeably with "religious tolerance." A quick glance at the popular press gives one the ready impression that freedom and toleration are one and the same thing. In sophisticated circles and the academic world, on the other hand, there has developed of late a decided preference for religious "diversity" or "toleration." [4] Indeed, "tolerance" and "toleration" especially have taken on the aura of some recent discovery, while "liberty" or "freedom"—the words traditionally used with respect to the status of religious faith in America—have been virtually abandoned.[5] One journal devoted to the subject proclaims in its editorial statement "that Universal Toleration of Religion is still the highest virtue a government can maintain."[6] Are we coming to think of our nation no longer as one that established religious liberty but as one that established religious toleration?

One need not think deeply about the matter to see that "toleration" is neither accurate nor sufficient. Who among us, after all, is doing the tolerating and whose particular faith or mode of worship is being tolerated? Or do we all mutually tolerate each other's religious preferences? If so, how far does toleration extend? Do we tolerate anything and everything? Is no religious practice—no matter how gruesome or obscene—intolerable? We might also ask why Washington, in his letter to the Reformed Congregation of New York cited above, to say nothing of the other founders, wrote not of religious toleration but of religious liberty? Somehow we have gotten off track with our choice of words, and must reconsider the matter with rather more care. How exactly did the founders understand religious "toleration" as opposed to religious "liberty"?

Religious Toleration in Western History

Any reader of *The Federalist*—or of any of the founders' writings—will note at once the extent of their knowledge of history, and the degree to which they drew upon it in coming to conclusions about the forms of government. This is no less true with respect to their understanding of religious faith and its relation to government.

The founders were well aware that religious toleration—the state and/or predominant religion *tolerating* one or more religious practices and forms—in the classical and medieval worlds was exceedingly rare, and religious freedom unknown. Religion was tied closely to government; frequently the two were one and the same. "Alternative religions" within a regime were proscribed.[7] In the ancient Roman republic, foreign religious expressions were tolerated—provided they were not subversive to the authority of the traditional Roman gods. During the empire, a sort of toleration allowed conquered nations to continue their local religious practices; some foreign gods were even incorporated into the imperial pantheon. And Rome was willing to tolerate the mystery cults of the later empire, for they presented no competition to one's loyalty to the emperor; they served to supplement emperor worship, rather than compete against it.[8] Christianity, in contrast, with its jealous God who demands that "thou shalt have no other gods before me" presented serious competition to the deified Roman emperor. And so it was that early Christians fell victim to a series of persecutions, beginning in earnest with the Emperor Nero (64-66 A.D.), and continuing intermittently for two and a half centuries.[9]

It comes often as a surprise to modern Christians that early church leaders were themselves not in general inclined toward tolerating offshoots of the Christian faith. The early Christians made no bones about excommunicating heretics, even while they themselves were suffering persecution at the hands of the Romans. One great exception to this, and an early voice arguing for religious toleration during Christianity's first years was Tertullian of Alexandria (d. 222 A.D.), whose letter to Scapula, a notable persecutor of Christians, aimed to persuade the Roman proconsul against further assaults on Christians:

> . . . it is a . . . privilege of nature, that every man should worship according to his own convictions: one man's religion neither harms nor helps another man. It is assuredly no part of religion to compel religion, to which free will and not force should lead us. You will render no real service to your gods by compelling us to sacrifice, for they can have no desire of offerings from the unwilling. . . . [10]

Constantine's conversion to Christianity early in the 4th century A.D. was quickly followed not by toleration toward non-Christians but by the persecution of paganism. Nevertheless, the rise of Christianity brought the first sense of a separation between religious devotion and government, in contrast to ancient religion, a distinction that would make possible, in time, state policies of toleration.

In medieval history, religious toleration again appears rarely. It is true that Jews were frequently tolerated in Jerusalem during the years when the city was ruled by Muslims, sometimes even fighting alongside each other against Christians during the Crusades. And Jews were famously tolerated in medieval Europe for their useful function as moneylenders. But in general, intolerance was the rule and toleration the exception, based on the widespread assumption that the Roman church was justified in demanding the allegiance of the entire community. Truly tolerant regimes—to say nothing of regimes enjoying religious freedom—could not come into being until matters of faith had been further removed from their long-standing connection with government.

The Reformation may be said to have redefined human salvation, taking it from the purview of the Roman church and making it dependent on the individual's faith and understanding of Scripture. And yet the Reformation marked no great immediate stride away from religious intolerance. Indeed, for the centuries immediately following the Reformation, "politics were to become not less but more theocratic than they were at the time of the outbreak of the Reformation."[11] Martin Luther, for example, held that the best regime a man might hope for was not a tolerant one, but government by a religious autocrat in a compact territory. He had no sympathy for ideas of representative government or several coexisting varieties of religious faith.[12] Calvin's Geneva is remembered as a hallmark of strict discipline and religious intolerance, with Calvin himself approving the burning of the heretic Michael Servetus in 1553.[13] Each of the early Protestant churches and their associated political regimes—from Calvin's Geneva to Zwingli in Zurich to John Knox in Scotland—operated on the assumption that any state's religious faith "must be uniform and that it was entitled to the cooperation of the civil power both for its maintenance and for the suppression of all variations."[14] What can be said for the Reformation, however, is that it opened the door for religious toleration in the reassertion that the individual must come to salvation by faith alone and by private reading of the Scriptures.

The Peace of Augsburg (1555) settled temporarily the first wave of religious warfare that the Reformation had brought to central Europe. Its doctrine of *cuius regio, eius religio* allowed princes or the holders of estates a limited religious choice between Lutheranism and Catholicism—but not Calvinism or Anabaptist doctrine. One might say that the Peace of Augsburg marks a first political step away from the past, yet it could hardly be described as having brought toleration, for it merely permitted each prince to announce the accepted form of faith for his regime. The best religious minorities could hope for was the freedom to emigrate without loss of property. Violence within the European principates toward religious minorities remained a feature. In Lutheran East Prussia in 1566, for instance, a man accused of Calvinist beliefs was executed in the marketplace to the cheers of a crowd. In 1570 Calvinist professors at the University of Heidelberg insisted on the execution of two men who questioned the divinity of Christ, while Chancellor Nikolas Krell was beheaded at Dresden in 1601 for including Calvinist themes in the Lutheran ritual."[15] And such persecutions were merely a foretaste of what was to come during the Thirty Years' War (1618-1648). In fact a series of four wars during which Bohemian, Danish, Swedish, and French armies devastated central Europe, the Thirty Years' War brought indescribable suffering:

> The Calvinists exhorted all true believers to violence and took special delight in the more bloodthirsty psalms. But the Catholics and Lutherans were not innocent and force was everywhere the proof of true faith. The Lutherans set upon the Calvinists in the streets of Berlin; Catholic priests in Bavaria carried firearms in self-defense; in Dresden the mob stopped the funeral of an Italian Catholic and tore the corpse to pieces; a Protestant pastor and a Catholic priest came to blows in the streets of Frankfurt on the Main. . . . In 1608 a riot between Catholics and Protestants at Donauwörth, a free city on the Danube, kept the Empire for some months on the edge of disaster.[16]

Acknowledging the horrors of the war, Publius writes simply in *Federalist* 19 that it left Germany "desolated." Indeed, approximately one-third of the population of central Europe died either as a direct result of the war or of the plagues and starvation that accompanied its widespread destruction. The Peace of Westphalia (1648), which marked the conclusion to the Thirty Years' War, expanded on the Peace of Augsburg by including Calvinism: A prince might now choose among three varieties of the Christian faith for himself and his subjects rather than just two. More important, the Peace of Westphalia limited the extent of the ruler's authority over his subjects' faith. Rulers now might do no more than impose regulations on the practice of public religion within their territory, making broad religious toleration possible for the first time. Persecution of Anabaptists and other lesser sects in central Europe, however, continued, forcing their followers to seek refuge abroad, often to Holland or North America.

Toleration in England

Renaissance and Enlightenment England provided the fertile soil for legal toleration of minority faiths, and served as the intellectual background for the American founders. Assisted by numerous contributing factors, including a general moderation of religious faiths, the growth of international trade and travel, and the development of the printing press, political pressure for a policy of toleration in England mounted steadily during the sixteenth and seventeenth centuries.[17] In the Toleration Act (1689), King William, the Whigs in Parliament, and moderate clergy pushed forward a law that permitted nonconformist Christians to worship as they pleased, yet, still was not to be interpreted "to extend to give any ease, benefit or advantage to any papist . . . or any person that shall deny in his preaching or writing the doctrine of the Blessed Trinity."[18] Moreover, the act disallowed those not observing the Church of England rite from partaking in local or national government.[19] The classic English argument for toleration was published (anonymously) that same year by John Locke—whose writings the framers knew intimately—in his *Letter Concerning Toleration*. Concurring with the authors of the Toleration Act, Locke held that toleration must necessarily be distinctly limited in scope.[20]

Of the policy of toleration, one prominent British historian writes that it was "limited in scope, somewhat ignoble in some of its sources, but constitutes, more or less, one of the most significant advances that the human race has ever achieved."[21] And indeed, for the first time in England, religious toleration had become the law of the land. Seventeenth-century England offered its citizens not only a government that was the world's most liberal, but also a regime that was among the most tolerant. On the other hand, while several strains of Christianity were permitted—and their adherents could worship safely in the knowledge that they would not be burned at the stake for their beliefs—they were not welcomed. Indeed, it was not until the late 1820s that the nation would come to terms with the idea of religious toleration. Only by that time could one say that anti-Catholic mobs were no longer a regular feature of English politics, and that Methodists, while still unpopular, were no longer subject to persecution.[22]

The Colonial Background

The Puritan colonists who settled in America along the northeastern seaboard were hardly a tolerant people. Puritanism in New England (1600-1700) brought to the Massachusetts Bay colony a Calvinist theocracy not far removed in spirit from Calvin's Geneva. Toleration on the part of the individual, wrote the Puritan minister Nathaniel Ward, was an indication that one "either doubts of his owne [faith], or is not sincere in it." As for toleration on the part of the state, he warned:

> That State that will give Liberty of Conscience in matters of Religion, must give Liberty of Conscience and Conversation in their Morall Lawes, or else the Fiddle will be out of tune, and some of the strings cracke.[23]

Historian Ralph Barton Perry writes that "Puritanism tended to theocracy. It was intolerant of other creeds—in this resembling its God, who might be merciful, but was not tolerant."[24] And yet Puritanism also produced the greatest single early critic of religious persecution and advocate of toleration, and even religious liberty, in Roger Williams. Founder of Rhode Island and author of *The Bloudy Tenent of Persecution,* Williams's writing decisively influenced the debate on religious toleration in England and the American colonies. Looking back on centuries of religious persecution, he asked, "Are all the thousands of millions . . . of consciences, at home and abroad, fuel only for a prison, for a whip, for a stake, for a gallows?"[25]

Other settlements in North America—even those founded on a principle of religious uniformity—found necessary the development of more liberal policies respecting matters of faith. The Maryland Toleration Act of 1649 offered a distinctly limited but precedent-setting toleration—chiefly directed at Roman Catholics—ensuring that no person within the colony, "professing to believe in Jesus Christ, shall from henceforth bee any waies troubled, Molested or discountenanced for or in respect of his or her religion nor in the free exercise thereof within this Province . . . nor any way compelled to the beleife or exercise of any other Religion against his or her consent." Blasphemy and denial of the trinity, however, "shal be punished with death and confiscation or forfeiture of all his or her lands and goods."

By the middle 1770s, as the colonists launched their War for Independence, the colonies had become home to Christians of every stripe. A majority of the American colonists were Protestant—and specifically Calvinist—in religious conviction.[26] Jews and Catholics were relatively few in number, the latter regarded as dangerously uncommitted to free government.[27] As the colonists began the work of writing their respective state constitutions, the question of religious establishment was considered anew. It was during this time—the same period that the colonists first began to refer to the rights of man rather than the rights of Englishmen—that a few of the founders began to champion the cause of religious liberty over and above mere religious toleration. And while it certainly cannot be said that the American founding settled the question of freedom of religious faith throughout all the land, the question received serious attention everywhere in the new nation before 1800. Several of the states, Virginia and Massachusetts in particular, served as the key battlegrounds in the controversy. In Boston, an article appearing in the *Massachusetts Spy* in 1776 reminded readers of Germany's bloody history of religious persecution, concluding that "to allow one part of a society to lord it over the faith and consciences of the other, in religious matters is the ready way to [lay] a foundation for persecution in the abstract."[28] In Virginia, where a long-standing debate over church establishment would rage, Madison and Jefferson championed the cause of religious liberty in the writing of the Virginia state constitution. Hammered out only weeks before Jefferson turned his full attention to the Declaration of Independence, the document holds as its final section,

> That religion, or the duty which we owe to our Creator, and the manner of discharging it, can be directed only by reason and conviction, not by force or violence; and therefore all men are equally entitled to the free exercise of religion, according to the dictates of conscience; and that it is the mutual duty of all to practise Christian forbearance, love, and charity towards each other.[29]

The liberality of the section is largely due to the efforts of Jefferson and Madison, at whose insistence proposed language guaranteeing "the free exercise of religion" replaced the previous guarantee offering merely "the fullest toleration."[30] But as Jefferson later observed in his *Notes on the State of Virginia,* the state's common law in fact included a number of provisions that were inconsistent with the principle of religious freedom as enshrined in the Constitution. Reflecting on this fact, Jefferson asked rhetorically what has been the historic aim of religious establishment. The answer, he determines, has been a "uniformity" of religious faith. But he asks,

> Is uniformity attainable? Millions of innocent men, women, and children, since the introduction of Christianity, have been burnt, tortured, fined, imprisoned; yet we have not advanced one inch towards uniformity. What has been the effect of coercion? To make one half the world fools, and the other half hypocrites. To support roguery and error all over the earth.[31]

That Jefferson understood the American founding as having taken the decisive step away from Lockean toleration, and toward religious freedom, is clear in his "Notes on Religion," written in 1782:

> Locke denies toleration to those who entertain opinions contrary to those moral rules necessary for the preservation of society, as for instance, that faith is not to be kept with those of another persuasion, that Kings excommunicated forfeit their crowns, that dominion is founded in grace, or that obedience is due to some foreign prince; or who will not own and teach the duty of tolerating all men in matters of religion; or who deny the existence of a god (it was a great thing to go so far—as he himself says of the parliament which framed the act of toleration—but where he stopped short we may go on).[32]

Madison in *Federalist* 10 concurs with Jefferson that uniformity is impossible to attain. Indeed, he identifies "a zeal for different opinions concerning religion" as one of the chief sources of faction, having "divided mankind into parties, inflamed them with mutual animosity, and rendered them much more disposed to vex and oppress each other, than to cooperate for their common good."

Nowhere in the new nation was the matter of religious establishment debated so fiercely as in Virginia.[33] In the state legislature a proposal made in 1785 by Patrick Henry and Richard Henry Lee to name Christianity the state religion was countered forcefully by Madison in the "Memorial and Remonstrance": "The religion of every man," he wrote, "must be left to the conviction and conscience of every man; and it is the right of every man to exercise it as these may dictate."[34] He went on to argue that while religious liberty offered no final guarantee against religious warfare, it did offer the best hope:

> Torrents of blood have been spilt in the Old World, by vain attempts of the secular arm to extinguish Religious discord, by proscribing all difference in Religious opinions. Time has at length revealed the true remedy. Every relaxation of narrow and rigorous policy, wherever it has been tried, has been found to assuage the disease. The American theatre has exhibited proofs, that equal and complete liberty, if it does not wholly eradicate it, sufficiently destroys its malignant influence on the health and prosperity of the state.[35]

What the founders did respecting government's stand toward religion was truly revolutionary. Instead of following the established pattern of religious toleration, they achieved an advanced principle to serve as the nation's guiding light with respect to matters of faith. That principle rests ultimately on the Declaration's most significant sentence: "We hold these truths to be self-evident, that all men are created equal, that they are endowed by their Creator with certain unalienable rights, that among these rights are life, liberty and the pursuit of happiness." For the first time in history, a nation's founding document had incorporated the principle that human beings—not just Englishmen—are endowed equally with particular rights. That founding principle demanded that the new regime would treat all faiths equally, with no one favored over the other, and hence avoiding the bloodshed of the past.

The Invention of Religious Liberty

The founders of the American regime laid no claim to new invention respecting government, but rather to the establishment of a regime embodying the great truths of Western philosophy. Central to all else is the establishment of a regime in which the individual rights of man would be observed. "The object of the Declaration of Independence," wrote Jefferson, was

> Not to find out new principles, or new arguments, never before thought of, not merely to say things which had never been said before; but to place before mankind the common sense of the subject, in terms so plain and firm as to command their assent, and to justify ourselves in the independent stand we are compelled to take. Neither aiming at originality of principle or sentiment, nor yet copied from any particular and previous writing, it was intended to be an expression of the American mind, and to give to that expression the proper tone and spirit called for by the occasion.

Religious liberty is a part of "the common sense of the subject." It is a part of that larger inalienable right to liberty that man has been endowed with by his Creator. And for the first time in history, a regime had been planned and constructed that would permit its citizens the enjoyment of their rights. The genius of the American founding lies, as Professor Harry Jaffa has observed, in the bonding together of civil and religious liberty.[36]

One might ask why the framers did not continue with the established course of action—religious toleration—a policy that amounted to the most liberal in the world at the time. The answer is that they could not, for toleration is incompatible with the idea of human equality, and amounts to one faith declaring itself and its adherents the natural superiors in terms of faith to all others. A prominent British historian has written of religious toleration in England that "it suggests at least latent disapproval of the belief or practice which is tolerated and refers to a somewhat limited or conditional freedom."[37] Clearly a regime grounded in equality could brook no such conditions if it was to be consistent with its principles. In an election sermon delivered at Boston in 1779, Samuel Stillman argued that there can be no establishment of religion because, "if the magistrate destroys the equality of the subjects of the state on account of religion, he violates a fundamental principle of a free government. . . . Happy are the inhabitants of that commonwealth . . . in which all are *protected*, but none *established*."[38]

No explanation of the difference between the old policy of toleration and the new one of religious liberty is more frequently recited than George Washington's remarkable letter to the Hebrew Congregation of Newport, Rhode Island, in reply to their letter of welcome in August 1790. For Washington, the American founding marked an end to the legitimacy of toleration:

> It is now no more that toleration is spoken of, as if it was by the indulgence of one class of people, that another enjoyed the exercise of their inherent natural rights. For happily the government of the United States, which gives to bigotry no sanction, to persecution no assistance, requires only that they who live under its protection should demean themselves as good citizens, in giving it on all occasions their effectual support. . . . May the children of the Stock of Abraham, who dwell in this land, continue to merit and enjoy the good will of the other inhabitants, while every one shall sit in safety under his own vine and fig tree, and there shall be none to make him afraid.[39]

Writing in *The Natural and Civil History of Vermont* (1794), Samuel Williams considers the manner in which the region's Episcopalians, Congregationalists, Presbyterians, Baptists, and Quakers have managed to get along. They understand that they are dependent on one another "in the common concerns and business of life." And all are persuaded "that government has nothing to do with their particular and distinguishing tenets." Respecting religion, he writes,

> It is not barely *toleration*, but *equality*, which the people aim at. Toleration implies either a power or a right in one party, to bear with the other; and seems to suppose, that the governing party are in possession of the truth, and that all

the others are full of errors. Such a toleration is the most that can be obtained by the minority, in any nation, where the majority assume the right and the power, to bind society, by established laws and forms in religion. The body of the people in this commonwealth, carry their ideas of religious liberty much further than this: That no party shall have any power to make laws or forms to oblige another; that each denomination may lay themselves under what civil contracts and obligations they please; but that government shall not make any distinctions between them; that all denominations shall enjoy equal liberty, without any legal distinction or preeminence whatever.[40]

How would religious faith fare under this revolutionary regime founded on the principle of equality? Years after the founding, James Madison wrote a letter in which he contrasted the old toleration with the new religious freedom, described the founders' understanding of the distinction between toleration and liberty, and answered those who wondered whether religious faith would wither away without the support of government:

It was the belief of all sects at one time that the establishment of Religion by law, was right and necessary; that the true religion ought to be established in exclusion of every other; And that the only question to be decided was which was the true religion. The example of Holland proved that a toleration of sects, dissenting from the established sect, was safe and even useful. The example of the Colonies, now States, which rejected religious establishments altogether, proved that all Sects might be safely and advantageously put on a footing of equal and entire freedom; and a continuance of their example since the Declaration of Independence, has shewn that its success in Colonies was not to be ascribed to their connection with the parent Country. If a further confirmation of the truth could be wanted, it is to be found in the examples furnished by the States, which have abolished their religious establishments. I cannot speak particularly of any of the cases excepting that of Virginia where it is impossible to deny that Religion prevails with more zeal, and a more exemplary priesthood than it ever did when established and patronised by Public authority. We are teaching the world the great truth that Governments do better without Kings and Nobles than with them. The merit will be doubled by the other lesson that Religion flourishes in greater purity, without than with the aid of Government.[41]

Despite Madison's optimism, it cannot be said that the step taken by some of the founders toward religious freedom ensured that all manner of faiths would henceforth coexist happily side by side. Just as slavery existed in the nation long after the Declaration had established the principle of equality, religious persecution of minority sects in the states was an occasional feature of the American political landscape. The infamous burning on August 11, 1834 of an Ursuline Convent only a stone's throw from Bunker Hill by an anti-Catholic mob is but one reminder that Americans did not always live up to the high principles of the founding.

Christians and Modern America

Regrettably, an occasional church burning is still heard of today. And Christians find intolerance regularly in decisions by federal judges and the Supreme Court. But a still greater challenge for Christians consists in this: that we are forgetting or confusing the meaning of religious freedom. It is essential that not only Christians but all Americans come to understand once again the remarkable step taken by the founders in advancing from religious toleration to religious freedom. However careless we may have become these many years later in our choice of words, we should recall that the founders were crystal clear about the distinction.

What are the practical implications of all this? First, Christians need to steer clear of the trend toward dividing our country into subsets and groups. This is particularly important in an age when "cultural diversity" is frequently emphasized in our universities and seminaries over and above what should unite all Americans, namely, our allegiance to the great principle of the Declaration, "that all men are created equal, and that they are endowed by their Creator with certain unalienable rights." It is our equality—what we hold in common with each other rather than our diversity—that serves as the foundation for our religious freedom. At the same time, Christians need to denounce vigorously the suggestion that one variety of Christianity or other should place itself in a position of merely tolerating other sects or faiths in the United States. Conservative and liberal Christians alike need to make themselves known as the champions of religious freedom.

Make no mistake: religious freedom is not to be confused with religious toleration, and those who so cavalierly do so put the former at risk. Christians of all stripes need to ride to the rescue, and to argue forcefully and without embarrassment—as did our nation's founders—for the principle of religious freedom.

NOTES

[1] Author's italics. "Letter to the Reformed German Congregation of New York" in *George Washington: A Collection,* ed. William B. Allen (Indianapolis: Liberty Press, 1988), 270. See also Washington's letter of November 16, 1782, to the Reformed Dutch Church in Kingston: "Convinced that our Religious Liberties were as essential as our Civil my endeavors have never been wanting to encourage and promote the one, while I have been contending for the other; . . ."

[2] Harold Laski, *A Defense of Liberty Against Tyrants* (London, 1924), cited in *Seedtime of the Republic,* Clinton Rossiter (New York: Harcourt, Brace & World, 1953), 36.

[3] Rossiter, *Seedtime of the Republic,* 36-37.

[4] See, for example, "Gore Urges Religious Tolerance, Activism," in *The Christian Century,* (February 16, 1994), 162-63.

[5] "Toleration" and "tolerance" are generally in style in the '90s. MTV ran a series promoting tolerance in the spring of 1993. In 1994, the United Nations announced that

the following year would be known as the "International Year of Tolerance," while the UN Tolerance Committee issued a "Tolerance Report." A museum in Los Angeles devoted to remembrance of the Holocaust and its victims is named The Museum of Tolerance. A tour of the museum, with press in tow, has become a popular act of penance for Southern California public figures guilty of intolerance.

[6] See *The Julian Review.*

[7] On the nature of ancient religion, see Fustel de Coulanges, *The Ancient City* (1874; reprint Garden City, N.Y.: Doubleday & Co., 1956): "We are not to suppose that . . . ancient religion resembled those founded when men became more enlightened. . . . Not only did [primitive religion] not offer only one god to the adoration of men, but its gods did not accept the adoration of all men . . ." (34) "Every city had gods which belonged to it alone. . . . The city which possessed a divinity of its own did not wish strangers to be protected by it, or to adore it.   More commonly a temple was accessible only to citizens . . . [T]he ancients never represented God to themselves as a unique being exercising his action upon the universe. Each of their innumerable gods had his little domain; to one a family belonged, to another a tribe, to a third a city. . . . As to the god of the human race, a few philosophers had an idea of him . . . but the vulgar never believed in such a god" (147-51). See also Winfred Ernest Garrison, *Intolerance* (New York: Round Table Press, 1934), and Simeon L. Guterman, *Religious Toleration and Persecution in Ancient Rome* (London: Aiglon Press, 1951).

[8] Garrison, *Intolerance*, 58-59.

[9] "Christianity" in *The Oxford Classical Dictionary,* N. G. L. Hammond and H. H. Scullard (Oxford: Clarendon Press, 1970), 231-33.

[10] "Ad Scapulam," trans. S. Thelwall, in *The Ante-Nicene Fathers,* ed. Alexander Roberts and Jacob Donaldson (Grand Rapids, Mich.: Wm. B. Eerdmans Publishing Co., 1957), vol. 3, 105.

[11] A. W. Ward et al., eds., *The Cambridge Modern History,* vol. 3, *The Wars of Religion* (Cambridge: Cambridge University Press, 1904), 740.

[12] Ward et al., *The Wars of Religion*, 740. See also Duncan B. Forrester, "Martin Luther and John Calvin," in *History of Political Philosophy*, ed. Leo Strauss and Joseph Cropsey, 3d ed., (Chicago: University of Chicago Press, 1987), 342-43.

[13] Jefferson makes note of his death in a letter of 1820: "The Presbyterian clergy are . . . the most intolerant of all sects, . . . ready at the word of the lawgiver, if such a word could be now obtained, to put the torch to the pile, and to rekindle in this virgin hemisphere, the flames in which their oracle Calvin consumed the poor Servetus, because he could not find in his Euclid the proposition which has demonstrated that three are one and one is three." Jefferson to William Short, April 13, 1820 in *The Writings of Thomas Jefferson,* ed. Andrew Lipscomb (Washington, D.C.: Thomas Jefferson Memorial Association, 1904), vol. 15, 246.

[14] Garrison, *Intolerance*, 121.

[15] Will and Ariel Durant, *The Age of Reason Begins* (New York: Simon and Schuster, 1961), 551-52.

[16] C. V. Wedgwood, *The Thirty Years' War* (Garden City, N.Y.: Anchor Books, 1961), 47 and 51.

[17] W. K. Jordan, *The Development of Religious Toleration in England* (London: George Allen & Unwin, Ltd., 1932), 17.

[18] George Burton Adams and H. Morse Stephens, eds., *Select Documents of English Constitutional History* (New York: The Macmillan Company, 1901), 462.

[19] Adams and Stephens, eds., *Select Documents*, 459-62.

[20] Locke writes: "Lastly, those are not at all to be tolerated who deny the being of a God. Promises, covenants, and oaths, which are the bonds of human society, can have no hold upon an atheist. The taking away of God, though but even in thought, dissolves all; besides also, those that by their atheism undermine and destroy all religion, can have no pretence of religion whereupon to challenge the privilege of a toleration. As for other practical opinions, though not absolutely free from all error, if they do not tend to establish domination over others, or civil impunity to the Church in which they are taught, there can be no reason why they should not be tolerated."

[21] Jordan, *The Development of Religious Toleration in England,* 17.

[22] Ursula Henriques, *Religious Toleration in England 1787-1833* (London: Routledge and Kegan Paul, 1961), 261-62.

[23] Perry Miller and Thomas H. Johnson, eds., *The Puritans: A Sourcebook of Their Writings* (New York: Harper & Row, 1938), vol. 1, 230.

[24] Ralph Barton Perry, *Puritanism and Democracy* (New York: The Vanguard Press, 1944), 115.

[25] As cited in W. K. Jordan, *The Development of Religious Toleration in England,* 127.

[26] Census figures from the period make note of churches including Congregational, Presbyterian, Anglican, Baptist, Quaker, German Reformed, Lutheran, Dutch Reformed, Methodist, Catholic, Moravian, Congregationalist-Separatist, Dunker, Mennonite, French Protestant, and more. Rossiter, *Seedtime of the Republic,* 38.

[27] Ibid., 36-37.

[28] "Worcestriensis" as reprinted in Charles S. Hyneman and Donald S. Lutz, *American Political Writing during the Founding Era 1760-1805* (Indianapolis: Liberty Press, 1983), vol. 1, 450.

[29] Richard L. Perry, ed., *Sources of Our Liberties* (Chicago: American Bar Foundation, 1978), 312.

[30] Leonard W. Levy, *Jefferson and Civil Liberties: The Darker Side* (Cambridge, Mass.: Harvard University Press, 1963), 4.

[31] Thomas Jefferson, "Notes on the State of Virginia" in *The Portable Thomas Jefferson,* ed. Merrill D. Peterson (New York: Viking Press, 1975), 212.

[32] Saul K. Padover, *The Complete Jefferson* (New York: Duell, Sloan & Pearce, 1943), 945. See also Sidney E. Mead, "Christendom, Enlightenment, and the Revolution" in *Religion and the American Revolution,* ed. Jerald C. Brauer (Philadelphia: Fortress Press, 1976), 48.

[33] On this debate, and the respective roles of both Madison and Jefferson, see Merrill D. Peterson and Robert C. Vaughan, *The Virginia Statute for Religious Freedom: Its Evolution and Consequences in American History* (Cambridge: Cambridge University Press, 1988).

[34] James Madison, "Memorial and Remonstrance" in *James Madison on Religious Liberty,* ed. Robert S. Alley (Buffalo, N.Y.: Prometheus Books, 1985), 56.

[35] Alley, ed., *James Madison on Religious Liberty,* 59.

[36] Harry V. Jaffa, *The American Founding as the Best Regime: The Bonding of Civil and Religious Liberty* (Claremont, Calif.: The Claremont Institute, 1990).

[37] Jordan, *The Development of Religious Toleration in England,* 17.

[38] Franklin Cole, ed., *They Preached Liberty* (Indianapolis: Liberty Press, n/d), 163.

[39] Allen, ed., *George Washington: A Collection,* 548.

[40] Samuel Williams, *The Natural and Civil History of Vermont* (1794) as reprinted in Hyneman and Lutz, *American Political Writing during the Founding Era 1760-1805* vol. 2, 959.

[41] Letter to Edward Livingston of July 10, 1822, in *The Mind of the Founder: Sources of the Political Thought of James Madison,* ed. Marvin Meyers (Hanover: Brandeis University Press, 1981), 341.

3

Are These Truths Now, or Have They Ever Been, Self-Evident?

Harry V. Jaffa

Leszek Kolakowski, professor at the University of Chicago and fellow of All Souls College, Oxford, began the fifteenth annual Jefferson lecture, in Washington, D.C., in April 1986, as follows:

> Consider what is probably the most famous single sentence ever written in the Western hemisphere. "We hold these truths to be self-evident, that all men are created equal, that they are endowed by their Creator with certain unalienable rights, that among these are Life, Liberty, and the Pursuit of Happiness." . . . Immediately, we notice that what seemed self-evident to Thomas Jefferson would appear either patently false or meaningless and superstitious to most great men who keep shaping our political imagination: to Aristotle, Machiavelli, Hobbes, Marx and all his followers, Nietzsche, Weber, and for that matter, to most contemporary political theorists.

I would not speak as confidently as Professor Kolakowski does of how those "great men" would have viewed the central proposition of the Declaration (or, for that matter, of the Gettysburg Address), but Thomas Jefferson, in his unsophisticated innocence, said that in the Declaration, he was placing "before mankind the common sense of the subject," and that what he wrote was an "expression of the American mind." He did not, he said, aim at originality of any kind, but sought to give expression to the "harmonizing sentiments of the day, whether expressed in conversations, in letters, in printed essays or in the elementary books of public right, as Aristotle, Cicero, Locke, Sidney, etc."[1] Aristotle, I might observe, although long known as "The Philosopher," was not a professional philosopher like Professor Kolakowski. And professional philosophers are notoriously incapable of understanding the language of ordinary human beings, above all the language of ordinary citizens, in the way that these human beings and citizens themselves understand it. But Jefferson expressed the convictions of his fellow citizens in language that, although extraordinary in its eloquence, was recognized instantly by them as representing their deepest convictions. These convictions were at once peculiarly and profoundly American, while peculiarly and profoundly representative of a natural law tradition—a belief in objective norms of conduct for both men and nations that lies at the root of everything making our human existence civilized. But this was in the days before professional philosophers or "contemporary political theorists" had mined and sapped the vitality of ordinary language and the common sense moral judgments upon which they, like Aristotle, had once relied.

Just before he died, Jefferson wrote that

> All eyes are opened, or opening, to the rights of man . . . [and to] the palpable truth, that the mass of mankind has not been born with saddles on their backs, nor a favored few, booted and spurred, ready to ride them. . . .[2]

A professional philosopher would, of course, set to work immediately to point out that horses are not born with saddles on their backs either. But Jefferson knew, and his fellow citizens knew, that the aristocrats of Paris on the eve of the French Revolution regarded their peasants in much the same light as human beings in general looked upon horses—as an inferior order in nature whose highest purpose in this world was to serve as beasts of burden to their masters. Jefferson's fellow citizens understood him to say, as we might still understand him once we shake off the miasma of the professional philosophers, that there is no such thing as a natural or divine right of any man or class of human beings to rule others. Legitimate government arises solely from a voluntary agreement embodied in laws binding rulers and ruled by which it is understood that all government exists to secure equally the natural rights of every citizen and the safety and happiness of all. Government is not for the private advantage of any self-anointed individual or class. Republican government, the only form of government intrinsically compatible with the rights of man, is government in which those who live under the law share equally in making the law they live under, and in which those who make the law are equally subject to the laws that they make.

Let me elaborate on the meaning of "all men are created equal," the proposition that Abraham Lincoln called the "father of all moral principle among us," and the "central idea" from which all the minor thoughts of our political tradition radiate. This proposition, although in terms no intelligent human being in 1776 failed to understand, is indeed elliptical. "Man equals man" would be true only because tautological. Much is owing to the word "created," which implies a "Creator," who is mentioned almost immediately. (No doubt this is what leads Professor Kolakowski to think that the sentence would be looked upon as "superstitious" by the cognoscenti.) "Created equal" implies a relationship between man and man as arises from a contemplation, not of man only, but of the whole Creation. In looking at man in the light of the whole Creation, we see him in comparison with what is lower than humankind and with what is higher.

Although the existence of God is certainly implied by the proposition that all men are created equal, it is not necessarily implied. What is necessarily implied is not the Creator, but Creation. In 1776 America, the language of the Bible was the language of the ordinary man. There were sophisticates, as Jefferson knew, who had considered that evolution, or the doctrine of the eternity of the universe, might offer alternative explanations to that of the Bible. To everyone, however, Creation meant the world whose existence is known to us by sense perception, and hence by such common nouns, or universals, as light an darkness, heaven and earth, land and water, the birds of the air, the fish of the sea, and the moving things, the animals, upon the land. Indeed, the world become an object of knowledge, the world accessible to the senses, and from the senses to the mind, was once familiar to most Americans as the world of which they had read in the first chapter of Genesis. To believe that this world actually exists is to believe nothing more than the evidence of our senses. (Professional philosophers, or most of them, at least since Hume, have systematically denied that our senses tell us anything reliable about the external world.) To believe that this same world is the work of the living God may be an act of faith. But for Jefferson and his fellow countrymen there was at least no disagreement that such a world existed. Nor was there any disagreement that the facts of this world, "these truths," held the key to the right ordering of man's moral and political life. In the twenty-sixth verse of the first chapter of Genesis, God said,

> Let us make man in our image, after our likeness, and let them have dominion over the sea, and over the birds of the air, and over the cattle, and over all the earth, and over every creeping thing that creeps upon the earth.

For Jefferson and his contemporaries, there was no question but that the differences in natures, differences inherent in the distinctions the Bible itself draws between man and beast, had implications (as in the Bible) that were no less moral than metaphysical. Man had both power and right to exercise the dominion that the Bible said had been given to him by God. With that power and right went, of course, responsibility. Man might not gratuitously destroy the resources of the lower nature (John Locke said that it would be foolish as well as dishonest to do so), but he might use them prudently for his own ends. There were no ends of the lower nature higher than the ends that they might serve in serving man. But the rule of a man over his horse or dog is by nature. Nature itself marks out which is to be master, and which is to be servant. This, believe it or not, is self-evident.

I recall a debate once with a prominent conservative who denied that the proposition that all men are created equal (or any other nonmathematical proposition) was in truth self-evident. Finally, I asked him, was it not self-evident to him that he was not a dog? His answer was no. To this I responded that, since he did not know that he was not a dog, he might not know that I was not a fire hydrant, and I warned him to keep his distance. I might have added that even if he did not know that he was not a dog, there was no dog living that was so ignorant. In truth, however, we have here an example of someone saying what he could not possibly have believed, unless of course he had become insane. But professional philosophers, and this man suffering from this delusion, make a point of pretending to forget what they actually know to maintain their credentials as professional skeptics. By this they disprove the possibility of philosophy itself as it was before the amateurs of wisdom were replaced by professionals. But such peculiarities should have no weight with normal human beings who can see instantly and without argument that men are really not dogs, or gods.

The equality of man proclaimed by the Declaration of Independence is to be understood first by comparison with the inequality that characterizes man's relationship with the lower orders of living beings. In comparison with this inequality there is nothing more evident, in the familiar words of John Locke, than that no human being is marked out by nature to rule, while others are marked out for subjection. This does not mean that human beings are not distinguished by such important marks as age, beauty, strength, intelligence, or virtue. Nor does it mean that these differences, or some of them, are not important in determining who should rule. But the question of who shall rule becomes relevant only after the recognition that it is the rights of the whole community, and of every member of that community, for whose sake the government is instituted. Who has courage, moderation, justice, and wisdom to best serve the community becomes a question only after the community is formed, and the rule of law enshrined within it. It becomes a question only after there is an agreement, voluntarily entered into, that the right each man has by nature to govern himself will become valuable to him only as he has transferred the exercise of that right to a government. And legitimate government is essentially the by-product of an understanding that henceforth the power of all will defend the right of each. Under the legitimate government of a civil society, every man obeys the law for the reason that in doing so he understands that he is enabling it to defend him, to secure his rights. This so-called social contract is the greatest of all practical applications of the golden rule: "Do unto others as you would have others do unto you."[3] Human virtue or excellence does indeed give some human beings, men or women, the right to hold office, the right to rule. But it is a right that can become valuable only as it is recognized as a right, not to privileges, but to service. It is a right that comes to light by virtue of the prior recognition of the equality of mankind and of the rule of law constructed on it premises.

That the political process by which such recognition is made may be an extremely defective one was recognized by Winston Churchill when he said that "democracy is the very worst form of government, except all those others forms that have been tried. . . ."[4] Its defects reflect the fact that if man is higher than the beasts, he is very far from God (or a god). The idea of God belongs to natural no less than to revealed theology. This idea is formed by reflecting on the resemblances, as well as the differences, between man and beast. Man is a compound of reason and passion. In beasts, instinct controls the mechanism of the passions. Beasts are controlled by reason only when they are controlled by human beings. But man, although possessed by the appetites of the instincts, knows that he has, by reason of his reason, the ability to control and direct instinct and passion alike. And he (that is, except professional philosophers) knows that with his reason he has been given the ability to know good and bad, just and unjust. That his reason is fallible is true; indeed, in nothing so much does man show that he is a rational animal than in recognizing such fallibility.

This fallibility is moreover twofold: first, in the difficulty in knowing amidst the complexity of human affairs what is just or right; second, in doing what is just or right. Knowing what is just or right also is exposed to a twofold difficulty: the one arising from the obscurity that sometimes lies in the subject; the other (and most common) arising, not from the subject, but from the influence of the passions on reason. King David did not see his sin when he seized the wife of Uriah the Hittite and compassed Uriah's death.[5] But when the prophet Nathan presented his own story to him disguised in a parable, he was exceedingly wrathful against the offender. Only then did the prophet tell him who the offender was. Then the king judged his own offense even as God judged it, showing that the faculty of judgment was in him, when his passion did not obscure the truth. It is precisely because the human soul is a compound of reason and passion that human wisdom prescribes the rule of law as fitting the human condition. For the glory of the rule of law is that it enables human reason to take into account the defects of human nature and to transcend those very defects by taking them into account. While human government needs human wisdom in the highest degree, even the wisest men may be subject to that partiality that endangers justice. And even assuming perfect impartiality, just judgments will be questioned by those against who the judgments are given. It is essential to the stability of government that those judgments be given, not as the personal wisdom of the wise, but as the law. Only thus can governments command the confidence of the governed.

The vote of the wise is then always for the rule, not of the wise, but of the law. It is in the making of laws that the highest wisdom of the race is manifested. The meaning of law is to be found, above all, in the understanding of the difference between man and God. It is this difference, the reciprocal so to speak of the difference between man and beast, that completes the meaning of what it is that we hold to be self-evident. For further evidence of its self-evidence to our ancestors, evidence that is as compelling today as it was in 1776, we turn to the good citizens of Malden, Massachusetts, who on May 27, 1776, instructing their representatives in the Continental Congress on a Declaration of Independence, wrote that an American republic

> is the only form of government which we wish to see established; for we can never be willingly subject to any other King than he who, being possessed of infinite wisdom, goodness, and rectitude, is alone fit to possess unlimited power.[6]

The equality of mankind is then to be understood in the light of this twofold inequality: the inequality of man and the lower order of Creation, on the one hand, and the inequality of man and God, on the other. The contemplation of the very differences between man and beast instructs us in what it is that makes man by nature the master of the beast. But the contemplation of these same differences instructs us in man's imperfections. Man's wisdom, goodness, and rectitude are forever limited by the fact that his passions are often at war with his reason, and his self-interest with his goodness and rectitude. Hence it is that no man is good enough, in Lincoln's words, to govern another without his consent.

For consent is the reciprocal of equality. And in the reciprocity of equality and consent we find that ground of morality that Lincoln found in the great proposition. The consent arising from equality ensures, as we said at the outset, that those who live under the law will share in making the law they live under, and that those who make the law must live under the law that they make. Constitutions are devices—inventions of prudence—to carry into practice these principles. But except in the light of these principles, a constitution is an empty vessel that can be a means to any ends whatever. The utopianism that lies at the root of all modern totalitarianism always presupposes the denial or abandonment of human nature and that "great chain of being" within which such nature is discovered. Unfortunately, such abandonment is equally characteristic of present-day conservatism and of present-day liberalism. A wise constitution— such as ours—ceases to be wise the moment it is separated from the principles that give it life. Man is by nature the master of what is below him in the order of Creation. But his ability to govern himself rests on his recognition of what God is, and hence of what he is not. That "all men are created equal" means then that man is neither beast nor God. This is indeed a self-evident truth. It is the ground of our Constitution, as it is the ground of all constitutionalism. It is the supreme justification for the rule of law and, as Abraham Lincoln said, the greatest barrier against despotism ever conceived by the human mind.[7]

NOTES

[1] Letter to Henry Lee (1825), *The Writings of Thomas Jefferson*, ed. Paul L. Ford (New York: G. P. Putnam's Sons, 1899), vol. 10, 343.

[2] Letter to Roger Weightman, June 24, 1826, Ford, ed., vol. 10, 390.

[3] Matt. 7:12.

[4] *The Oxford Dictionary of Quotations,* 3d ed., (Oxford: Oxford University Press, 1979), 150.

[5] 2 Sam. 12:1-13.

[6] Henry Steele Commager, *Documents of American History* (Englewood Cliffs, N. J.: Prentice-Hall, 1973), vol. 1, 97-98.

[7] Roy P. Basler, ed., *The Collected Works of Abraham Lincoln* (Rutgers, N.J.: Rutgers University Press, 1953), vol. 3, 376.

4

The Christian and Rebellion against Authority

Glen E. Thurow

Is it proper for a Christian to rebel against political authority? The American Revolution forced Christians to confront this question. The Declaration of Independence was a decision to disobey the law and constituted authority; but did not Christ advise obedience to rulers, even to Caesar? The decision to revolt against Great Britain was a decision to go to war to defeat and expel the British soldiers; but did not Christ come to bring peace, not war? It was also a decision to take responsibility for, and to dedicated one's energies to, overthrowing one government and instituting a new one; but did not Christ counsel that we be not concerned with the things of this world? And when Christians and their churches chose sides in the momentous conflict, was that not a clear violation of the principle that church and state ought to be separate, one of the central doctrines for which the Revolution was fought?

All of these questions were examined and answered by Christians of the revolutionary generation. Possessed of a Christianity deeply rooted in the Bible, and fearless in their reasoning from its texts, the leading clergy—especially the non-Anglican clergy—gave clear and forceful answers to these questions. They saw rebellion and war against the law and political authority of Geat Britain not only as permissible but, indeed, as a positive duty and requirement for the Christian. Far from believing that Christians should avoid politics or war, or that the proper separation of church and state should lead churches not to take sides, they thought the pulpit should spearhead the cause of American liberty. What was their view of Christianity's relationship to political authority that led them to this resolute conclusion?

The answer to this question is not a mere historical curiosity. Today our circumstances are very different. We are not a colony seeking independence. We are not contemplating a radical alteration in our form of government. Our "lives, liberty, and sacred honor" are not at stake when we take a stand for liberty. Yet the same underlying issues faced by the Christians of the founding generation face Christians in America today. If we do not need to wonder whether we should disobey British law and authority, we still have laws and authorities that sometimes allow or command un-Christian actions and threaten liberty. When ought we as Christians disobey the law or political authority? If the issues agitating our politics are different, we still must consider when to engage in or

forbear from political action. Is the Christian commanded to leave politics to
Caesar? If we are not engaged in a revolutionary war, we still have wars. What
ought to be the Christian response to this warfare?

How often have we heard that it is a violation of the separation of church
and state for Christians to apply their religious principles to political issues? It
has even been suggested that Christian ministers and churches should express no
opinions about any issue of political dispute, even when an issue may touch a
central tenet of Christianity, such as the sanctity of innocent human life. Yet such
was not the view of the very men who fought to bring about the separation of
church and state. For them, there were clear political and moral principles taught
by Christianity which, far from endangering political life, provided the foundation of free government. They thought it the duty of the Christian to bring these
to bear on political life. We have much to learn about obedience to, and rebellion
against, authority from the Christians of the revolutionary and founding period.
These were men and women who were close to the fountainhead of our
democratic liberty. They had to make hard choices and had much to lose. And
they were prepared for those choices because they were steeped both in the Bible
and in the texts of political liberty in a way that few are today. They did not
merely act to defend liberty; they also knew why they were risking all, and were
convinced that they were moved by their love of Christ as well as by their love of
liberty.

By the 1770s, the various political issues faced by Christians in the
revolutionary period coalesced in one decisive question: Was it proper for
Christians to revolt against the law and authority of Great Britain? The
overwhelming answer given by the Puritan, Baptist, and other non-Anglican
clergy was "yes," and their pulpits became a center of revolutionary teaching.
Why were they so certain that revolution was proper? By seeing how they
understood the relationship of Christianity to political authority, we may
understand why they were such enthusiastic supporters and leaders of the
patriots' cause, and better understand how Christians should act politically
today.

The view of the Christians of the revolutionary period can best be seen by
looking at their response to three oft-made arguments about the Christian attitude
toward authority. These contentions were used by those opposing the revolution
to suggest that Christians should not support the move to independence, just as
they are used today to argue that Christians should not carry a Christian view
into politics.

The first contention is that the Christian should be aloof from politics. It is
argued that Christ points us toward higher and more important things than
political action, which is necessarily an arena of sin. According to this view, the
proper object of the Christian is the salvation of one's soul, not the order of
society. After all, Christ in the wilderness rejected the temptation of becoming a
political leader.

The second argument is that it is the duty of the Christian to obey whoever
is in power. Christ said, "Render unto Caesar the things that are Caesar's," thus

advocating obedience in civil matters even to an absolute dictator. How much more, the opponents of the Revolution could say, should one obey the parliamentary monarchy of Great Britain.

The third argument is that resistance to law and political authority inevitably leads to un-Christian acts. Christianity counsels peace, which can only be achieved by obedience to the law. The opponents of rebellion pointed out that resistance to authority meant war. In war force replaces persuasion, and human misery, deceit, and injustice follow.

The revolutionary era Christians rejected all of these arguments. Let us see why.

Christianity and Political Action

Should Christian churches and pastors be concerned with politics, or is such a concern improper because it diverts people from attention to their salvation? In what the historian Bernard Bailyn has called the "most famous sermon preached in pre-Revolutionary America,"[1] Jonathan Mayhew, the great Puritan minister, answered this question by contending not only that Christians may properly be concerned with politics but also that their Christian duty demands it. While acknowledging that there is a "very plain and important sense in which Christ's kingdom is not of this world,"[2] Mayhew argues that one would have to deny the divine origin of Christianity to deny Christians the power to inquire into political subjects. The Bible itself enjoins attention to politics. Recalling that all of Scripture is, in the words of 2 Pet. 3:16, "profitable for doctrine, for reproof, for correction, for instruction in righteousness," he reasoned that those parts of Scripture that "relate to civil government" ought to be examined and explained just as other passages. If obedience to the civil magistrate is a Christian duty, he contends, then it is proper for a minister to examine the "nature, grounds, and extent of it."[3]

Mayhew finds that the Bible does indeed address the issues of politics. Christ's "inspired apostles have . . . laid down some general principles concerning the office of civil rulers, and the duty of subjects, together with the reason and obligation of that duty." Therefore, there is a Christian teaching about such matters, and it is proper for all Christians, and the duty of "Christian magistrates," to examine this doctrine and learn what their religion teaches about the nature and design of political office.[4]

Mayhew derives the Christian's concern with politics from the very fountainhead of Christianity itself. The Bible—indeed, the very center of the Bible found in the teachings of Christ and his apostles—is the source of the Christian's concern for politics. The Christian cannot be faithful to that center of his faith without attempting to understand the political teaching the Scriptures manifestly contain.

Mayhew's view is but the common sense of the matter. For all know that the Bible teaches many things about what is the right or wrong way to act, and that many of these actions may affect, or be affected, by government. All of the great revolutionary era clergy spoke about politics, and all who examined the question thought such speech proper and even required.

If it is difficult for us today to accept this straightforward defense of a Christian's concern with politics, it is because it seems to contradict the separation of church and state. But it only seems so because we have accepted a contemporary misunderstanding of the meaning of this doctrine, forgetting its true significance.

Today the separation of church and state is often taken to mean that religion should have nothing to do with politics. Twentieth-century secularists have invited us to think that the separation of power means that Christians who are good citizens must close their eyes to the biblical teachings about politics when they speak as citizens. No doctrine derived from one's faith can legitimately be put forward in politics, it is said, for such a faith is not shared by all citizens.

This was not the understanding of the revolutionary era clergy. These clergymen thought the separation of church and state a vitally important principle, yet spoke constantly about politics. They agreed that the union of church and state was a central aspect of tyranny. Their fervor against Roman Catholicism, for example, in part rested on their conviction that the Catholic Church violated this principle, combining political and religious authority in the pope. Benjamin Colman, pastor of the Brattle Street Church in Boston, wrote, "It is one evident mark of the Romish imposture, and of the spirit of the Antichrist, that it has invaded, usurp'd upon and subverted the authority of kings and princes. . . ."[5]

But their understanding of the separation of church and state differed from the contemporary secularist opinion in two important respects. First, they did not think that the separation of church and state was a secularist doctrine. Rather, they thought that the Bible itself teaches that church and state ought to be separated. Colman noted that it was an oracle of God, as Paul had written, that there should be civil authority:

> Rom. xiii. 1-5. Let every Soul be subject unto the higher Powers: For there is no Power but of God; the Powers that be are ordained of God: Whosoever therefore resisteth the Power, resisteth the Ordinance of God. Wherefore ye must needs be subject, not only for Wrath (or fear of punishment) but also for Conscience sake. Render therefore unto all their Dues, Tribute to whom Tribute is due, Custom to whom Custom, Fear to whom Fear, and Honour to whom Honour.[6]

Since the separation of church and state was a principle derived from the Bible itself, it could not be interpreted as an anti-Christian doctrine.

Second, they believed that, although politics was not to be governed by church authority, it could not thrive unless suffused with Christian moral teaching. Particular religious groups or sects should not govern political life, nor should government favor some of these over others, but Christian moral teaching should guide political life. Phillips Payson, pastor of a church in Chelsea, in a sermon delivered in 1778 noted the connection between Christian morality and good citizenship and commented, "Hence a people formed upon the morals and principles of the gospel are capacitated to enjoy the highest degree of civil liberty, and will really enjoy it, unless prevented by force or fraud."[7] For this reason government might properly assist the cause of religion in general while not favoring particular denominations. This view was memorably expressed in Washington's Farewell Address: "Of all the dispositions and habits which lead to political prosperity, religion and morality are indispensable supports. In vain would that man claim the tribute of patriotism who should labor to subvert these great pillars of human happiness, these firmest props of the duties of men and citizens."[8]

Those who were instrumental in helping to found our free society saw no contradiction between the separation of church and state and the Christian concern with politics. There are human needs that can only be satisfied through the authority of civil government, and God made man free to establish such authority. To those Christians who thought that they did not owe subjection to any non-Christian prince but only to religious authority, Mayhew replied that this was to mistake the nature of Christ's kingdom. Precisely because Christ's kingdom is not of this world, it does not usurp the authority of civil powers.[9]

But the Bible and good politics also require the Christian to bring his Christian moral principles into the political order. The doctrine of the separation of church and state does not have the object of excluding the moral concerns of religion from politics. Its aim is not to create a wholly secular politics, but to prevent religious as well as political tyranny. To bring Christian moral and political teaching to bear on politics is not to threaten tyranny, the revolutionaries thought, but, on the contrary, to help provide the foundation for free government. This becomes even more clear when one sees what the Christian teaching about politics is, as I shall show in the next section.

Obedience to Rulers

If the Christian is properly concerned as a citizen with the Christian teaching about politics, what is that teaching? Does Christianity teach that we should obey whatever form of government is in power? Does it support monarchy, as many of the opponents of the Revolution thought? What does the Bible teach us about politics?

The clergy of the revolutionary period addressed these issues first by examining the biblical passages that seemed to counsel unlimited submission to government. The way in which they understood these passages can be seen by looking at the interpretation of two of the most famous of these by Samuel West, another leading New England clergyman. In an election day sermon in 1776, West examines 1 Pet. 2:13, 14:

> "Submit yourselves to every ordinance of man,"—or, rather, as the words ought to be rendered from the Greek, submit yourselves to every human creation, or human constitution—"for the Lord's sake, whether it be to the king as supreme, or unto governors, as unto them that are sent by him for the punishment of evil-doers, and for the praise of them that do well."[10]

West interprets this passage (1) by noting exactly what it says, and (2) by looking at its counsel in the light of the reason it gives or implies for this counsel. West notes that the passage specifies that the "magistery is of human creation or appointment." This means that magistrates receive their power from the people and, by implication, are accountable to them. He further notes that the passage indicates the reason for the counsel of submission to the magistrate: the power of the magistrate is designed to punish evildoers and to encourage and honor the virtuous and obedient. Magistrates who act in this manner fulfill the will of God, and, therefore, one ought to submit to them as a divine command. But if they do not do these things, but rather "punish the virtuous and encourage the vicious, we have a right to refuse yielding any submission or obedience to them."[11] 1 Peter teaches that the duty of obedience is conditional upon the magistrate's doing God's work.

Similarly, West's interpretation of Rom. 13:1-6 reaches the same conclusion. Paul says,

> Let every soul be subject to the higher powers; for there is no power but of God. The powers that be are ordained of God. Whosoever therefore resisteth the power, resisteth the ordinance of God; and they that resist shall receive to themselves damnation; for rulers are not a terror to good works, but to the evil.

West notes that neither God nor his apostles appointed a particular family or person to rule over people. Magistrates can be considered ministers of God only insofar as they carry out God's purposes, "the preservation and safety of mankind." Therefore, resistance to magistrates,

> must be criminal only so far forth as they are the ministers of God, i.e., while they act up to the end of their institution, and ceases being criminal when they cease being the ministers of God, i.e., when they act contrary to the general good, and seek to destroy the liberties of the people.

In fact, West goes on to argue that when magistrates cease to do God's will and instead "become a terror to good works," they are

> so far from being the powers that are ordained of God that they become the ministers of the powers of darkness, and it is so far from being a crime to resist them, that in many cases it may be highly criminal in the sight of Heaven to refuse resisting and opposing them to the utmost of our power. . . . [just as we should] oppose and resist the ordinance of Satan.[12]

Not only does the Bible not counsel unlimited submission, but, to the contrary, it supports liberty. In a sermon delivered to a Boston artillery company in 1773, another prominent clergyman, Simeon Howard, examined the Bible's support for liberty. Preaching on Gal. 5:1, "Stand fast therefore in the liberty wherewith Christ hath made us free," Howard identifies the liberty to which Paul refers with the natural liberty given equally to all by God. Although Paul's particular concern was with the restricting effects of Jewish law, his exhortation is generalized to "any other real and valuable liberty which men have a right to." Since men are naturally free by God's decree, just government can only be that government to which men consent.[13]

Liberty, according to Howard, "is a trust committed to us by heaven: we are accountable for the use we make of it. . . ." To allow oneself or others to lose that liberty, to become slaves of another, "is worse than hiding his talent in a napkin." If we are not to suffer the doom of the slothful servant, we "should endeavour to defend our rights and liberties." But since the happiness of others, as well as our own, depends on the defense of liberty, it is not only our right, but also our duty to defend liberty.[14]

Howard's sermon embodies another feature that is characteristic of the way in which the revolutionary era clergy understood the commands of Christ. They did not believe that God created man's reason to mislead him and do the work of the devil. On the contrary, they regarded man's reason to be one of God's great gifts. To use reason was not to undermine God's revelation but to fulfill and confirm it.

Howard's sermon draws out the teaching of reason—a teaching that is succinctly summarized in the Declaration of Independence: Men are born free and, therefore, just government derives from the consent of the governed. "God has given to every one liberty to pursue his own happiness in whatever way, and by whatever means he pleases, without asking the consent or consulting the inclination of any other man, provided he keeps within the bounds of the law of nature." But the need to secure peace gives rise to civil society, so that men living in civil society have their natural liberty but limited by "what they have expressly given up for the good of the whole society."[15]

This teaching of natural reason is the biblical teaching as well, as Howard attempts to show through his interpretation of Galatians. But reason has the same authority as revelation, precisely because it is a gift of God to mankind to be used for its good. As Samuel West states,

> Now, whatever right reason requires as necessary to be done is as much the will and law of God as though it were enjoined us by an immediate revelation from heaven, or commanded in the sacred scriptures.[16]

When Howard finds that revelation and reason agree, he can be more certain that he is interpreting revelation rightly and that he is reasoning well. Near the end of his sermon, Howard concludes that "reason, humanity and religion, all conspire to teach us, that we ought in the best manner we can, to provide for the happiness of posterity." Both nature and heaven's decree support political freedom and happiness.

This conclusion is further bolstered by the fact that bad government harms religion. Political slavery "exposes to many temptations to vice," "debases and weakens the mind," and "creates a dependance upon, and subjection to wicked men, highly prejudicial to virtue." The loss of liberty, he concludes is "soon followed by the loss of all virtue and religion."[17]

To summarize the view of the revolutionary era clergy: The teaching of Christianity is not a teaching of passive submission to those in power. While the need of men for government requires of them obedience to political authority, it does not require an unlimited obedience. When governments become tyrannical, Christians properly rebel.

The Christian and Resistance to Authority

We have already seen that the biblical commands which some have read to counsel unlimited obedience instead were read as counseling obedience only to good rulers. Christians were not compelled to consent to a tyrant's enslavement of them or their posterity. But does not forceful resistance inevitably lead to un-Christian conduct?

In recent American history the most famous answer given to this question was that of Martin Luther King, Jr., who answered that it does. The only proper response of a Christian—indeed of any moral man—according to King was nonviolent resistance: we ought to disobey improper authority but not exercise force in return. Only nonviolent resistance can bring about "the creation of the beloved community," while violence ends only in "tragic bitterness." Through the power of redemptive suffering, love substitutes for hate, a love that seeks "to preserve and create community"—the very goal of the cross and the resurrection.[18] Nonviolent resistance is the proper stance of the Christian.

The answer given by the revolutionary era clergy was very different. They argued that there were circumstances in which force was justified, in which it was indeed the Christian response. Force was understood in some sense to be the last resort, but a resort that was sometimes—perhaps not infrequently—justified, and sometimes even required of the Christian.

These pastors thought that there is a natural desire in all of us to defend our lives and liberty, so that if we are attacked we will be inclined to resist. They also understood that, although creation is good, men have done evil since the time of Cain, and that "the same practice is still to be expected, while human nature continues what it is."[19] This teaching about human nature is confirmed by the Bible, and means that men will often be in a position where our natural inclination to defend ourselves comes into play.

But to defend ourselves in these circumstances is not to return "evil for evil." Although our actions may hurt another, it is an unavoidable hurt if we are to prevent the "mischief he endeavors to do us." Our action hurting another is needed to stop evil, and is, therefore, just. The action of our attacker "proceeds from malice and revenge"; our own "merely from self-love, and a just concern for our own happiness, and argues no ill will against any man." It is evil to unjustly hurt another; but it is righteous to stop evil, even if one has to hurt the evildoer to stop him. War, Howard summarizes succinctly, is "consistent with the spirit of the gospel."[20]

At the level of tactics, the difference between Martin Luther King and the revolutionary era clergy turns on the effectiveness of the two methods. Martin Luther King did not counsel martyrdom; he believed that nonviolent resistance would be a politically effective tactic. His view rests on the contention that the humans confronted will back down because of the compelling appeal a just cause will make to their consciences. In King's circumstances this was not a wholly unreasonable assumption. America was already publicly committed in its most solemn documents to the principle of human equality. To end racial segregation, they needed to be confronted with the disjunction between what they proclaimed and the reality of segregation. A powerful appeal could be made to most people's consciences in these circumstances. But in the Revolution, the situation was very different. One could not appeal to the consciences of Englishmen because they had no such public commitment to the principles underlying the Revolution: they did not believe that all men are created equal or that it was just that America should be independent. Furthermore, England appeared in the shape of armies, not as individual citizens or even as local sheriffs who could be called to account by courts and higher political authorities.

At the level of Christian principle, the revolutionary era clergy also disagreed with King's later view. They did not believe that war meant either that one denied the possibility of the redemption of the souls of Englishmen or that one's own soul would be harmed. One hated the tyranny the English sought to impose, and had to stop them, but to act from this just motive was not to reduce oneself to the level of the oppressor acting from unjust motives.

In fact, they thought that the fight against oppression makes us better human beings and better Christians. Virtues such as courage are cultivated in resisting tyranny by force. To fight in a just cause also displays our confidence in God that he will protect the righteous. To fail to defend ourselves is to erase the law God has written in our hearts. "Providence seems plainly to point to us the expediency, and even necessity, of our considering ourselves as an independent state."[21] Mayhew goes so far as to say that when one tolerates an unreasonable, ambitious, and cruel man to rule, it would "be more rational to suppose that they that did not resist, than that they who did, would receive to themselves damnation."[22]

Since defensive war is justified, when one should strike is simply a matter of prudence. One needs to judge whether one has the means of resisting before making the attempt, on the one hand. On the other, it should be realized that the first incursions on liberty are the easiest to resist, and, if they are allowed to go unchecked, frequently make later incursions harder to resist. In fact, Howard goes so far as to argue that Christians may strike first.

> An innocent people threatened with war are not always obliged to receive the first attack. This may frequently prove fatal, or occasion an irreparable danger. When others have sufficiently manifested an injurious or hostile intention, and persist in it, notwithstanding all the admonition and remonstrance we can make, we may, in order to avoid the blow they are meditating against us, begin the assault.[23]

Not only is such resistance, even taking the initiative, allowed, but it also is positively enjoined upon men. This is because God intends and requires men to be free. Howard notes that men can not properly give up all their liberty to authority. They cannot "give up the liberty of private judgment in matters of religion, or convey to others a right to determine of what religion he shall be, and in what way he shall worship God." Similarly, if a man agreed to let another treat him as a slave, that agreement would be invalid because it "would be inconsistent with that submission which he owes to the authority of God, and his own conscience."[24]

Because failure to resist is contrary to God's wishes, there is a positive injunction upon men to resist. Says West, "It is an indispensable duty, my brethren, which we owe to God and our country, to rouse up and bear ourselves, and, being animated with a noble zeal for the sacred cause of liberty, to defend our lives and fortunes, even to the shedding of the last drop of blood." West is not using hyperbole in calling the cause of liberty "sacred." It is sacred because it is a cause required of us by God. To give up our liberty is to cease to be good Christians and human beings. West calls those who would not join the resistance against oppression "savage beasts."[25]

This right to rebel against authority is not an unlimited right. It is limited in its very nature to those who would defend liberty against tyrants. And liberty is not to be confused with licentiousness. In defining the liberty for which one may fight, Howard notes "that the most desirable liberty, and which we should be ready to defend, is that of a well governed society, which is as essentially different from the licentiousness, which is without law or government, as it is from an absolute subjection to the arbitrary will of another."[26]

This right is also limited by the requirement that the people at large endorse the rebellion. The decision that a government is tyrannical and that rebellion is justified is not to be made by "a few disaffected individuals" but, as Samuel West put it, by the "collective body of the state." "The public is always willing to be rightly informed, and when it has proper matter of conviction laid before it, its judgment is always right."[27]

One should also investigate other possibilities before resorting to force. "He is first to try gentle methods for his safety, to reason with, and persuade the adversary to desist, if there be opportunity for it; or get out of his way, if he can; and if by such means he can prevent the injury, he is to use no other."[28]

Furthermore, Howard argues, only defensive war is justified, even if such a war might require us to act first. And small injuries should be endured rather than resisted with the sword. Even after entering the war, a people ought "to set reasonable bounds to their resentment." Their aim ought to be to repel injury, obtain reparation for damages, and secure their future security. If they wage war to distress their enemies or to reduce them under their power, their war is unjust.[29]

But these are all qualifications—albeit important qualifications—on the basic point: a free people needs to be prepared for war given the inclinations of men to engage in evil. Howard does not flinch from saying that the depravity of human nature obliges men "to keep up the idea of blood and slaughter, and expend their time and treasure to acquire the arts and instruments of death."[30] This spirit of defensive warfare is not contrary to the spirit of Christianity; indeed, they go hand in hand. Men need both the art of war and religion and virtue, and they reinforce one another. For it is religion that best makes men courageous, and that courage is in turn cultivated by warfare.[31] Political and religious liberty go together, and sometimes require that men be willing to fight and die for them.

Conclusion

The revolutionary era clergy taught that the Christian should be obedient to civil authority. God had created the church to assist in man's salvation and guidance; the state to bring about his safety and advance his earthly happiness. These different objects required that church and state be separated. But this separation did not mean that religion had nothing to teach the state or men about the state. God had created man free, and his freedom enabled him to be the master of civil authority. The principles of the Declaration of Independence stemmed from an understanding of what it meant for men to be free with regard to their civil and political lives. These standards were the standards of the Christian religion, as well as the standards of civil society.

Consequently, the obedience of the Christian to government is not unlimited; it is obedience to a properly constituted and acting government. If that government should turn tyrannical, it is equally the duty of the Christian to resist and rebel against that government. In rebelling, the extent of the action taken is a prudential question, to be measured by the strength of one's resources and the strength of the enemy, and to be judged by what is necessary to preserve God's desired freedom for man. When that necessity requires the use of force, it is not only men's right, but it is also their Christian duty, to fight.

In these views we find an alternative to the view of those who would relegate Christianity to a subsidiary place in our politics. They display both the right and the responsibility of Christians to help shape the future of our country, and reveal some of the resources the Christian tradition possesses for directing our political actions.

NOTES

[1] Bernard Bailyn, ed., *Pamphlets of the American Revolution: 1750-1776* (Harvard University Press, Cambridge, Mass., 1965), vol. 1, 204.

[2] Jonathan Mayhew, "A Discourse Concerning Unlimited Submission and Non-Resistance to the Higher Powers" (1750), in *The Pulpit of the American Revolution,* ed. John Wingate Thornton (Boston: Gould and Lincoln, 1860), 53.

[3] Mayhew, *A Discourse,* 47. See also Samuel West, "On the Right to Rebel against Governors" (1776), infra, 125.

[4] Mayhew, *A Discourse,* 53-54.

[5] Benjamin Colman, "Government the Pillar of the Earth" (1730) in *Political Sermons of the American Founding Era: 1730-1805,* ed. Ellis Sandoz (Indianapolis: Liberty Press, 1991), 20.

[6] Colman, "Government the Pillar of the Earth," 21. For a thorough discussion of the importance to true Christianity of the separation of church and state, see Isaac Backus, "An Appeal to the Public for Religious Liberty," in Sandoz, *Political Sermons,* esp. 335-48.

[7] Phillips Payson, "A Sermon Preached before the Honorable Council and the Honorable House of Representatives, of the State of Massachusetts-Bay" (1778) in *The Pulpit of the American Revolution,* ed. John Wingate Thornton (Boston: Gould and Lincoln, 1860), 330.

[8] George Washington, "Farewell Address," (1796), infra, 191.

[9] Mayhew, *A Discourse*, 217.

[10] West, "On the Right to Rebel," infra, 131.

[11] West, "On the Right to Rebel," infra, 131.

[12] West, "On the Right to Rebel," infra, 131-32. This was the common interpretation of Romans xiii among the American clergy. See, among many such statements, that of Elisha Williams in Sandoz, 79-80.

[13] Simeon Howard, "A Sermon Preached to the Ancient and Honorable Artillery Company in Boston," (1773), infra, 99.

[14] Howard, "A Sermon Preached to the Ancient and Honorable Artillery Company in Boston," infra, 111.

[15] Howard, "A Sermon," infra, 101.

[16] West, "On the Right to Rebel," infra, 125.

[17] Howard, "A Sermon," infra, 112.

[18] Martin Luther King, Jr., "Nonviolent Resistance to Evil", in *Negro Protest Thought in the Twentieth Century,* ed. Francis L. Broderick, August Meier (Indianapolis & New York: Bobbs-Merrill, 1965), 264-67.

[19] Howard, "A Sermon," infra, 102.

[20] Howard, "A Sermon," infra, 104-105.

[21] West, "On the Right to Rebel," infra, 144.

[22] Mayhew, 88.

[23] Howard, "A Sermon," infra, 106.

[24] Howard, "A Sermon," infra, 101.

[25] West, "On the Right to Rebel," infra, 143.

[26] Howard, "A Sermon," infra, 116.

[27] West, "On the Right to Rebel," infra, 176. For another statement of this same principle, see that of Samuel Cooke (pastor of the Second Church in Cambridge), in Thornton, *The Pulpit of the American Revolution,* 158-59.

[28] Howard, "A Sermon," infra, 102-3.

[29] Howard, "A Sermon," infra, 106.

[30] Howard, "A Sermon," infra, 108. For one of the most exhaustive defenses of the right to resist tyranny by force of arms, see the sermon "Defensive Arms Vindicated" by Stephen Case in Sandoz, *Political Sermons*, 715-770.

[31] Howard, "A Sermon," infra, 110. See also the statement by William Gordon, pastor of the Third Church in Roxbury, of the great good to be accomplished by victory in the impending war. In Thornton, *The Pulpit of the American Revolution,* 225-26.

5

Civil Rights and Liberties in the Vocabulary of the American Founding

James R. Rogers

Religious sentiment both informs a people's political vocabulary and is informed by their vocabularies. Among other influences, the vocabulary of the American founding was naturally informed by Christian theism. Few dispute that. What this influence was on the development and understanding of American political thought and institutions, however, is a different matter. Sketching a claim to the ongoing importance of that vocabulary in understanding American civil liberties and rights is the concern of this essay.

From the outset this claim needs to be understood for what it is and for what it is not. It is not a claim that most, or even many, of the American founders were theologically orthodox Christians. It is not a claim that they were personally pious men. It is not a claim that they collectively adopted political institutions—such as slavery—that were Christian institutions. It is not a claim that America is a uniquely "chosen" nation.[1] Rather the claim is this: that the founding was constituted within a predominantly Christian vocabulary, and understanding that vocabulary is critical to understanding the sensibleness of American political institutions. And, unlike sterile debates over whether Jefferson was really a deist or merely a naturalistic Christian, this claim matters today. For if true, American political institutions may "make sense" only within such a vocabulary, and its neglect may entail that these institutions are not working as well as they should. Furthermore, if true, not only may Christians be "permitted" to participate in American political discourse, but Christian participation, provided it intelligently reappropriates this vocabulary, may be critical to renewing its successful working.[2]

Nonetheless, it must be acknowledged that the vocabulary of the American founding was also indebted to an intellectual tradition incorporating Greek and Roman thought.[3] Unfortunately, no satisfactory outline of the intersecting contours of Athens and Jerusalem in the American project can be taken up here. Rather, because Aristotle "leaves the question of the content" of human ends "largely open,"[4] it is assumed here, as an empirical and linguistic matter, that this content was significantly filled out in the American context by the assumptions and vocabulary of its predominant theistic religion. Thus, with a nod to the appropriate caveats, this essay refers to a "Christian" vocabulary of the founding.

The argument here revolves around four claims:

1. American civil rights and liberties were understood at the time of the American founding in a vocabulary that drew heavily on classical Christian theism. The vocabulary nested liberty in moral relation to particular understandings of "life" and "happiness."

2. A vocabulary of individual autonomy replaced the older religious vocabulary. This vocabulary understands liberty to imply that the state must be neutral between rival versions of the good. It is reflected in modern constitutional jurisprudence where "liberty" is no longer conceived in relation to other ends, but is conceived as the singular dimension of the American political project.

3. When applied by the judiciary to understand and interpret institutions and practices of a Constitution constructed in the context of the older vocabulary, the vocabulary of autonomy distorts those institutions and practices, and promotes socially dysfunctional outcomes.

4. The founding vocabulary is the natural environment of American constitutional jurisprudence. It represents a largely coherent vocabulary. The vocabulary of individual autonomy is incoherent, generating a distorted jurisprudence. Therefore, a commitment to original public understandings of American rights and liberties should constitute a privileged approach to constitutional interpretation.

The importance of the vocabulary in which liberty is understood is not limited, however, to the judicial realm. While most Americans do not hang onto every word published by the Supreme Court, constitutional jurisprudence does affect popular discourse and practices. First, because law—and particularly constitutional law—expresses and forms the aspirations of a society.[5] The most controversial Supreme Court decisions attract attention precisely because they forbid expression of deeply and widely held public aspirations. But more than simply serving as an outlet for reifying popular sentiment, changing the law changes who we are as a people. This is particularly true for constitutional law in the United States because Americans project constitutional principles aimed at regulating governmental conduct onto generally applicable social conventions stipulating nongovernmental conduct. ("I got rights." "It's a free country.")

Constitutional jurisprudence also has any number of indirect connections to public sentiment. In fact, these indirect connections may be far more important than the direct connections: Individuals may imbibe judicial philosophies without ever having read a judicial opinion because legal rules shape human practices, which, in turn, shape how we think. Even little noticed changes in legal "technicalities" can foster significant changes in social habits and outcomes. Although an example derived from American property law, Alexis de Tocqueville's discussion of the elimination of "primogeniture" comes immediately to mind.[6] The right of primogeniture permitted property to be entailed on only one person in each generation, usually the eldest son. In so doing, it required that estates be kept intact, thus effectively preventing their sale or transfer.[7] Tocqueville pointed out that when estates no longer pass down intact to one child, but are equally divided between all children, even huge family fortunes dissipate within a few generations. The circulation and instability of family wealth and, hence, the absence of great families and what that implies, play a central role in Tocqueville's telling of the story of American democracy—all of which was induced by a technical change in property law. Constitutional jurisprudence forms American culture directly and indirectly. What judges do affects us all, hence, what judges think is important to us all.

Liberty and Happiness in the Founding Vocabulary

This essay traces the changing conceptions of liberty through changes in the vocabulary in which liberty is understood. The argument here is corollary to Alasdair MacIntyre's broader historical argument in *After Virtue*:

> Up to the present in everyday discourse the habit of speaking of moral judgments as true or false persists; but the question of what it is in virtue of which a particular moral judgment is true or false has come to lack any clear answer. That this should be so is perfectly intelligible if the historical hypothesis which I have sketched is true: that moral judgments are linguistic survivals from the practices of classical theism which have lost the context provided by these practices. . . . Moral judgments lose any clear status and the sentences which express them in a parallel way lose any undebatable meaning. Such sentences become available as forms of expression for an emotivist self which lacking the guidance of the context in which they were originally at home has lost its linguistic as well as its practical way in the world.[8]

This short essay traces the implication of MacIntyre's dictum through the lens of one pivotal word of the founding era—"happiness." The change in the public understanding of happiness, and its implications for American notions of liberty, is itself a case study of the historical evolution MacIntyre sketches in movement from a public vocabulary organically linked with substantive religious and moral content to a modern vocabulary in which the same words are used but in which their meaning has collapsed into subjective, emotive expressions.

In the vocabulary of the founding, "happiness"—as in a right to "life, liberty, and the pursuit of happiness"—had an external reference, as well as an emotional reference. Today, Americans are wont to take the Declaration's assertion of a right to pursue happiness simply as a well-wishing appendage to the right to liberty. In the modern reading, the right to pursue happiness means little more than a right to do what makes you feel happy. More sophisticated readers, recalling that John Locke asserted inalienable rights to "life, liberty, and property," may think that Thomas Jefferson did not want baldly to plagiarize Locke and so replaced the affirmation of a right to property with a less materialistic assertion of a right to pursue happiness.

In the vocabulary of the founding, happiness meant much more than emotional joy or enjoyment of property. The argument below is that the term was used in early American political discourse with a generally accepted meaning along the lines of "the enjoyment of good order, both private and public." If true, then founding notions of liberty point to something different from modern notions of individual autonomy, where individuals are thought to choose their own ends and the government is supposed to be neutral between rival notions of the good.

We should start with what is well-known about the well-known phrase. The Declaration asserts that there are "unalienable rights" and that "governments are instituted" to "secure these rights." The Declaration asserts a right not only to liberty, but to life and happiness also.[9] It asserts that the rights to life and happiness are co-equal with the right to liberty: liberty cannot be sacrificed to life or happiness, nor can life or happiness be sacrificed to liberty.

We will return to this point in a moment, but we should not too easily glide over the Declaration's assertion that these rights are *inalienable* rights. Borrowing a word from property law, items that are inalienable are items or rights to property that cannot be transferred. An estate entailed through primogeniture, to take Tocqueville's example again, is an *inalienable* estate: it cannot be permanently sold or given away. Thus, if certain political rights are inalienable, it means that these rights may not be even consensually transferred or disposed of. While one of the Declaration's very familiar statements, the implications of certain rights being "unalienable" are widely unappreciated. Inalienability plays a very practical role in consent theories of government.

In Locke's theory of civil government, for example, evidence need not be adduced that a tyrant holds despotic powers unjustly precisely because no person enjoys the initial right to transfer rights to his own life or liberty. In contrast, if these rights were alienable, then the actual, historical trail of consent and transfer would need to be reviewed prior to any conclusion that a tyrant was wielding despotic powers unjustly. If rights were alienable, then a despot just might hold good title to the lives and property of his subjects. In *The Social Contract*, for example, Rousseau explains:

> If a private citizen, says Grotius, can alienate his liberty and make himself another man's slave, why should not a whole people do the same, and subject themselves to the will of a King? The argument contains a number of ambiguous words which stand in need of explanation. But let us confine our attention to one only— *alienate*. To alienate means to give or to sell.[10]

Locke's theory of political authority does not rest on the premise of human self-ownership, as do modern libertarian theories. Rather, Locke begins with the proposition that God owns humans; we do not have a property right in ourselves. Because God owns each person, no one has the initial authority to transfer—or alienate—certain rights in themselves to another person. Hence, any assertion that despotic power had been arrived at justly, according to this view, is known to be false without any need to investigate the actual history of political consent. This contrasts with modern assertions of self-ownership such as that forwarded by Robert Nozick in *Anarchy, State, and Utopia*.[11] Nozick's doctrine of self-ownership permits people individually to alienate their life and liberty, thus permitting a "just" form of slavery.[12] Tyrannical government *may* justly arise, according to his scheme, depending on the actual history of consent.[13] Nozick asserts *alienable* rights to life and liberty. Locke, and Jefferson, assert *inalienable* rights.

Thus far, the difference between the two views may sound purely academic. But even at this broad level there are implications for modern public policy. For example, policy arguments advancing legal recognition of a "right to die" or statutory permission for "assisted suicide" are based squarely on the idea that human life is an *alienable* right; that one may permissibly consent to end one's own life. Thus, such proposals are explicitly contrary to the articulated ideals of the American founding. But note also that these proposals carry with them wider, philosophical implications. The assumptions inherent in "right to die" proposals are the philosophical postulates of despotism. Their significance is that they strike at the very center of the philosophical commitment of the American project. Because life is an inalienable right in the argument of the founding, there can be no "right to die" found in guarantees of individual liberty.[14]

Just as the inalienable right to life encapsulates the proper domain of American liberty, so does the inalienable right to pursue happiness. Unlike the word "life," however, modern ears are less attuned to the founding era's use of the word "happiness," even though it is sprinkled liberally throughout the political discourses of the era. While not intended to provide a comprehensive survey of its use, the selected texts reproduced in part 2 do provide a sample of how "happiness" was used in the political discourse of the founding. The sample is sufficient to underscore that the term pointed to something much broader and less subjective than emotional pleasure. I now turn to consider several passages.

In his first inaugural address, George Washington asserted that "there is no truth more thoroughly established, than that there exists in the economy and course of nature, an indissoluble union between virtue and happiness." Linking this with divine law, Washington explained that this connection existed because "the propitious smiles of Heaven, can never be expected on a nation that disregards the eternal rules of order and right, which Heaven itself has ordained." Almost eight years later Washington closed his administration by reminding Americans that he deemed "religion and morality" to be "great pillars of human happiness." Echoing the sentiment, the first Congress asserted in the Northwest Ordinance that "religion, morality and knowledge" are "necessary" to "the happiness of mankind."

Washington and Congress asserted a more objective basis for happiness than idiosyncratic emotion—happiness has a common root in submission to God and in the development of mature character. Still, its scope of reference was not limited to the individual but included the link between the well-ordered soul and the well-ordered society. Samuel West spoke directly to the relationship between liberty, individual happiness, and social happiness in his 1776 sermon:

> [I]f we consult our happiness and real good, we can never wish for an unreasonable liberty, viz., a freedom to do evil, which, according to the apostle, is the only thing that the magistrate is to refrain us from. To have a liberty to do whatever is fit, reasonable, or good, is the highest degree of freedom that rational beings can possess. And how honorable a station are those men placed in, by the providence of God, whose business it is to secure to men this rational liberty, and

to promote the happiness and welfare of society, by suppressing vice and immorality, and by honoring and encouraging everything that is honorable, virtuous, and praiseworthy.

Like Washington and the first Congress, West underscored that human happiness is rooted in doing good and that this is the purpose of liberty. He harkened to objective standards of right and wrong in locating this "happiness and real good" for individuals. Political liberty does not include "a freedom to do evil"; it is a liberty afforded to rational beings to pursue "whatever is fit." There is thus no infringement on liberty when the government seeks to promote social happiness by "suppressing vice and immorality."

While some modern Americans are wont to think of vice and immorality as quaint, if not repressive, terms, commentators around the time of the founding point again and again to a linkage between individual virtue and social happiness. Washington cited an obvious example in his Farewell Address when he asked what would happen to the American judicial process if an oath would not suffice to guarantee that a sworn individual told the truth. To be sure, oath breaking evidences a disordered soul, but the ramifications would imperil civil society as well.

In his 1773 sermon, Simeon Howard suggested a similar line of thought, asserting that "civil liberty" does not mean a right to pursue licentiousness, rather "it is a freedom restrained by beneficial laws, and living and dying with public happiness." More generally, Howard argued that laws "requiring the subjects to do things immoral" are "destructive of public happiness." Similarly, Nathaniel Whittaker asserted in his sermon that the wicked "endeavor to destroy the happiness of society."[15] Happiness had both a personal and social reference, and pointed to a relation between the two spheres.

This relationship was assumed in speaking of liberty at the time. Thus, when Howard asserted that, in a state of nature, "God has given to every one liberty to pursue his own happiness in whatever way he pleases," he immediately added, "provided he keeps within the bounds of the law of nature," which "bounds this liberty, forbids all injustice and wickedness, allows no man to injure another in his person or property, or to destroy his own life."[16] Even the state of nature, according to Howard, could not be a "state of licentiousness." Licentious behavior has no right founding in liberty. Nonetheless, liberty played an important role in happiness: Individuals who enjoyed personal and social order, being mature and self-governing, therefore had the privilege and right to order their own lives and that of their community as they saw fit.

Based on this admittedly partial survey,[17] we can nonetheless reach for a more accurate understanding of "happiness" as employed at the time of the American founding. Happiness has at least two dimensions. The first dimension is that of the internal rewards of virtue, or self-governing maturity, which each individual enjoys. This harkens to Christian concepts of blessedness and to Aristotelian notions of *eudaimonia*, meaning something along the lines of being in right relationship within oneself and to the divine. This personal dimension seems to be in primary view when the Declaration asserts that "all men" are endowed by their Creator with the inalienable right to pursue happiness.

The second dimension is that of public happiness. The Declaration seems to have this public domain more in view when it refers to governments being instituted and organized by "the people" in a way "as to them shall seem most likely to effect their safety and happiness." The public dimension of human happiness seems to comprehend—to borrow a phrase from economics—externalities generated by the actions of some people and imposed on third parties. For example, a licentious individual might sow public disorder through theft or assault. The external or public cost of his licentiousness is felt by his innocent victims. To provide a more current example, an individual breaking his marriage vow in seeking divorce may be individually disordered, thus imperiling his personal well-being, but to the extent that his wife requires public support or that his children will not be nurtured in an intact family, his behavior also imperils public happiness by imposing negative social externalities on third parties to the marriage.[18]

Whichever dimension is primarily considered, the conclusion will be much the same: We saw, as with the right to life, that inalienability not only denies a person the right to take another's life arbitrarily, but also denies the right of a person to take his own life. With liberty, inalienability not only denies a person the right to reduce another person to slavery, but also denies that any person has the right himself to consent to despotic rule. So, too, with happiness: Not only is there no right of one person to require that another act licentiously—and so to prevent the pursuit of virtue's felicity—but the inalienability of this right also means that no person has the right to separate himself from this happiness.[19]

Speeches and texts of the time indicate that the new national Constitution was understood to provide concrete legal expression to this relationship between life, liberty, and happiness. In his Thanksgiving Proclamation of 1789, Washington expressly pointed to "the peaceable and rational manner in which we have been enabled to establish constitutions of government for our safety and happiness, and particularly the national one now lately instituted." In asking Washington to make the proclamation, Congress had openly acknowledged that the new Constitution "establish[ed] a form of government for [the people's] safety and happiness." Earlier that year Washington noted in his inaugural address that the new constitutional government was "instituted" by the "people of the United States" for the "essential purposes" of "libert[y] and happiness." These appeals bespeak a common vocabulary linking the public discourse of the founding with the purposes of the Constitution.

The judiciary early on incorporated this vocabulary in interpreting the Constitution. For example, in the "first and leading"[20] federal court case interpreting the Constitution's "privileges and immunities" clause (Art. IV, § 2), the judge wrote that the clause protected only "fundamental" privileges and immunities, meaning those "which belong of right to the citizens of all free governments." The court summarized these "fundamental principles" under these general headings: "protection by the government, with the right to acquire and possess property of every kind, and to pursue and obtain happiness and safety, subject, nevertheless, to such restraints as the government may prescribe for the general good of the whole."[21] Even as late as the 1920s the older vocabulary still echoed in the Supreme Court's constitutional jurisprudence. In *Meyer v. Nebraska* (1923), Justice James McReynold's wrote that "liberty" included the right "generally to enjoy those privileges long recognized at common law as essential to the orderly pursuit of happiness by free men."[22]

Reducing the American project to any one dimension—life, liberty, *or* happiness—effectively ends that project. The genius of the American project is its multidimensional commitment. If life becomes the universe of political ends, then liberty and happiness are endangered by an emergent maternalistic state.[23] If virtue becomes the universe of political ends, then liberty is endangered by a grim, infantalizing moralism.[24] And if liberty becomes the universe of the American project, then licentiousness endangers safety and happiness. Note that the burden of licentiousness takes its toll on society's weakest members—those who do not have the resources to protect themselves from criminal predators and those who do not have the resources to extricate themselves from the consequences of their debauchery. For these, life begins to approach the Hobbesian state of nature in which life is "nasty, brutish, and short." The Declaration commits the American government to preventing that outcome and asserts that "whenever any form of government becomes destructive of these ends"—including safety and happiness— "it is the right of the people to alter or to abolish it."

A Change in the Constitutional Vocabulary of Liberty

We have seen that the founding vocabulary bespoke a notion of civil liberty and rights that afforded the pursuit of individual and public happiness, and that this notion of happiness had substantive moral content. The vocabulary informed the jurisprudence of the time. Change vocabularies and you change jurisprudences. More specifically, change how one understands the particular words of the Constitution and, without changing one word in the Constitution, you change the Constitution. This is what has occurred, particularly as the Supreme Court replaced the vocabulary of the founding with the vocabulary of individual autonomy.

Over the last century of Supreme Court adjudication, many of the Court's most controversial judgments have issued as it rejected the old vocabulary of the founding in favor of a new vocabulary of individual autonomy. The general historical evolution that MacIntyre traces in philosophy could also be traced in American jurisprudence. From First Amendment issues of free speech and religious exercise, to Fourth Amendment search and seizure doctrines, to Fourteenth Amendment doctrines of substantive due process and the liberty guarantee, to nontextual privacy rights, all are now articulated in a vocabulary alien to the "safety and happiness" the founders understood the Constitution to be securing.

No comprehensive review of modern Supreme Court jurisprudence can be attempted here. But, that the modern Court embraces autonomy as a singular virtue in the constitutional jurisprudence of liberty is hardly a novel or controversial claim.[25] Indeed, the Court has been explicit about it. Writing for the Court in the 1992 *Casey* decision, for example, Justices O'Connor, Kennedy, and Souter, in announcing their explicit embrace of substantive due process in the social realm, write that the philosophical backdrop for the "reasoned judgment" they assert in the case is that "choices central to personal dignity and autonomy, are central to the liberty protected by the Fourteenth Amendment."[26] By 1992, "liberty" had long been scrubbed of corresponding ends in life and happiness, rejected in favor of the idea that the state must be neutral between rival versions of the good.

Of course, the founding vocabulary linking the substantive content of happiness to liberty had begun to give way much earlier. Thus, in a 1927 opinion Justice Louis Brandeis averred that the founders "believed liberty to be the secret of happiness."[27] Happiness no longer enjoyed substantive content independent of liberty, rather, in the language of autonomy, happiness became a tautological footnote to liberty. The rich, multidimensional commitment of the founding to life and happiness—as well as liberty—had been flattened to the single, unvariegated dimension of liberty. In understanding liberty, the vocabulary of autonomy had been substituted for the vocabulary of Christian theism.

When it does not ignore the founding, the modern Court does little but sneer at the commitments of the founding and at any jurisprudence that frankly acknowledges the earlier vocabulary. In *Lynch v. Donnelly* (1984), for example, Justice Brennan, in dissent, chastised the majority for what he thought was "a long step backwards to the days when Justice [David] Brewer could arrogantly declare for the Court that 'this is a Christian nation.'"[28] There undoubtedly was some untoward and parochial triumphalism among nineteenth century American Protestants. But as a recognition of fact—that American institutions developed in a public environment freighted with the assumptions and commitments of Christian theism—Justice Brewer's declaration hardly appears arrogant. It need not be triumphalism or arrogance, but simply empirical reflection on the vocabulary of the judiciary and the existing state of the American people that prompted Justice Brewer's statement. The same sentiments could have prompted Justice Joseph Story's 1844 conclusions that "the Christian religion is part of the common law of Pennsylvania" and that the United States is "a Christian nation."[29] Do we doubt what the polls would have shown? Do we doubt that the predominant vocabulary of the time drew heavily on Christian theism?

To be sure, the assertion that the United States was a "Christian nation" cannot be left unexplicated. It does not mean that American institutions have the status of revealed truth; nor does it mean that to be "un-American" is also to be "un-Christian"; nor does it mean that every policy adopted by the nation has been consistent with Christian principles. Rather, it points to a common source of judgment. For example, Americans disagreed violently on the status of slavery. Christians argued on both sides of the dispute. But they shared, in large measure, a common vocabulary; a common standard by which all agreed their beliefs and behavior should be judged. This contrasts with the interminable debates of modern societies which MacIntyre attributes to the working out of the emotivist vocabulary of individual autonomy. What is important about the founding is not, for example, the substantive truth of the childhood fable that George Washington in fact cut down a cherry tree, but that *if* he had cut it down, we all agree that he *should* have told his father the truth of the matter. The common standard of judgment and moral discourse is what matters. To return to the slavery question, Americans object to it as an American institution not only because all slavery is wrong, but also because we believe that the early Americans were not true to the ideals they expressed in founding the nation. Those who share or understand the vocabulary of the founding censure American slavery in the context of that shared vocabulary, not in spite of it.[30]

It should also be underscored that viewing American liberty and rights through the lens of philosophical autonomy does not entail only "liberal" distortion. Indeed, doctrines of substantive due process first arose in the economic realm around the turn of the century by a Court seemingly determined to write doctrines of economic autonomy into the text of the Fourteenth Amendment's liberty guarantee. In those cases the Court drew on a language that understood individuals to be discrete and isolated economic actors engaged solely in arms-length transactions with one another and interacting only in the terms of explicit contract. Attempts by states to regulate these transactions were thus unconstitutional intrusions on individual autonomy. There is, at bottom, little philosophical difference between the vision of individual autonomy that informed the rise of substantive due process in the economic realm in the early 1900s and the vocabulary of individual autonomy that informs the modern Court's doctrines of substantive due process in the social realm.

Modern Constitutional Jurisprudence and the Privileged Vocabulary of the Founding

We have seen, albeit briefly, that liberty did not constitute the single dimension along which the American project was conceived. In the vocabulary of the founding, liberty stood in relationship also to life and happiness, forming a multidimensional American commitment. Within this framework American liberties were conceived and articulated, and American institutions were built. That vocabulary constitutes the natural environment for those liberties and institutions. We have seen, also briefly, that the modern Court has substituted a vocabulary of autonomy for the Christian vocabulary of the American founding. In doing this, the Court has distorted constitutional principles in application to American life. The American judiciary has followed a broader trend in American and Western culture, being neither the primary instigator of this trend nor the least significant reflection of the practical consequence of this trend.

MacIntyre could have been summarizing the philosophical movement in modern constitutional jurisprudence in his summary of the broader political implications of liberal individualism—by which he means a commitment, on either side of the political spectrum, to individual autonomy:

> For liberal individualism a community is simply an arena in which individuals
> each pursue their own self-chosen conception of the good life, and political

institutions exist to provide that degree of order which makes such self-determined activity possible. Government and law are, or ought to be, neutral between rival conceptions of the good life for man, and hence, although it is the task of government to promote law-abidingness, it is on the liberal view no part of the legitimate function of government to inculcate any one moral outlook.[31]

The working out of this ideological commitment to autonomy results in personal and public *un*happiness. Again, our discussion must be more suggestive than comprehensive. Nonetheless, the theme is not new or unknown. Over a century and a half ago, Tocqueville predicted the consequences that might follow if American individualism were permitted fully to work out its logic. His discussion touches on numerous aspects of American life—personal, cultural, and political. He argued that it would alter our relationship to the government, to one another, and within ourselves. In pointing to the rise of "bureaucratic individualism" MacIntyre identified outcomes similar to those Tocqueville predicted, now an accomplished fact, apparently unaware of the Frenchman's prescience. Charles Taylor also identified dislocations in modern understandings of the self issuing from notions of the self's fundamental autonomy.[32]

Along a more public dimension, A. James Reichley, in his study of religion in American public life for the Brookings Institution, concluded that "if left unleashed for an extended time, as some on both the left and the right seem anxious to do, egoism"—his term for philosophical autonomy—"is practically guaranteed to cause social disaster."[33] Conceptions of liberty that are deaf to important conceptions of happiness and life hinder the achievement of public and personal happiness. Theories of autonomy have contributed in most practical ways to very real changes in American culture.

If my sketch of the founding vocabulary of rights and liberties, its replacement by a vocabulary of autonomy, and of the practical outcomes of this replacement are correct, then this also points us toward a positive theory of constitutional originalism. American institutions were created with a certain vocabulary in mind and with certain ends in view. Replacing that vocabulary with the incompatible rival of individual autonomy succeeds only in collapsing the possibility of considering, let alone sustaining, moral judgments in the public square. For better or for worse, when the Court weighs in on questions of liberty and rights, it cannot help but employ a moral vocabulary. The question, therefore, is not whether the Court will bring a philosophical commitment to the Constitution, but *which* commitment it will bring.

The American founders established a Constitution within a public vocabulary richly informed by Christian theism. That vocabulary formed and made sense of the sort of liberty and rights to which the American regime was committed. The broader experiment to replace that vocabulary with the truncated vocabulary of autonomy has not worked. There are no other rivals on the scene.[34] The choice before the Court, and the wider culture, is to continue to initiate substantial constitutional revisions by imposing a defective vocabulary of autonomy on constitutional texts or to privilege the Christian vocabulary of the founding, recognizing that its vocabulary was the environment for this particular set of institutions and is the only one in which they make sense.

A final note: Modern Christians may legitimately recognize that a vocabulary rich with Christian commitments and concepts is not as alien to the American political scene as they may believe. Still, this is not to say that modern Christians can simply pick up where things were left. In addition to facing residual hostility among anti-Christian elites, Christians—particularly evangelical Christians—must face and own up to a century in which their world view was narrowed and crabbed by anti-intellectualism, cultural withdrawal, and a continuing lack of intellectual seriousness. Furthermore, a century or more of revivalism, popular Pelagianism, and the concomitant success of anabaptist ecclesiologies expressing little more than baptized versions of individual autonomy, are serious obstacles to a wider, more serious public engagement on the part of Christians.[35] If the Christian vocabulary of the founding has been ignored, it has as much to do with Christian neglect as it does with secularist exorcism.

NOTES

[1] Mark A. Noll, Nathan O. Hatch, and George Marsden, *The Search for Christian America* (Westchester, Ill.: Crossway Books, 1983), for example, eschew a sensitive treatment of the relationship of Christian theism to American political institutions by reducing the question to superficial issues of Protestant triumphalism and exceptionalism, the heterodoxy of many of the founders, and the imperfection of the political forms they adopted.

[2] Cf., Richard John Neuhaus, *The Naked Public Square* (Grand Rapids: Eerdmans, 1984).

[3] Carl Richard, *The Founders and the Classics: Greece, Rome, and the American Enlightenment* (Cambridge: Harvard University Press, 1994).

[4] Alasdair MacIntyre, *After Virtue*, (2d ed.) (Notre Dame, Ind.: University of Notre Dame Press, 1984), 148.

[5] Robert E. Rodes, Jr., "On Law and Virtue," in *Virtue—Public and Private*, ed. R. J. Neuhaus (Grand Rapids: Eerdmans, 1986). Cf. Susan S. Silbey, "A Sociological Interpretation of the Relationship between Law and Society," in *Law and the Ordering of Our Life Together,* ed. R. J. Neuhaus (Grand Rapids: Eerdmans, 1989).

[6] Alexis de Tocqueville, *Democracy in America,* trans. George Lawrence (New York: Perennial Library, 1988).

[7] Much of the dramatic tension in Jane Austen's novels is motivated by entailed estates and a family's lack of a male heir.

[8] MacIntyre, *After Virtue*, 60.

[9] I drop the "pursuit of" for the sake of economy. Cf. the Declaration's later assertion that governments are instituted "to effect [a people's] safety and happiness."

[10] Jean-Jacques Rousseau, *Social Contract: Essays by Locke, Hume, and Rousseau* (London: Oxford University Press, 1947), 173-74. Thomas Hobbes also asserts alienable rights to life and liberty, *Leviathan* (New York: Macmillian Publishing Co., 1962), 151-58. Cf., the beginning of the Egyptian despotism recorded in Genesis 47, especially verses 20-26.

[11] Robert Nozick, *Anarchy, State, and Utopia* (New York: Basic Books, 1974).

[12] Nozick, *Anarchy, State, and Utopia,* 331.

[13] Although Nozick claims this possibility to be *empirically* unlikely, he does admit it as a logical possibility. Nozick, *Anarchy, State, and Utopia,* 292.

[14] Locke, for example, is explicit on this point: because life is an inalienable right, no person has the right to dispose of his own life through suicide. See, e.g., § 6 and § 135 in Locke's Second Treatise. Peter Laslett, ed., *Two Treatises of Government* (New York: New American Library, 1965).

[15] Cf., West's comments: "This plainly shows that the highest state of liberty subjects us to the law of nature and the government of God."

[16] Many of the references to licentiousness in the appended readings comprehend not simply a general immorality, although some do that, but appear to have as their particular reference attacks on the order of civil society.

[17] For a more general treatment of virtue in the American Republic, see Richard Vetterili and Gary Bryner, *In Search of the Republic* (Totowa, N.J.: Rowman & Littlefield, 1987).

[18] See, e.g., Barbara Dafoe Whitehead, "Dan Quayle was Right," *The Atlantic Monthly* (April 1993): 47-50ff.

[19] Barry Shain has an excellent discussion of these relationships in chapter 5 of *The Myth of American Individualism* (Princeton, N.J.: Princeton University Press, 1994), concluding that: "Liberty as individual autonomy or self-creation was not described, or even hinted at, in these definitions [of liberty]" (163).

[20] This according to Justice Samuel Freeman Miller's majority opinion in the *Slaughter-House Cases,* 16 Wall. (83 U.S.) 36 (1873).

[21] 6 Fed. Cas. No. 3,230, at 551-52 (C.C.E.D. Pa. 1823).

[22] *Meyer v. Nebraska,* 262 U.S. 390 (1923).

[23] Tocqueville, *Democracy in America,* 690-702.

[24] A modern variant is the inquisitional spirit of "political correctness."

[25] See, generally, Gerald Gunther, *Individual Rights in Constitutional Law* (Westbury, N.Y.: Foundation Press, 1991).

[26] *Planned Parenthood of Southeastern Pennsylvania v. Casey,* 505 U.S. 833, 112 S.Ct. 2791 (1992).

[27] 274 U.S. 357 (1927) (concurring).

[28] 465 U.S. 668 (1984), *citing, Church of Holy Trinity v. United States,* 143 U.S. 457 (1892).

[29] *Vidal v. Girard's Executors,* 143 U.S. 126 (1844).

[30] All this is to say that the vocabulary of the founding embraced a vocabulary of "moral realism." For a recent articulation, see, e.g., Ruth Shively, *Compromised Goods* (Madison: University of Wisconsin Press, 1997) (forthcoming).

[31] MacIntyre, *After Virtue,* 195. Justice Oliver Wendell Holmes' dissent in *Lochner v. New York,* 198 U.S. 45 (1905), provides an instructive contrast with the modern Court's jurisprudence of autonomous liberty. He argues that *because* the Constitution "is made for people of fundamentally differing views" that *therefore* courts should refrain from imposing their views on democratic outcomes. This is precisely the opposite conclusion the modern Court reaches from the same premise. For a treatment of the role of democratic prudence in the constitutional scheme, see Gary L. Young, "When Rights Clash: Applying Our Principled and Prudential Constitution," *Regent University Law Review* (Fall 1996, Vol. 7, 61-101).

[32] Charles A. Taylor, *Sources of the Self* (Cambridge: Harvard University Press, 1989).

[33] A. James Reichely, *Religion in American Public Life* (Washington, D.C.: Brooking Institution, 1985), 343.

[34] While many of the founding Americans did attempt to synthesize these traditions, Reichley argues that the classical tradition has piggybacked on Christian theism as an important intellectual source in the American political tradition. He concludes that the "fundamental flaw of secular civil humanism"—his phrase for the classical tradition—"as a basis for democratic values is that it fails to meet the test of intellectual credibility." Op. cit., 348. In a distantly related context, R. R. Reno argues in *The Ordinary Transformed: Karl Rahner and the Christian Vision of Transcendence* (Grand Rapids: Eerdmans, 1995), that the both/and nature of the Christian view of transcendence is necessary to sustain a vocabulary that can discern and judge in the world. Immanentistic theories, as well as radical forms of transcendent thought, are unable to do so. Hence, moral realism must be a distinctly *Christian* moral realism.

[35] I very briefly discuss how theories of individual autonomy have warped modern evangelical theology and practice in my own critical reflections on the Religious Right in "The Necessity of Christendom: Toward a Christian Social Theory," *Common Practice: A Monthly Newsletter on the Church and Society*, vol. 2, no. 1 (November 1993).

Part II: Selected Documents and
Sermons from the Founding Era

6

"A Discourse Concerning Unlimited Submission and Non-Resistance to the Higher Powers"

Jonathan Mayhew

Harvard graduate and Congregationalist minister, Jonathan Mayhew (1720-1766) served the West Church in Boston from his ordination in 1747 until his death. The Discourse *was first published in Boston in 1750.*

. . . Let us now trace the apostle's reasoning in favor of submission to the *higher powers*, a little more particularly and exactly. For by this it will appear, on one hand, how good and conclusive it is, for submission to those rulers who exercise their power in a proper manner: And, on the other, how weak and trifling and unconnected it is, if it be supposed to be meant by the apostle to show the obligation and duty of obedience to tyrannical, oppressive rulers in common with others of a different character.

The apostle enters upon his subject thus—*Let every soul be subject unto the higher powers; for there is no power but of God: the powers that be, are ordained of God.*[*] Here he urges the duty of obedience from this topic of argument, that civil rulers, as they are supposed to fulfill the pleasure of God, are the ordinance of God. But how is this an argument for obedience to such rulers as do not perform the pleasure of God, by doing good; but the pleasure of the devil, by doing evil; and such as are not, therefore, *God's ministers*, but the devil's! *Whosoever, therefore, resisteth the power, resisteth the ordinance of God; and they that resist, shall receive to themselves damnation.* Here the apostle argues, that those who resist a reasonable and just authority, which is agreeable to the will of God, do really resist the will of God himself; and will, therefore, be punished by him. But how does this prove, that those who resist a lawless, unreasonable power, which is contrary to the will of God, do therein resist the will and ordinance of God? Is resisting those who resist God's will, the same thing with resisting God? Or shall those who do so, *receive to themselves*

---

[*] Rom. 13:1—*Ed.*

77

damnation! For rulers are not a terror to good works, but to the evil. Wilt thou then not be afraid of the power? Do that which is good; and thou shalt have praise of the same. For he is the minister of God to thee for good. Here the apostle argues more explicitly than he had before done, for revering, and submitting to, magistracy, from this consideration, that such as really performed the duty of magistrates, would be enemies only to the evil actions of men, and would befriend and encourage the good: and so be a common blessing to society. But how is this an argument, that we must honor, and submit to, such magistrates as are not enemies to the evil actions of men; but to the good: and such as are not a common blessing, but a common curse, to society! *But if thou do that which is evil, be afraid: For he is the minister of God, a revenger, to execute wrath upon him that doth evil.* Here the apostle argues from the nature and end of magistracy, that such as did evil, (and such only) had reason to be afraid of the higher powers; it being part of their office to punish evildoers, no less than to defend and encourage such as do well. But if magistrates are unrighteous; if they are *respecters of persons*; if they are partial in their administration of justice; then those who do well have as much reason to be afraid, as those that do evil: there can be no safety for the good, nor any peculiar ground of terror to the unruly and injurious. So that, in this case, the main end of civil government will be frustrated. And what reason is there for submitting to that government, which does by no means answer the design of government? *Wherefore ye must needs be subject not only for wrath, but also for conscience sake.* Here the apostle argues the duty of a cheerful and conscientious submission to civil government, from the nature and end of magistracy as he had before laid it down, i.e. as the design of it was to punish evildoers, and to support and encourage such as do well; and as it must, if so exercised, be agreeable to the will of God. But how does what he here says, prove the duty of a cheerful and conscientious subjection to those who forfeit the character of rulers? to those who encourage the bad, and discourage the good? The argument here used no more proves it to be a sin to resist such rulers, than it does, to *resist the devil*, that he may *flee from us.* For one is as truly the *minister of God* as the other. *For, for this cause pay you tribute also; for they are God's ministers, attending continually upon this very thing.* Here the apostle argues the duty of paying taxes, from this consideration, that those who perform the duty of rulers, are continually attending upon the public welfare. But how does this argument conclude for paying taxes to such princes as are continually endeavoring to ruin the public? And especially when such payment would facilitate and promote this wicked design! *Render therefore to all their dues; tribute, to whom tribute is due; custom, to whom custom; fear, to whom fear; honor, to whom honor.* Here the apostle sums up what he had been saying concerning the duty of subjects to rulers. And his argument stands thus—"Since magistrates who execute their office well, are common benefactors to society; and may, in that respect, be properly stiled *the ministers and ordinance of God*; and since they are constantly employed in the service of the public; it becomes you to pay them tribute and custom; and to reverence, honor, and submit to, them in the execution of their respective offices." This is apparently good reasoning. But does this argument conclude for the duty of paying tribute, custom, reverence, honor and obedience, to such persons as (although they bear the title of rulers) use all their power to hurt and injure the public? such as are not *God's ministers*, but *satan's*? such as do not take care of, and attend upon, the public interest, but their own, to the ruin of the public? that is, in short, to such as have no natural and just claim at all to tribute, custom, reverence, honor and obedience? It is to be hoped that those who have any regard to the apostle's character as an inspired writer, or even as a man of common understanding, will not represent him as reasoning in such a loose incoherent manner; and drawing conclusions which have not the least relation to his premises. For what can be more absurd than an argument thus framed? "Rulers are, by their office, bound to consult the public welfare and the good of society: therefore you are bound to pay them tribute, to honor, and to submit to them, even when they destroy the public welfare, and are a common pest to society, by acting in direct contradiction to the nature and end of their office."

Thus, upon a careful review of the apostle's reasoning in this passage, it appears that his arguments to enforce submission, are of such a nature, as to conclude only in favor of submission to *such rulers as he himself describes*; i.e., such as rule for the good of society, which is the only end of their institution. Common tyrants, and public oppressors, are not intitled to obedience from their subjects, by virtue of any thing here laid down by the inspired apostle.

I now add, farther, that the apostle's argument is so far from proving it to be the duty of people to obey, and submit to, such rulers as act in contradiction to the public good,[*] and so to the design of their office, that it proves *the direct contrary*. For, please to observe, that if the end of all civil government, be the good of society; if this be the thing that is aimed at in constituting civil rulers; and if the motive and argument for submission to government, be taken from the apparent usefulness of civil authority; it follows, that when no such good end can be answered by submission, there remains no argument or motive to enforce it; if instead of this good end's being brought about by submission, a *contrary end* is brought about, and the ruin and misery of society effected by it, here is a plain and positive reason against submission in all such cases, should they ever happen. And therefore, in such cases, a regard to the public welfare, ought to make us withhold from our rulers, that obedience and subjection which it would, otherwise, be our duty to render to them. If it be our duty, for example, to obey our king, merely for this reason, that he rules for the public welfare, (which is the only argument the apostle makes use of) it follows, by a parity of reason, that when he turns tyrant, and makes his subjects his prey to devour and to destroy, instead of his charge to defend and cherish, we are bound to throw off our allegiance to him, and to resist; and that according to the tenor of the apostle's argument in this passage. Not to discontinue our allegiance, in this case, would be to join with the sovereign in promoting the slavery and misery of that society, the welfare of which, we ourselves, as well as our sovereign, are indispensably

---

[*] This does not intend, their acting so in a few particular instances, which the best of rulers may do through mistake, &c. but their acting so habitually; and in a manner which plainly shows, that they aim at making themselves great, by the ruin of their subjects.

obliged to secure and promote, as far as in us lies. It is true the apostle puts no case of such a tyrannical prince; but by his grounding his argument for submission wholly upon the good of civil society; it is plain he implicitly authorizes, and even requires us to make resistance, whenever this shall be necessary to the public safety and happiness. Let me make use of this easy and familiar *similitude* to illustrate the point in hand—Suppose God requires a family of children, to obey their father and not to resist him; and enforces his command with this argument; that the superintendence and care and authority of a just and kind parent, will contribute to the happiness of the whole family; so that they ought to obey him for their own sakes more than for his: Suppose this parent at length runs distracted, and attempts, in his mad fit, to cut all his children's throats: Now, in this case, is not the reason before assigned, why these children should obey their parent while he continued of a sound mind, namely, *their common good*, a reason equally conclusive for disobeying and resisting him, since he is become delirious, and attempts their ruin? It makes no alteration in the argument, whether this parent, properly speaking, loses his reason; or does, while he retains his understanding, that which is as fatal in its consequences, as any thing he could do, were he really deprived of it. This similitude needs no formal application.

But it ought to be remembered, that if the duty of universal obedience and nonresistance to our king or prince, can be argued from this passage, the same unlimited submission under a republican, or any other form of government; and even to all the subordinate powers in any particular state, can be proved by it as well: which is more than those who alledge it for the mentioned purpose, would be willing should be inferred from it. So that this passage does not answer their purpose; but really overthrows and confutes it. This matter deserves to be more particularly considered.—The advocates for unlimited submission and passive obedience, do, if I mistake not, always speak with reference to kingly or monarchical government, as distinguished from all other forms; and, with reference to submitting to the will of the king, in distinction from all subordinate officers, acting beyond their commission, and the authority which they have received from the crown. It is not pretended that any person besides kings, have a divine right to do what they please, so that no one may resist them, without incurring the guilt of factiousness and rebellion. If any other supreme powers oppress the people, it is generally allowed, that the people may get redress, by resistance, if other methods prove ineffectual. And if any officers in a kingly government, go beyond the limits of that power which they have derived from the crown, (the supposed original source of all power and authority in the state) and attempt, illegally, to take away the properties and lives of their fellow subjects, they may be forcibly resisted, at least till application can be made to the crown. But as to the sovereign himself, he may not be resisted in any case; nor any of his officers, while they confine themselves within the bounds which he has prescribed to them. This is, I think, a true sketch of the principles of those who defend the doctrine of passive obedience and nonresistance. Now there is nothing in Scripture which supports this scheme of political principles. As to the passage under consideration, the apostle here speaks of civil rulers in *general*; of all persons in *common*, vested with authority for the good of society, without any particular reference to one form of government, more than to another; or to the supreme power in any particular state, more than to subordinate powers. The apostle does not concern himself with the different forms of government.* This he supposes left entirely to human prudence and discretion. Now the consequence of this is, that unlimited and passive obedience, is no more enjoined in this passage, under monarchical government; or to the supreme power in any state, than under all other species of government, which answer the end of government; or, to all the subordinate degrees of civil authority, from the highest to the lowest. Those, therefore, who would from this passage infer the guilt of resisting kings, in all cases whatever, though acting ever so contrary to the design of their office, must, if they will be consistent, go much farther, and infer from it the guilt of resistance under all other forms of government; and of resisting *any petty officer* in the state, tho' acting beyond his commission, in the most arbitrary, illegal manner possible. The argument holds equally strong in both cases. All civil rulers, as such, are the *ordinance* and *ministers of God*; and they are all, by the nature of their office, and in their respective spheres and stations, bound to consult the public welfare. With the same reason therefore, that any deny unlimited and passive obedience to be here enjoined under a republic or aristocracy, or any other established form of civil government; or to subordinate powers, acting in an illegal and oppressive manner; (with the same reason) others may deny, that such obedience is enjoined to a king or monarch, or any civil power whatever. For the apostle says nothing that is *peculiar to kings*; what he says, extends equally to *all* other persons whatever, vested with any civil office. They are all, in exactly the same sense, the *ordinance of God*; and the *ministers of God*; and obedience is equally enjoined to be paid to them all. For, as the apostle expresses it, *there is* NO POWER *but of God*: And we are required to *render to* ALL *their* DUES; and not MORE than their DUES. And what these *dues* are, and to *whom* they are to be *rendered*, the apostle *sayeth not*; but leaves to the reason and consciences of men to determine.

---

* The essence of government (I mean *good* government; and this is the *only* government which the apostle treats of in this passage) consists in the *making* and *executing of good laws*—laws attempered to the common felicity of the *governed*. And if this be, *in fact*, done, it is evidently, in it self, a thing of no consequence at all, what the *particular* form of government is;—whether the legislative and executive power be lodged in *one and the same* person, or in different persons;—whether in *one* person, whom we call an *absolute monarch*;—whether in a *few*, so as to constitute an *aristocracy*;—whether in *many*, so as to constitute a *republic*; or whether in *three co-ordinate branches*, in such manner as to make the government *partake* something of *each* of these forms; and to be, at the same time, *essentially different* from them *all*. If the *end* be attained, it is enough. But no form of government seems to be so unlikely to accomplish this *end*, as *absolute monarchy*— Nor is there any one that has so little pretence to a *divine original*, unless it be in this sense, that God *first* introduced it into, and thereby overturned, the common wealth of *Israel*, as a *curse* upon that people for their *folly* and *wickedness*, particularly in *desiring* such a government. (See I *Sam*. viii. chap.) Just so God, before, sent *Quails* amongst them, as a *plague*, and a *curse*, and not as a *blessing*. *Numb*. chap. xi.

Thus it appears, that the common argument, grounded upon this passage, in favor of universal, and passive obedience, really overthrows itself, by proving too much, if it proves any thing at all; namely, that no civil officer is, in any case whatever, to be resisted, though acting in express contradiction to the design of his office; which no man, in his senses, ever did, or can assert.

If we calmly consider the nature of the thing itself, nothing can well be imagined more directly contrary to common sense, than to suppose that *millions* of people should be subjected to the arbitrary, precarious pleasure of *one single man*; (who has *naturally* no superiority over them in point of authority) so that their estates, and every thing that is valuable in life, and even their lives also, shall be absolutely at his disposal, if he happens to be wanton and capricious enough to demand them. What unprejudiced man can think, that God made ALL to be thus subservient to the lawless pleasure and frenzy of ONE, so that it shall always be a sin to resist him! Nothing but the most plain and express revelation from heaven could make a sober impartial man believe such a monstrous, unaccountable doctrine, and, indeed, the thing itself, appears so shocking—so out of all *proportion*, that it may be questioned, whether all the *miracles* that ever were wrought, could make it credible, that this doctrine *really* came from God. At present, there is not the least syllable in Scripture which gives any countenance to it. The hereditary, indefeasible, divine right of kings, and the doctrine of nonresistance which is built upon the supposition of such a right, are altogether as fabulous and chimerical, as transubstantiation; or any of the most absurd reveries of ancient or modern visionaries. These notions are fetched neither from divine revelation, nor human reason; and if they are derived from neither of those sources, it is not much matter from *whence they come, or whither they go.* Only it is a pity that such doctrines should be propagated in society, to raise factions and rebellions, as we see they have, in fact, been both in the *last*, and in the *present*, REIGN.

But then, if unlimited submission and passive obedience to the *higher powers*, in all possible cases, be not a duty, it will be asked, "HOW far are we obliged to submit? If we may innocently disobey and resist in some crises, why not in all? Where shall we stop? What is the measure of our duty? This doctrine tends to the total dissolution of civil government; and to introduce such scenes of wild anarchy and confusion, as are more fatal to society than the worst of tyranny."

After this manner, some men object; and, indeed, this is the most plausible thing that can be said in favor of such an absolute submission as they plead for. But the worst (or rather the best) of it, is, that there is very little strength or solidity in it. For similar difficulties may be raised with respect to almost every duty of natural and revealed religion.—To instance only in two, both of which are near akin, and indeed exactly parallel, to the case before us. It is unquestionably the duty of children to submit to their parents; and of servants, to their masters. But no one asserts, that it is their duty to obey, and submit to them, in all supposable cases; or universally a sin to resist them. Now does this tend to subvert the just authority of parents and masters? Or to introduce confusion and anarchy into private families? No. How then does the same principle tend to unhinge the government of that larger family, the body politic? We know, in general, that children and servants are obliged to obey their parents and masters respectively. We know also, with equal certainty, that they are not obliged to submit to them in all things, without exception; but may, in some cases, reasonably, and therefore innocently, resist them. These principles are acknowledged upon all hands, whatever difficulty there may be in fixing the exact limits of submission. Now there is at least as much difficulty in stating the measure of duty in these two cases, as in the case of rulers and subjects. So that this is really no objection, at least no reasonable one, against resistance to the *higher powers*: Or, if it is one, it will hold equally against resistance in the other cases mentioned.—It is indeed true, that turbulent, vicious-minded men, may take occasion from this principle, that their rulers may, in some cases, be lawfully resisted, to raise factions and disturbances in the state; and to make resistance where resistance is needless, and therefore, sinful. But is it not equally true, that children and servants of turbulent, vicious minds, may take occasion from this principle, that parents and masters may, in some cases be lawfully resisted, to resist when resistance is unnecessary, and therefore, criminal? Is the principle in either case false in itself, merely because it may be abused; and applied to legitimate disobedience and resistance in those instances, to which it ought not to be applied? According to this way of arguing, there will be no true principles in the world; for there are none but what may be wrested and perverted to serve bad purposes, either through the weakness or wickedness of men.*

---

* We may very safely assert these two things in general, without undermining government: One is, That no civil rulers are to be obeyed when they enjoin things that are inconsistent with the commands of God: All such disobedience is lawful and glorious; particularly, if persons refuse to comply with any legal establishment of religion, because it is a gross perversion and corruption (as to doctrine, worship and discipline) of a pure and divine religion, brought from heaven to earth by the Son of God, (the only King and Head of the Christian church) and propagated through the world by his inspired apostles. All commands running counter to the declared will of the supreme legislator of heaven and earth, are null and void: And therefore disobedience to them is a duty, not a crime. —Another thing that may be asserted with equal truth and safety, is, That no government is to be submitted to, at the expense of that which is the sole end of all government,—the common good and safety of society. Because, to submit in this case, if it should ever happen, would evidently be to set up the means as more valuable, and above, the end: than which there cannot be a greater solecism and contradiction. The only reason of the institution of civil government; and the only rational ground of submission to it, is the common safety and utility. If therefore, in any case, the common safety and utility would not be promoted by submission to government, but the contrary, there is no ground or motive for obedience and submission, but, for the contrary.

Whoever considers the nature of civil government must, indeed, be sensible that a great degree of *implicit confidence*, must unavoidably be placed in those that bear rule: this is implied in the very notion of authority's being originally a *trust*, committed by the people, to those who are vested with it, as all just and righteous authority is; all besides, is mere lawless force and usurpation; neither God nor nature, having given any man a right of dominion over any society, independently of that society's approbation, and

A people, really oppressed to a great degree by their sovereign, cannot well be insensible when they are so oppressed. And such a people (if I may allude to an ancient *fable*) have, like the *hesperian* fruit, a DRAGON for their *protector* and *guardian*: Nor would they have any reason to mourn, if some HERCULES should appear to dispatch him—For a nation thus abused to arise unanimously, and to resist their prince, even to the dethroning him, is not criminal; but a reasonable way of indicating their liberties and just rights; it is making use of the means, and the only means, which God has put into their power, for mutual and

---

consent to be governed by him—Now as all men are fallible, it cannot be supposed that the public affairs of any state, should be always administered in the best manner possible, even by persons of the greatest wisdom and integrity. Nor is it sufficient to legitimate disobedience to the *higher powers* that they are not so administered; or that they are, in some instances, very ill-managed; for upon this principle, it is scarcely supposeable that any government at all could be supported, or subsist. Such a principle manifestly tends to the dissolution of government: and to throw all things into confusion and anarchy.—But it is equally evident, upon the other hand, that those in authority may abuse their *trust* and power *to such a degree*, that neither the law of reason, nor of religion, requires, that any obedience or submission should be paid to them: but, on the contrary, that they should be totally *discarded*; and the authority which they were before vested with, transferred to others, who may exercise it more to those good purposes for which it is given.—Nor is this principle, that resistance to the *higher powers*, is, in some extraordinary cases, justifiable, so liable to abuse, as many persons seem to apprehend it. For although there will be always some petulant, querulous men, in every state—men of factious, turbulent and carping dispositions,—glad to lay hold of any trifle to justify and legitimate their caballing against their rulers, and other seditious practices; yet there are, comparatively speaking, but few men of this *contemptible character*. It does not appear but that mankind, in general, have a disposition to be as submissive and passive and tame under government as they ought to be.—Witness a great, if not the greatest, part of the known world, who are now groaning, but not murmuring, under the heavy yoke of tyranny! While those who govern, do it with any tolerable degree of moderation and justice, and, in any good measure act up to their office and character, by being public benefactors; the people will generally be easy and peaceable; and be rather inclined to flatter and adore, than to insult and resist, them. Nor was there ever any *general* complaint against any administration, *which lasted long*, but what there was good reason for. Till people find themselves greatly abused and oppressed by their governors, they are not apt to complain; and whenever they do, in fact, find themselves thus abused and oppressed, they must be stupid not to complain. To say that subjects in general are not proper judges when their governors oppress them, and play the tyrant; and when they defend their rights, administer justice impartially, and promote the public welfare, is as great treason as ever man uttered;—'tis treason,—not against one single man, but the state—against the whole body politic;—'tis treason against mankind;—'tis treason against common sense;—'tis treason against God. And this impious principle lays the foundation for justifying all the tyranny and oppression that ever any prince was guilty of. The people know for what end they set up, and maintain, their governors; and they are the proper judges when they execute their *trust* as they ought to do it;—when their prince exercises an equitable and paternal authority over them;—when from a prince and common father, he exalts himself into a tyrant—when from subjects and children, he degrades them into the class of slaves;—plunders them, makes them his prey, and unnaturally sports himself with their lives and fortunes.

self-defense. And it would be highly criminal in them, not to make use of this means. It would be stupid tameness, and unaccountable folly, for whole nations to suffer *one* unreasonable, ambitious and cruel man, to wanton and riot in their misery. And in such a case it would, of the two, be more rational to suppose, that they that did NOT *resist*, than that they who did, would *receive to themselves damnation*. And,

This naturally brings us to make some reflections upon the resistance which was made about a century since, to that unhappy prince, KING CHARLES I; and upon the ANNIVERSARY of his death. This is a point which I should not have concerned myself about, were it not that *some men* continue to speak of it, even to this day, with a great deal of warmth and zeal; and in such a manner as to undermine all the principles of LIBERTY, whether civil or religious, and to introduce the most abject slavery both in church and state: so that it is become a matter of universal concern.—What I have to offer upon this subject, will be comprised in a short answer to the following *queries*; *viz.*

For what reason the resistance to king *Charles* the *First* was made?

By whom it was made?

Whether this resistance was REBELLION,[*] or not?

How the *Anniversary* of king *Charles's* death came at first to be solemnized as a day of fasting and humiliation?

And lastly,

Why those of the episcopal clergy who are very high in the principles of *ecclesiastical authority*, continue to speak of this unhappy man, as a great SAINT and a MARTYR?

For what reason, then, was the resistance to king *Charles*, made? The general answer to this inquiry is, that it was on account of the *tyranny* and *oppression* of his reign. Not a great while after his accession to the throne, he married a *French Catholic*; and with her seemed to have *wedded* the politics, if not the religion of France, also. For afterwards, during a reign, or rather a tyranny of many years, he governed in a perfectly wild and arbitrary manner, paying no regard to the constitution and the laws of the kingdom, by which the power of the crown was limited; or to the solemn oath which he had taken at his coronation. It would be endless, as well as needless, to give a particular account of all the illegal and despotic measures which he took in his administration;— partly from his own natural lust of power, and partly from the influence of wicked councellors and ministers.—He committed many illustrious members of both houses of parliament to the *tower*, for opposing his arbitrary schemes.—He levied many taxes upon the people without consent of parliament;—and then imprisoned great numbers of the principal merchants and gentry for not paying them.—He erected, or at least revived, several new and arbitrary courts, in which the most unheard-of barbarities were committed with his knowledge and approbation.—He supported that more than fiend, arch-bishop *Laud* and the

---

[*] N.B. I speak of rebellion, treason, saintship, martyrdom, &c. throughout this discourse, only in the *scriptural* and *theological* sense. I know not how the *law* defines them; the study of *that* not being my employment.

clergy of his stamp, in all their church-tyranny and hellish cruelties.—He authorized a book in favor of *sports* upon the *Lord's day*; and several clergymen were persecuted by him and the mentioned *pious* bishop, for not reading it to the people after *divine service.*—When the parliament complained to him of the arbitrary proceedings of his corrupt ministers, he told that *august body*, in a rough, domineering, unprincely manner, that he wondered anyone should be so foolish and insolent as to think that he would part with the meanest of his servants *upon their account.*—He refused to call any parliament at all for the space of twelve years together, during all which time, he governed in an absolute lawless and despotic manner.—He took all opportunities to encourage the *papists*, and to promote them to the highest offices of honor and trust.—He (probably) abetted the horrid massacre in *Ireland*, in which two hundred thousand Protestants were butchered by the Roman Catholics.—He sent a large sum of money, which he has raised by his arbitrary taxes, into *Germany*, to raise foreign troops, in order to force more arbitrary taxes upon his subjects.—He not only by a long series of actions, but also in *plain terms*, asserted an absolute uncontrollable power; saying even in one of his speeches to parliament, that as it was blasphemy to dispute what God might do; so it was sedition in subjects to dispute what the king might do.—Towards the end of his tyranny, he came to the house of commons with an armed force,* and demanded five of its principal members to be delivered up to him—And this was a prelude to that unnatural war which he soon after levied against his own dutiful subjects; whom he was bound by all the laws of honor, humanity, piety, and I might add, of *interest* also, to defend and cherish with a paternal affection—I have only time to hint at these facts in a general way, all which, and many more of the same tenor, may be proved by good authorities: So that the *figurative* language which St. *John* uses concerning the just and beneficent deeds of our blessed Saviour, may be applied to the unrighteous and execrable deeds of this prince, *viz. And there are also many other things which king Charles did, the which, if they should be written every one, I suppose that even the world itself, could not contain the books that should be written.* Now it was on account of king *Charles's* thus assuming a power above the laws, in direct contradiction to his coronation oath, and governing the greatest part of his time, in the most arbitrary oppressive manner; it was upon this account, that that resistance was made to him, which, at length, issued in the loss of his crown, and of *that head* which was unworthy to wear it.

But by whom was this resistance made? Not by a private *junta*;—not by a small seditious *party*;—not by a *few desperadoes*, who, to mend their fortunes, would embroil the state;—but by the LORDS and COMMONS of *England*. It was they that almost unanimously opposed the king's measures for overturning the constitution, and changing that free and happy government into a wretched, absolute monarchy. It was they that when the king was about levying forces against his subjects, in order to make himself absolute, commissioned officers,

---

* Historians are not agreed what number of soldiers attended him in this monstrous invasion of the privileges of parliament. Some say 300, some 400: And the author of *The History of the Kings of Scotland*, says 500.

and raised an army to defend themselves and the public: And it was they that maintained the war against him all along, till he was made a prisoner. This is indisputable. Though it was not properly speaking the parliament, but the army, which put him to death afterwards. And it ought to be freely acknowledged, that most of their proceeding, in order to get this matter effected; and particularly the court by which the king was at last tried and condemned, was little better than a mere mockery of justice.—

The next question which naturally arises, is, whether this resistance which was made to the king *by the parliament*, was properly *rebellion*, or not? The answer to which is plain, that it was not; but a most righteous and glorious stand, made in defense of the natural and legal rights of the people, against the unnatural and illegal encroachments of arbitrary power. Nor was this a rash and too sudden opposition. The nation had been patient under the oppressions of the crown, even to *long suffering*;—for a course of many years; and there was no rational hope of redress in any other way—Resistance was absolutely necessary in order to preserve the nation from slavery, misery and ruin. And who so proper to make this resistance as the lords and commons;—the whole representative body of the people:—guardians of the public welfare; and each of which was, in point of legislation, vested with an equal, co-ordinate power, with that of the crown? * Here were *two* branches of the legislature against *one*;—two, which had

---

* The *English* constitution is originally and essentially *free*. The character which *J. Caesar* and *Tacitus* both give of the ancient Britons so long ago, is, That they were extremely *jealous of their liberties*, as well as a people of a *martial* spirit. Nor have there been wanting frequent instances and proofs of the same glorious spirit (in both respects) remaining in their posterity ever since,—in the struggles they have made for liberty, both against foreign and domestic tyrants.—Their kings hold their title to the throne solely by grant of parliament; i.e. in other words, by the voluntary consent of the people. And, agreeably hereto, the prerogative and rights of the crown are stated, defined and limited by law; and that as truly and strictly as the rights of any inferior officer in the state; or indeed, of any private subject. And it is only in this respect that it can be said, that "the king can do no wrong." Being restrained by the law, he cannot, while he confines himself within those just limits which the law prescribes to him as the measure of his authority, injure and oppress the subject.—The king in his coronation oath, swears to exercise only such a power as the constitution gives him. And the subject, in the oath of allegiance, swears only to obey him in the exercise of such a power. The king is as much bound by his oath, not to infringe the legal rights of the people, as the people are bound to yield subjection to him. From whence it follows, that as soon as the prince sets himself up above law, he loses the king in the tyrant: he does to all intents and purposes, unking himself, by acting out of, and beyond, that sphere which the constitution allows him to move in. And in such cases, he has no more right to be obeyed, than any inferior officer who acts beyond his commission. The subjects' obligation to allegiance then ceases of course: and to resist him is no more *rebellion*, than to resist any foreign invader. There is an essential difference betwixt *government and tyranny*; at least under such a constitution as the *English*. The former consists in ruling according to law and equity; the latter, in ruling contrary to law and equity. So also, there is an essential difference betwixt resisting a tyrant, and rebellion; The former is a just and reasonable self-defense; the latter consists in resisting a prince whose administration is just and legal; and this is what

law and equity and the constitution on their side, against one which was impiously attempting to overturn law and equity and the constitution; and to exercise a wanton licentious *sovereignty* over the properties, consciences and lives of all the people:—Such a *sovereignty* as some inconsiderately ascribe to the supreme Governor of the world.—I say, inconsiderately; because God himself does not govern in an absolutely arbitrary and despotic manner. The power of this Almighty King (I speak it not without caution and reverence; the power of this Almighty King) is *limited by law*; not, indeed, by *acts of parliament*, but by the eternal *laws* of truth, wisdom and equity; and the everlasting *tables* of right reason;—tables that cannot be *repealed*, or *thrown down* and *broken* like those of *Moses*.—But king *Charles* sat himself up above all these, as much as he did above the written laws of the realm; and made mere humor and caprice, which are no rule at all, the only rule and measure of his administration. And now, is it not perfectly ridiculous to call resistance to such a tyrant, by the name of *rebellion?—the grand rebellion*? Even that—parliament, which brought king *Charles* II to the throne, and which run *loyally mad*, severely reproved one of their own members for condemning the proceedings of that parliament which first took up arms against the former king. And upon the same principles that the proceedings of this parliament may be censured as wicked and rebellious, the proceedings of those who, since, opposed King *James* II, and brought the prince of *Orange* to the throne, may be censured as wicked and rebellious also. The cases are parallel.—But whatever *some* men may *think*, it is to be hoped that, for their own sakes, they will not dare to *speak* against the REVOLUTION, upon the justice and legality of which depends (in part) his present MAJESTY'S right to the throne.

    If it be said, that although the parliament which first opposed king *Charles's* measures, and at length took up arms against him, were not guilty of rebellion; yet certainly those persons were, who condemned, and put him to death: even this perhaps is not true. For he had, in fact, *unkinged* himself long before, and had forfeited his title to the allegiance of the people. So that those who put him to death, were, at most only guilty of *murder*; which, indeed, is bad enough, if they were really guilty of *that*; (which is at least disputable.) *Cromwell*, and those who were principally concerned in the (*nominal*) king's death, might possibly have been very wicked and designing men. Nor shall I say any thing in vindication of the reigning *hypocrisy* of those times; or of *Cromwell's* mal-administration during the *interregnum*: (for it is *truth*, and not a *party*, that I am speaking for.) But still it may be said, that *Cromwell* and his adherents were not, properly speaking, guilty of *rebellion*; because he, whom they beheaded was not, properly speaking, *their king*; but a *lawless tyrant.*—much less, are the whole

---

denominates it a crime. Now it is evident, that king *Charles's* government was illegal, and very oppresive, through the greatest part of his reign: And, therefore, to resist him, was no more rebellion, than to oppose any foreign invader, or any other domestic oppressor.

body of the nation at that time to be charged with rebellion on that account; for it was no *national act*; it was not done by a *free* parliament. And much less still, is the nation at present, to be charged with the great sin of rebellion, for what their *ancestors* did, (or rather did NOT) a century ago.

But how came the *anniversary* of king *Charles's* death, to be solemnized as a day of fasting and humiliation? The true answer in brief, to which inquiry, is, that this fast was instituted by way of *court* and *complement* to king *Charles* II, upon the *restoration*. All were desirous of making their court to him: of ingratiating themselves; and of making him forget what had been done in opposition to his *father*, so as not to revenge it. To effect this, they ran into the most extravagant professions of affection and loyalty to him, insomuch that he himself said, that it was a *mad* and *hair brain'd loyalty* which they professed. And amongst other strange things, which his first parliament did, they ordered the *Thirtieth* of *January* (the day on which his father was beheaded) to be kept as a day of solemn humiliation, to deprecate the judgments of heaven for the rebellion which the nation had been guilty of, in that which was no national thing; and which was not rebellion in them that did it—Thus they soothed and flattered their new king, at the expense of their liberties:—And were ready to yield up freely to *Charles* II, all that enormous power, which they had justly resisted *Charles* I, for usurping to himself.

The last query mentioned, was, Why those of the *Episcopal clergy* who are very high in the principles of *ecclesiastical authority*, continue to speak of this unhappy prince as a *great Saint* and a *Martyr*? This, we know, is what they constantly do, especially upon the 30th of *January*;—a day sacred to the *extolling* of *him*, and to the *reproaching* of those who are not of the *established church. Out of the same mouth* on this day, *proceedeth blessing and cursing; there with bless they their God, even* Charles, *and therewith curse they* the dissenters: And their *tongue can no man tame; it is an unruly evil, full of deadly poison*. King *Charles* is, upon this solemnity, frequently compared to our Lord Jesus Christ, both in respect of the holiness of his life, and the greatness and injustice of his *sufferings*; and it is a wonder they do not add something concerning the *merits* of his death also—But *blessed Saint* and *royal martyr*, are as humble titles as any that are thought worthy of him.

Now this may, at first view, well appear to be a very strange *phenomenon*. For king *Charles* was really a man black with guilt and *laden with iniquity*, as appears by his crimes before mentioned. He lived a tyrant; and it was the oppression and violence of his reign, that brought him to his untimely and violent end at last. Now what of saintship or martyrdom is there in all this! What of saintship is there in encouraging people to profane the Lord's Day? What of saintship in falsehood and perjury? What of saintship in repeated robberies and patriots, into gaols? What of saintship in overturning an excellent civil constitution:—and proudly grasping at an illegal and monstrous power? What of saintship in the murder of thousands of innocent people: and involving a nation in all the calamities of a civil war? And what of martyrdom is there, in a man's bringing an immature and violent death upon himself, by being wicked overmuch? Is there any such thing as grace, without goodness! As being a follower of Christ, without following him? As being his disciple, without learning of him to be just and beneficent? Or, as saintship without sanctity? If not, I fear it will be hard to prove this man a saint. And verily one would be apt to suspect that that church must be but poorly stocked with saints and martyrs, which is forced to adopt such enormous sinners into her calendar, in order to swell the number.

But to unravel this *mystery* of (*nonsense* as well as of) *iniquity*, which has *already worked* for a *long time* amongst us; or, at least, to give the most probable solution of it; it is to be remembered, that king *Charles*, this *burlesque* upon saintship and martyrdom, though so great an oppressor, was a true friend to the *Church*; so true a friend to her, that he was very well affected towards the *Roman Catholics*; and would, probably, have been very willing to unite *Lambeth* and *Rome*. This appears by his marrying a true daughter of that true *mother of harlots*; which he did with a dispensation from the Pope, that supreme BISHOP; to whom when he wrote he gave the title of MOST HOLY FATHER. His queen was extremely bigoted to all the follies and superstitions, and to the *hierarchy*, of *Rome*; and had a prodigious ascendancy over him all his life. It was, in part, owing to this, that he (probably) abetted the massacre of the protestants in *Ireland*; that he assisted in extirpating the *French* protestants at *Rochelle*; that he all along encouraged *papist*, and popishly effected *clergymen*, in preference to all other persons, and that he upheld that monster of wickedness, ARCH-BISHOP LAUD, and the bishops of his stamp; in all their church-tyranny and diabolical cruelties. In return to his kindness and indulgence in which respects, they caused many of the pulpits throughout the nation, to ring with the divine absolute, indefeasible right of kings; with the praises of Charles and his reign; and with the damnable sin of resisting the Lord's anointed, let him do what he would. So that not Christ, but Charles, was commonly preached to the people.— In *plain English*, there seems to have been an impious bargain struck up betwixt the *scepter* and the *surplice,* for enslaving both the *bodies* and *souls* of men. The king appeared to be willing that the clergy should do what they would,—set up a monstrous hierarchy like that of Rome—a monstrous inquisition like that of Spain or Portugal,—or any thing else which their own pride, and the devil's malice, could prompt them to: *Provided always*, that the clergy would be tools to the crown; that they would make the people believe, that kings had God's authority for breaking God's law; that they had a commission from heaven to seize the estates and lives of their subjects at pleasure; and that it was a damnable sin to resist them, even when they did such things as deserved more than damnation.—This appears to be the true key for explaining the *mysterious* doctrine of king *Charles's* saintship and martyrdom. He was a saint, not because he was in his life, a good *man*, but a good *churchman*; not because he was a lover of *holiness*, but the *hierarchy*; not because he was a friend to *Christ*, but the *Craft*. And he was a martyr in his death, not because he bravely suffered death in the cause of truth and righteousness, but because he died an enemy to liberty and the rights of conscience; i.e. not because he died an enemy to *sin,* but *dissenters.* For these reasons it is that all bigoted clergymen, and friends to church-power, paint this man as a saint in his life, though he was such a mighty, such a *royal sinner*; and as a martyr in his death, though he fell a sacrifice only to his own ambition, avarice, and unbounded lust of power. And from prostituting their praise upon king *Charles*, and offering him that incense which is not his due, it is natural for them to make a transition to the dissenters, (as they commonly do) and to load them with that reproach which they do not deserve; they being generally professed enemies both to civil and ecclesiastical tyranny. WE are commonly charged (upon the *Thirtieth of January*) with the guilt of putting the king to death, under a notion that it was our ancestors that did it; and so we are represented in the blackest colors, not only as scismaticks, but also as traitors and rebels and all that is bad. And these *lofty* gentlemen usually rail upon this head, in such a manner as plainly shows, that they are either grossly ignorant of the history of those times which they speak of; or, which is worse, that they are guilty of the most shameful prevarication, slander and falsehood.—But every *petty priest*, with a *roll* and a *gown,* thinks he must do something in imitation of his betters, in lawn, and show himself a true son of the church: And thus, through a foolish ambition to appear *considerable*, they only render themselves *contemptible.*

But suppose *our* fore-fathers did kill their *mock* saint and martyr a century ago, what is that to *us* now? If I mistake not, these gentlemen generally preach down the doctrine of the *imputation of Adam's sin to his posterity*, as absurd and unreasonable, notwithstanding they have solemnly subscribed what is equivalent to it in *their own articles of religion.* And therefore one would hardly expect that they would lay the guilt of the king's death upon US, altho' *our fore-fathers* had been the only authors of it. But this conduct is much more surprising, when it does not appear that *our* ancestors had any more hand in it than *their own.*— However, bigotry is sufficient to account for this, and many other *phenomena,* which cannot be accounted for in any other way.

Although the observation of this *anniversary* seems to have been (at least) superstitious in its *original*; and although it is often abused to very bad purposes by the established clergy, as they serve themselves of it, to perpetuate strife, a party spirit, and divisions in the Christian church; yet it is to be hoped that one good end will be answered by it, quite contrary to their intention: It is to be hoped that it will prove a standing *memento*, that *Britons* will not be *slaves*; and a warning to all corrupt *councellors* and *ministers*, not to go too far in advising to arbitrary, despotic measures—

To conclude: Let us all learn to be *free*, and to be *loyal*. Let us not profess ourselves vassals to the lawless pleasure of any man on earth. But let us remember, at the same time, government is *sacred*, and not to be *trifled* with. It is our happiness to live under the government of a PRINCE who is satisfied with ruling according to law; as every other *good prince* will—We enjoy under his administration all the liberty that is proper and expedient for us. It becomes us, therefore, to be contented, and dutiful subjects. Let us prize our freedom; but not *use our liberty for a cloak of maliciousness.* There are men who strike at *liberty* under the term *licentiousness*. There are others who aim at *popularity* under the disguise of *patriotism.* Be aware of both. *Extremes* are dangerous. There is at present amongst *us*, perhaps, more danger of the *latter*, than of the *former*. For which reason I would exhort you to pay all due Regard to the government over us; to the KING and all in authority; and to *lead a quiet and peaceable life.*— And while I am speaking of loyalty to our *earthly Prince,* suffer me just to put you in mind to be loyal also to the supreme RULER of the universe, *by whom kings reign, and princes decree justice.* To which king eternal immortal, invisible, even to the ONLY WISE GOD, be all honor and praise, DOMINION and thanksgiving, through JESUS CHRIST our LORD. AMEN.

7

"The Curse of Cowardice"

Samuel Davies

A renowned Virginia orator and educator, Samuel Davies preached this sermon to the militia of Hanover County, Virginia, on May 8, 1758, as that body sought new recruits for the war against French and Indian forces. Following are excerpts from that sermon.

Cursed be he that doth the Work of the Lord deceitfully; and cursed be he that keepeth back his Sword from Blood. Jer. 48:10

Nothing can be more agreeable to the God of Peace than to see universal harmony and benevolence prevail among His creatures; and He has laid them under the strongest obligations to cultivate a pacific temper toward one another, both as individuals and as nations. "Follow peace with all men," is one of the principal precepts of our holy religion. And the great Prince of Peace has solemnly pronounced, "Blessed are the peacemakers."

But when, in this corrupt, disordered state of things, where the lusts of men are perpetually embroiling the world with wars and fightings and throwing all into confusion; when ambition and avarice would rob us of our property, for which we have toiled and on which we subsist; when they would enslave the freeborn mind and compel us meanly to cringe to usurpation and arbitrary power; when they would tear from our eager grasp the most valuable blessing of Heaven, I mean our *religion*; when they invade our country, formerly the region of tranquillity, ravage our frontiers, butcher our fellow subjects, or confine them in a barbarous captivity in the dens of savages; when our earthly all is ready to be seized by rapacious hands, and even our eternal all is in danger by the loss of our religion; when this is the case, what is then the will of God?

Must peace then be maintained? Maintained with our perfidious and cruel invaders? Maintained at the expense of property, liberty, life, and everything dear and valuable? Maintained, when it is in our power to vindicate our right and do ourselves justice? Is the work of peace then our only business? No; in such a time even the God of Peace proclaims by His providence, "To arms!"

Then the sword is, as it were, consecrated to God; and the art of war becomes a part of our religion. Then happy is he that shall reward our enemies, as they have served us. Blessed is the brave soldier; blessed is the defender of his country and the destroyer of its enemies. Blessed are they who offer themselves willingly in this service, and who faithfully discharge it. But, on the other hand, "Cursed is he that doth the work of the Lord deceitfully; and cursed is he that keepeth back his sword from blood." . . .

"Cursed be he that keepeth back his sword from blood." This denunciation, like the artillery of heaven, is leveled against the mean, sneaking coward who, when God, in the course of His providence, calls him to arms, refuses to obey and consults his own ease and safety more than his duty to God and his country.

"Cursed be he that doth the work of the Lord deceitfully." This seems leveled against another species of cowards—sly, hypocritical cowards who undertake the work of the Lord, that is, take up arms; but they do the work of the Lord *deceitfully*, that is, they do not faithfully use their arms for the purposes they were taken. They commence soldiers, not that they may serve their country and do their duty to God but that they may live in ease, idleness, and pleasure, and enrich themselves at the public expense. "Cursed be he that doth the work of the Lord deceitfully," and serves himself under pretense of serving his country.

Need I inform you what barbarities and depredations a mongrel race of Indian savages and French Papists have perpetrated upon our frontiers? How many deserted or demolished houses and plantations! How wide an extent of country abandoned! How many poor families obliged to fly in consternation and leave their all behind them! What breaches and separations between the nearest relations! What painful ruptures of heart from heart! What shocking dispersions of those once united by the strongest and most endearing ties!

Some lie dead, mangled with savage wounds, consumed to ashes with outrageous flames, or torn and devoured by the beasts of the wilderness, while their bones lie whitening in the sun and serve as tragical memorials of the fatal spot where they fell. Others have been dragged away captives and made the slaves of imperious and cruel savages. Others have made their escape and live to lament their butchered or captivated friends and relations. In short, our frontiers have been drenched with the blood of our fellow subjects, through the length of a thousand miles; and new wounds are still opening.

We, in these inland parts of the country, are as yet unmolested, through the unmerited mercy of Heaven. But let us glance a thought to the western extremities of our body politic; and what melancholy scenes open to our view! Now, perhaps, while I am speaking; now, while you are secure and unmolested, our fellow subjects there may be feeling the Calamities I am describing. Now, perhaps, the savage shouts and whoops of Indians, and the screams and groans of some butchered family, may be mingling their horrors and circulating their horrendous echoes through the wilderness of rocks and mountains. Now, perhaps, some tender, delicate creature may be suffering an involuntary prostitution to savage lust; and perhaps debauched and murdered by the same hand. Now, perhaps, some miserable Briton or Virginian may be passing through a tedious process of experiments in the infernal art of torture. Now, some helpless children may be torn from the arms of their murdered parents and dragged away weeping and wringing their hands, to receive their education among barbarians and to be formed upon the model of a ferocious Indian soul.

And will these violences cease without a vigorous and timely resistance from us? Can Indian revenge and thirst for blood be glutted? Or can French ambition and avarice be satisfied? No, we have no method left but to repel force with force, and to give them blood to drink in their turn who have drunk ours. If we sit still and do nothing, or content ourselves, as alas we have hitherto, with feeble, dilatory efforts, we may expect these barbarities will not only continue but that the Indians, headed by the French, those eternal enemies of peace, liberty, and Britons, will carry their inroads still farther into the country and reach even to us.

By the desertion of our remote settlements, the frontiers are approaching every day nearer and nearer to us; and if we cannot stand our ground now, when we have above 100 miles of a thick-settled country between us and the enemy, much less shall we be able when our strength is weakened by so vast a loss of men, arms, and riches, and we lie exposed to their immediate incursions. Some cry, "Let the enemy come down to us, and then we will fight them." But this is the trifling excuse of cowardice or security, and not the language of prudence and fortitude. Those who make this plea, if the enemy should take them at their word and make them so near a visit, would be as forward in flight as they are now backward to take up arms.

Such, my brethren, such, alas! is the present state of our country. It bleeds in a thousand veins; and, without a timely remedy, the wound will prove mortal. And, in such circumstances, is it not our duty, in the sight of God, is it not a work to which the Lord loudly calls us, to take up arms for the defense of our country? . . .

Our countrymen, in general, have acted as if beings of their importance and merit might certainly rest in the quiet, unmolested possession of their liberty and property without anyone daring to disturb them, and without their doing anything for their own defense; or as if neither God nor man could strip them of their enjoyments. What vain, self-confident presumption, what intolerable insolence is this, in a sinful nation, a people laden with iniquity, who have forfeited every blessing, even the ground they tread upon and the air they breathe in, and who live merely by the unmerited grace and bounty of God?

Is not cowardice and security, or an unwillingness to engage with all our might in the defense of our country, in such a situation an enormous wickedness in the sight of God and worthy of His curse, as well as a scandalous, dastardly meanness in the sight of men, and worthy of public shame and indignation? Is it not fit that those who so contemptuously depreciate the rich and undeserved bounties of Heaven, and who swell so insolently with a vain conceit of their own importance and worth, should be punished with the loss of these blessings? . . .

Ye young and hardy men, whose very faces seem to speak that God and nature formed you for soldiers, who are free from the encumbrance of families depending upon you for subsistence, and who are perhaps but of little service to society while at home, may I not speak for you and declare as your mouth, "Here we are, all ready to abandon our ease and rush into the glorious dangers of the field, in defense of our country"? Ye that love your country, enlist; for honor will follow you in life or death in such a cause. You that love your religion, enlist; for your religion is in danger. Can Protestant Christianity expect quarters from heathen savages and French Papists? Sure in such an alliance, the power of hell make a third party. Ye that love your friends and relations, enlist; lest ye see them enslaved or butchered before your eyes. Ye that would catch at money, here is a proper bait for you—£10 for a few months' service, besides the usual pay of soldiers.

I seriously make the proposal to you, not only as a subject of the best of kings and a friend to your country but as a servant of the most high God; for I am fully persuaded what I am recommending is His will; and disobedience to it may expose you to His curse.

This proposal is not liable to the objections that have been urged against former measure for raising men. You can no longer object "that you are dragged away like slaves against your wills, while others are without reason exempted"; for now it is left to your own honor, and you may act as free men. Nor can you object "that you are arbitrarily thrust under the command of foreign, unknown, or disagreeable officers"; for the gentleman that has the immediate command of this company and his subordinate officers are of yourselves, your neighbors' children, and, perhaps, your old companions.

And I hope, I may add, you need not object that you shall be badly used, for, Gentlemen Officers, may I not promise for you that no one man in your company shall be treated with cruelty or injustice as far as your authority or influence can prevent? May I not be your security that none but the guilty shall be punished, and they only according to the nature of the offense?

Perhaps some may object that should they enter the army their morals would be in danger of infection, and their virtue would be perpetually shocked with horrid scenes of vice. This may also be a discouragement to parents to consent to their children's engaging in so good a cause. I am glad to hear this objection, when it is sincere and not an empty excuse. And I wish I could remove it by giving you a universal assurance that the army is a school of religion and that soldiers, as they are more exposed to death than other men, are proportionably better prepared for it than others. But, alas! the reverse of this is too true; and the contagion of vice and irreligion is perhaps nowhere stronger than in the army; where, one would think, the Supreme Tribunal should be always in view, and it should be their chief care to prepare for eternity, on the slippery brink of which they stand every moment.

But, Gentlemen Officers, I must again appeal to you that, as for this company, you will not willingly allow any form of vice to be practiced in it with impunity, but will always endeavor to recommend and enforce religion and good morals by your example and authority and to suppress the contrary. May I not give the public the satisfaction of such an assurance concerning you, that, whatever others do, as for you and your company you will serve the Lord? Do you not own yourselves bound to this in honor and duty? Such a conduct, I can assure you, will render you popular among the wise and good; though perhaps it may expose you to the senseless contempt of fools who *make a mock of sin*, and who esteem it bravery to insult that God in whose hand their breath is and whose are all their ways. Such a conduct will afford you pleasure in the review, when the terrors of the bloody field are spread round you and death starts up before you in a thousand shocking forms. Such a conduct will be a source of true courage and render you nobly indifferent about life or death in a good cause. And let me honestly warn you that, if you do not maintain such a conduct, you will bitterly repent it, either in time or eternity. . . .

Everyone can complain of the bad management of our public undertakings, and lament the general security and inactivity that prevails. Everyone can wish that something were effectually done and that this and that person would enlist. Everyone can tell what great achievements he *would* perform were it not for this and that and a hundred obstructions in his way. But this idle complaining, wishing and lamenting, and boasting will answer no end. SOMETHING MUST BE DONE! must be done BY YOU! Therefore, instead of assuming the state of patriots and heroes at home, TO ARMS! and away to the field and prove your pretensions sincere. Let the thunder of this imprecation rouse you out of your ease and security—"Cursed be he that doth the work of the Lord deceitfully; and cursed be he that keepeth back his sword from blood." . . .

Thus far have I addressed you as soldiers, or at least as persons concerned in your stations to do all in your power to save your country. But we must not part thus. It is possible we may never meet more till we mingle with the assembled universe before the Supreme Tribunal. Therefore, before I dismiss you, I must address myself to you as sinners and as candidates for eternity. You are concerned to save your souls as well as your country; and should you save or gain a kingdom, or even the whole world, and lose your souls, your loss will be irreparable.

None of you, I hope, will reply, "I am now a soldier and have nothing more to do with religion." What! Has a soldier nothing to do with religion? Is a soldier under no obligations to the God that made him and that furnishes him with every blessing? Is not a soldier as much exposed to death as other men? May not a soldier be damned for sin as well as other sinners? And will he be able to dwell with devouring fire and everlasting burnings? Are these things so? Can any of you be so stupid as to think them so? If not, you must own that even a soldier has as much concern with religion as another. Therefore, hear me seriously upon this head.

You are about entering into the school of vice; for such the army has generally been. And are any of you already initiated into any of the mysteries of iniquity there practiced? Must I so much as suppose that some of you, who have bravely espoused the cause of your country, are addicted to drunkenness, swearing, whoredom, or any gross vice? I cannot now take time to reason with you for your conviction; it may suffice to appeal to your own reason and conscience. Do you do well in indulging these vices? Will you approve of it in the honest hour of death? Will this conduct prove a source of courage to you, when the arrows of death are flying thick around you and scores are falling on every side? No, you are self-condemned; and may I not reasonably hope you will endeavor to reform what you cannot but condemn?

Soldiers, indeed, are too commonly addicted to such immoralities; but are they the better soldiers on that account? Can an oath or a debauch inspire them with a rational fortitude against the fears of death? Would not prayer and a life of holiness better answer this purpose? Their courage, if they have any, must be the effect, not of thought but of the want of thought; it must be a brutal stupidity or ferocity, but not the rational courage of a man or a Christian.

Some of you, I doubt not, are happily free from these gross vices; and long may you continue so! But I must tell you, this negative goodness is not enough to prepare you for death, or to constitute you true Christians. The temper of your minds must be changed by the power of divine grace; and you must be turned from the love and practice of all sin to the love and practice of universal holiness. You must become humble, brokenhearted penitents and true believers in Jesus Christ. You must be enabled to live righteously, soberly, and godly in this present evil world.

This is religion; this is religion, that will keep you uncorrupted in the midst of vice and debauchery; this is religion, that will befriend you when cannons roar and swords gleam around you, and you are every moment expecting the deadly wound; this is religion, that will support you in the agonies of death and assure you of a happy immortality. . . .

Here I thought to have concluded; but I must take up a few minutes more to ask this crowd—Is there nothing to be done by us who stay at home toward the defense of our country and to promote the success of the expedition now in hand? Shall we sin on still impenitent and incorrigible? Shall we live as if we and our country were *self-dependent* and had nothing to do with the Supreme Ruler of the universe? Can an army of saints or of heroes defend an obnoxious people, ripe for destruction, from the righteous judgment of God?

The cause in which these brave men, and our army in general, are engaged is not so much their own as *ours*. Divine Providence considers them not so much in their private, personal character as in their public character as the representatives and guardians of their country; and, therefore, they will stand or fall, not so much according to their own personal character as according to the public character of the people whose cause they have undertaken. Be it known to you, then, their success depends upon *us* even more than upon themselves.

Ye that complain of the burden of our public taxes; ye that love ease and shrink from the dangers of war; ye that wish to see peace restored once more; ye that would be happy beyond the grave and live forever—attend to my proposal. It is this: A THOROUGH NATIONAL REFORMATION. This will do what millions of money and thousands of men, with guns and swords and all the dreadful artillery of death, could not do—it will procure us peace again, a lasting, well-established peace.

8

A Sermon Preached to the Ancient and Honorable Artillery Company in Boston

Simeon Howard

Successor to Jonathan Mayhew at Boston's West Church, Harvard-educated minister Simeon Howard delivered this sermon to an artillery company in the city in 1773, at a time when its population remained predominately loyal to Great Britain.

GALATIANS V:1
Stand fast therefore in the liberty wherewith
Christ hath made us free.

Mankind are generally averse to innovations both in religion and government. Laws and constitutions to which they have been long used, they are fond of retaining, even though better are offered in their stead. This appeared in the Jews. Their law required a burdensome and expensive service: Christianity set them free from this law. Nevertheless, many of them were desirous of continuing the observation of it, after they became Christians; and of having the gentile converts also submit to it. Accordingly there were some Judaising teachers who endeavored to persuade the Galatians to this submission. The Apostle, therefore, in this epistle, particularly in the immediately foregoing chapter, asserts and proves, that Christians have nothing to do with the ceremonial law of the Jews, they being freed by Christ, from this burden. And then as an inference from what he had said, and by way of admonition to the Galatians, he subjoins the exhortation in the text; stand fast therefore in the liberty wherewith Christ hath made us free.

But though the words originally refer to that freedom from the Jewish law which the gospel confers on the church of God, yet the reason of the inference holds good in the case of any other real and valuable liberty which men have a right to: So that this observation is plainly deducible from the text; vis. that it is the duty of all men to stand fast in such valuable liberty, as providence has confered upon them.

This observation I shall endeavor, by the help of God, to illustrate and improve: In order to which, I shall shew;

I. What I intend by that liberty in which men ought to stand fast.

II. In what way they ought to stand fast in this liberty, or what they may and ought to do in defence of it.

III. The obligations they are under to this duty.

After which, I shall subjoin some reflections, and apply the subject to the present occasion.

I. I am to shew what is intended in this discourse by the liberty in which men ought to stand fast.

Though this word is used in various senses, I mean by it here, only that liberty which is opposed to external force and constraint, and to such force and constraint only, as we may suffer from men. Under the term liberty, taken in this sense, may naturally be comprehended all those advantages which are liable to be destroyed by the art or power of men; every thing that is opposed to temporal slavery.

This liberty has always been accounted one of the greatest natural blessings which mankind can enjoy. Accordingly, the benevolent and impartial Father of the human race, has given to all men a right, and to all naturally an equal right to this blessing.

In a state of nature, or where men are under no civil government, God has given to every one liberty to pursue his own happiness in whatever way, and by whatever means he pleases, without asking the consent or consulting the inclination of any other man, provided he keeps within the bounds of the law of nature. Within these bounds, he may govern his actions, and dispose of his property and person, as he thinks proper.[1] Nor has any man, or any number of men, a right to restrain him in the exercise of this liberty, or punish, or call him to account for using it. This however is not a state of licentiousness, for the law of nature which bounds this liberty, forbids all injustice and wickedness, allows no man to injure another in his person or property, or to destroy his own life.

But experience soon taught that, either thro' ignorance of this law, or the influence of unruly passions, some were disposed to violate it, but encroaching upon the liberty of others; so that the weak were liable to be greatly injured by the superior power of bad men, without any means of security or redress. This gave birth to civil society, and induced a number of individuals to combine together for mutual defence and security; to give up a part of their natural liberty for the sake of enjoying the remainder in greater safety; to agree upon certain laws among themselves to regulate the social conduct of each individual, or to intrust to one or more of their number, in whose wisdom and goodness they could confide, a power of making such laws, and putting them in execution.

---

[1] See Locke on government.

In this state, the liberty which men have is all that natural liberty which has been mentioned, excepting what they have expressly given up for the good of the whole society; a liberty of pursuing their own happiness governing their actions, and disposing of their property and persons as they think fit, provided they transgress no law of nature, and keep within those restrictions which they have consented to come under.

This liberty will be different in different communities. In every state, the members will, probably, give up so much of their natural liberty, as they think will be most for the good of the whole. But different states will judge differently upon this point, some will give up more, some less, though still with the same view, the public good. And every society have doubtless a right to act according to their own judgment and discretion in this matter, this being only an exercise of that natural liberty in which all are bound.

When a society commits to one or a few a power to govern them, the general practice is to limit this power by certain prescribed rules and restrictions. But sometimes this is omitted, and it does not appear from any act of the people, but that the power, with which they have intrusted their rulers, is unlimited. In this case common sense will tell us that the power granted to rulers is to be limited by the great end and design of society and government, and he must be destitute of common sense, who does not know that this is the general good, the happiness and safety of the whole society. So that though a people should, through inadvertency, neglect to prescribe any bounds to the power of their rulers, this power would nevertheless be limited, and they would be at liberty to refuse submission to such restraints or laws, as were plainly inconsistent with the public good.

There are some natural liberties or rights which no person can divest himself of, without transgressing the law of nature. A man cannot, for instance, give up the liberty of private judgment in matters of religion, or convey to others a right to determine of what religion he shall be, and in what way he shall worship God. A grant of this nature would destroy the foundation of all religion in the man who made it, and must therefore be a violation of the law of nature; nor would he be obliged to abide by it, if in consequence of it, he should be required to act contrary to the dictates of his conscience. Or should a man pretend to grant to others a power to order and govern all his actions that were not of a religious nature, so that in all cases he must act agreeable to their direction; this would be inconsistent with that submission which he owes to the authority of God, and his own conscience. The grant would be in itself void, and he would, notwithstanding, be at liberty to act according to his own conscience, though contrary to the command of those to whom he had made so extravagant a donation.

Should therefore the legislature of a state make laws requiring the subjects to do things immoral, and which they knew to be SO, such, for instance, as were apparently destructive of public happiness, though it was in consequence of an express grant of unlimited power, the subjects would be at liberty to refuse obedience, and not violate conscience or destroy their own happiness.[2] So that only such laws of society as are not plainly inconsistent with the end of society, or, in any other respect, inconsistent with the law of nature, the eternal rules of mortality, can restrain and limit the natural liberty of those who belong to it.

It is to be further observed here, that states or communities, as such, have naturally the same liberty which individuals have in the state of nature: but this liberty is restrained, in some measure, by what are called the laws of nations, which are certain rules, that by a tacit consent are agreed upon among all communities, at least among those who are accounted the polite and civilized part of mankind. These, nations are not at liberty to violate.

What has been said may be sufficient to shew what that liberty is in which men ought to stand fast. In a state of nature it is all that liberty which is consistent with the law of nature; under civil government, it is all which is consistent with the law of nature, and with such restrictions as they have consented to come under consistently with the law of nature and the end of society: and when we consider one independent state in reference to another, it is all that natural liberty which is consistent with the laws of nations.

And whatever share men enjoy of this liberty, we may properly say in the words of the text, that Christ has made them free with it, since after his resurrection and exaltation to the right hand of the Majesty on high, all power in heaven and in earth was committed to him, and he now sits, and is to continue at the head of God's providential government, till he hath put all enemies under his feet, after which, he shall deliver up the kingdom to God, even the Father—that God may be all in all.

II. I am in the next place to shew in what way men are to stand fast in their liberty, or what they may and ought to do in defence of it.

It is here supposed that some attempts are made to injure it. And it has been found in all ages and places that such attempts have been made by unreasonable and wicked men. The history of mankind is filled with instances of this; insomuch that if from the great number of historical books that have been written, we should leave out those parts that relate to their encroachments upon one another, their injuries and injustice, most of those huge volumes would shrink to a very small size. Cain began this practice very soon after the creation: and it has been continued ever since, both among kingdoms and individuals. And the same practice is still to be expected, while human nature continues what it is.

Now for men to stand fast in their liberty means, in general, resisting the attempts that are made against it, in the best and most effectual manner they can.

When any one's liberty is attacked or threatened, he is first to try gentle methods for his safety, to reason with, and persuade the adversary to desist, if

---

[2] "All conveyance of absolute power, whether to prince or a senate, with a preclusion of all rights of resistance, must be a deed originally invalid, as founded in an error about what is most essential in such transactions, the tendency of such power to the general good." Dr. Hutcheson's system of moral philosophy, vol. 2, page 271.

there be opportunity for it; or get out of his way, if he can; and if by such means he can prevent the injury, he is to use no other.

But the experience of all ages has shewn, that those, who are so unreasonable as to form designs of injuring others, are seldom to be diverted from their purpose by argument and persuasion alone. Notwithstanding all that can be said to shew the injustice and inhumanity of their attempt, they persist in it, till they have gratified the unruly passion which set them to work. And in this case, what is to be done by the sufferer? Is he to use no other means for his safety, but remonstrance or flight, when these will not secure him? Is he patiently to take the injury and suffer himself to be robbed of his liberty or his life, if the adversary sees fit to take it? Nature certainly forbids this tame submission, and loudly calls to a more vigorous defence. Self-preservation is one of the strongest, and a universal principle of the human mind: And this principle allows of every thing necessary to self-defence, opposing force to force, and violence to violence. This is so universally allowed that I need not attempt to prove it.

But since it has been supposed by some that Christianity forbids all violent resisting of evil, or defending ourselves against injuries in such a manner as will hurt, or endanger those who attack us; it may not be amiss to enquire briefly, whether defensive war be not allowed by the gospel of Christ, the Prince of peace.

And there are, if I mistake not, several passages in the new testament, which shew, that, it was not the design of this divine institution to take away from mankind the natural right of defending their liberty, even by the sword.

I will not alledge the words of John the baptist when in answer to the demand which the soldiers made; *What shall we do?—he said unto them, do violence to no man, neither accuse any falsely, and be content with your wages.*[3] For though they plainly imply, that, at that time, the military profession was not unlawful, and, consequently, that men might use the sword when there was occassion for it, yet it does not follow from hence, that the religion which Jesus was to institute, would allow of that profession and the use of the sword.

But there are other passages proper to be here alledged.

The first that I shall mention is our Lord's own words to Pilate, when under examination before that Governor. The chief charge bro't against Jesus was, that he was going to set up a temporal kingdom inconsistent with the sovereignty of the Roman Emperor. In answer to which he declared, that his *kingdom was not of this world;* and then offered the following argument to prove the assertion: *If my kingdom were of this world, then would my servants fight, that I should not be delivered to the Jews: But now is my kingdom not from hence.*[4] There is an ellipsis in the latter clause; but the sense of the whole is obviously what follows. You know that those who aim at temporal dominion, endeavor to establish their authority and defend themselves, by force of arms, when it is necessary: If this had been my aim I should have taken the same method, and ordered my servants to fight against the Jews when they came to apprehend me: Wherefore, since I

---

[3] Luke 3:14.
[4] John 18:36.

have made no violent resistance, but, on the contrary, "hindered one of my disciples from fighting who fought to rescue me," it must now be evident to you, that the kingdom which I claim is not of this world. Our Lord here, plainly allows that it is fit and proper to temporal kingdoms to fight in defence of their liberty. His own kingdom is not, indeed, to be defended in this way, which being wholly spiritual, consisting of the obedience of men's wills and affections to the laws of God, is incapable of being directly either injured or defended by the sword, as the kingdoms of this world, and men's temporal interest may.

Cornelius, a centurion of the Italian band, was directed by an angel of God to send for Peter, who should tell him "what he ought to do."[5] But we do not find that the apostle directed him to quit his military profession, or intimated that it was inconsistent with the spirit of Christianity; which he certainly would have done, had the character of a soldier and a good Christian been incompatible.

The apostle Paul exhorts the Romans thus: *If it be possible, as much as lieth in you, live peaceably with all men.*[6] Which words plainly imply, that notwithstanding all their endeavors to preserve peace, it might be impossible for them to live peaceably with all men, or not to contend and be at strife with some; i.e. impossible in a moral sense, improper, unlawful, for they do not require us to do all which we have a natural power to do for the sake of peace, but only all that we can do consistently with higher obligations, with our duty in other respects.

Once more—let me observe that in the apocalypse of St. John, where we have a prophetic account of the future state of the church on earth, till the consummation of all things, there are several passages which intimate, that the saints of the Most High, will fight in their defence against their enemies; and that though they shall in various instances be overcome, yet that they shall at length, by an amazing slaughter of their persecutors, obtain for themselves the peaceable enjoyment of that liberty, wherewith Christ hath made them free.[7] Now it cannot reasonably be supposed that the spirit of God would have represented his faithful servants, as thus fighting against their enemies, and being so favored by divine providence, as finally to prevail over them, if defensive war was inconsistent with the spirit of the gospel.

It is not, however, to be denied that there are some passages in the New Testament which seem to forbid all war: particularly, our Saviour's own words in his sermon on the mount. *I say unto you that ye resist not evil—love your enemies, do good to them that hate you,* etc. And those of the apostle Paul; *Recompence to no man evil for evil.*—Avenge not your selves: and some others of the like import. And from such passages some have supposed that Christians are not allowed to defend themselves by force of arms, how violently soever they may be attacked.

---

[5] Acts 10.

[6] Chap. 12. 18

[7] Chap. XI, ver. 7. XII. 7. XIV. 19, 20. XVII. 14. XIX. 14-21. ‡ Matthew 5. Romans 12, 17, 19.

Give me leave then, to offer a few remarks to take off the force of this objection.

1. When our Saviour forbids us to resist evil, he seems to have had in view only small injuries, for such are those which he mentions in the following words, as an illustration of the precept; smiting on the cheek, taking away one's coat, or compelling him to go a mile. And to such injuries it is oftentimes a point of prudence, as well as duty to submit, rather than contend. But it does not follow, that because we are forbidden to resist such slight attacks, we may not defend ourselves when the assault is of a capital kind. But,

2. Supposing our Lord's words to refer only to small injuries, they ought not to be taken in an absolute sense. Expressions of this nature frequently occur in Scripture, which are universally understood with certain restrictions and limitations. For instance; *Love not the world, nor the things that are in the world.*[8] *Lay not up for yourselves treasure on earth.*[9] *Give to him that asketh thee, and from him that would borrow of thee, turn not thou away.*[10] Now, I believe, no body ever supposed, not even the honest Quakers, that these precepts were to be understood so literally, as to forbid all love of the world, and all care to provide the good things of it; or to oblige us "to give to every idle fellow all he may think fit to ask, whether in charity or loan." And we have as good a right to limit the precept which forbids our resisting evil, by the nature and reason of things, as we have to limit these other indefinite expressions.

3. Defending ourselves by force of arms against injurious attacks, is a quite different thing from rendering evil for evil. The latter implies doing hurt to another, because he has done hurt to us; the former implies doing hurt to another, if he is hurt in the conflict, only because there is no other way of avoiding the mischief he endeavors to do us: the one proceeds from malice and revenge; the other merely from self-love, and a just concern for our own happiness, and argues no ill will against any man.

And therefore it is to be observed,

4. That necessary self-defence, however fatal it may prove to those who unjustly attack us, implies no principle inconsistent with that love to our enemies which Christ enjoins. For, at the same time that we are defending ourselves against their assaults, we may bear good-will towards them, wish them well, and pray God to befriend them: All which we doubtless ought to do in respect to our bitterest enemies.

Enough has been said to shew the consistency of war with the spirit of the gospel.

But it is only defensive war that can be justified in the sight of God. When no injury is offered us, we have no right to molest others. And Christian meekness, patience and forbearance, are duties that ought to be practiced both by kingdoms and individuals. Small injuries, that are not likely to be attended with any very pernicious consequences, are rather to be submitted to, than resisted by

---

[8] John 2: 5.

[9] Matt. 6:19.

[10] Matt. 5: 42.

the sword. Both religion and humanity strongly forbid the bloody deeds of war, unless they are necessary. Even when the injury offered is great in itself, or big with fatal consequences, we should, if there be opportunity, endeavor to prevent it by remonstrance, or by offering to leave the matter in dispute to indifferent judges, if they can be had. If these endeavors are unsuccessful, it then becomes proper to use more forceable means of resistance.

A people may err by too long neglecting such means, and shamefully suffer the sword to rust in its scabbard when it ought to be employed in defending their liberty. The most grasping and oppressive power will commonly let its neighbors remain in peace, if they will submit to its unjust demands. And an incautious people may submit to these demands, one after another, till its liberty is irrecoverably gone, before they saw the danger. Injuries small in themselves, may in their consequences be fatal to those who submit to them; especially if they are persisted in. And, with respect to such injuries, we should ever act upon that ancient maxim of prudence; *obsta principiis*. The first unjust demands of an encroaching power should be firmly withstood, when there appears a disposition to repeat and increase such demands. And oftentimes it may be both the right and duty of a people to engage in war, rather than give up to the demands of such power, when they could, without any inconvenience, spare in the way of charity. War, though a great evil, is ever preferable to such concessions, as are likely to be fatal to public liberty. And when such concessions, are required and insisted upon, as the conditions of peace, the only consideration to be attended to by the abused state, is that which our Saviour intimates common prudence will always suggest in such cases: *What king going to make war against another king, sitteth not down first and consulteth whether he be able, etc.*[11]

An innocent people threatened with war are not always obliged to receive the first attack. This may frequently prove fatal, or occasion an irreparable damage. When others have sufficiently manifested an injurious or hostile intention, and persist in it, notwithstanding all the admonition and remonstrance we can make, we may, in order to avoid the blow they are meditating against us, begin the assault.

After a people have been forced into war for their own security, they ought to set reasonable bounds to their resentment, or they may become as guilty as the first aggressors. They should aim at nothing more than repelling the injury, obtaining reparation for damages sustained, and security against future injuries. If, after these ends are obtained, they continue the war, in order to distress their enemies, or reduce them under their power, they become offenders, and the war on their side is unjust.

Submitting the foregoing general observations to your candor, I go on to hint at some things proper to be attended to, by every people, in order to their being in a capacity to defend themselves against encroachments on their liberty.

1. They should endeavor to be united and at peace among themselves. The strength of a society, as well as its honor and happiness, depends much upon its union. Our Saviour's maxim is founded in reason, and has been confirmed by the

---

[11] Luke 14:31.

experience of all ages: Every kingdom divided against itself is brought to desolation. When the body politic is divided into parties, and the members make a business of opposing each other, it is in a fair way to ruin. They are not likely to unite in measures of defence against a common enemy, and will therefore lie open to the encroachments of violence and oppression, and become an easy prey to every invader. The tyrants of the earth, sensible of this, have commonly acted upon this maxim, *divide et impera*: let us first divide the people, whom we mean to enslave, into parties, and we shall then easily bring them under our power.

2. They should endeavor to maintain among themselves a general disposition to submit to government. Society cannot subsist without government; and there can be no government without laws, and a submission to laws. If a licentious spirit prevails among a people, a general disposition to trample upon laws and despise government, they will probably make but a poor figure in defending themselves against a common enemy, for, in making this defence, there must be leaders and followers, some to command and some to obey: And, other things being equal, the more a disposition to submit to rule and order prevails among a people, the more likely will they be to defend their liberty against foreign invasions. Indeed without any enemy from abroad, the general prevalence of a licentious spirit may as effectively destroy the liberty of a people, as the most despotic government, for civil "liberty is something as really different from that licentiousness which supposeth no government, as from that slavery which supposeth tyranny: it is a freedom restrained by beneficial laws, and living and dying with public happiness."[12]

3. That people that would be in a capacity to defend themselves successfully against encroachments, should take care that their internal government be free and easy; allowing all that liberty to every one which is consistent with the necessary restraints of government; laying no burdens upon any, but what are for the good of the whole, and to which the whole society has actually or virtually consented. Though the contrary evil takes its rise from the weakness or wickedness of rulers, yet in every free state it is the right and duty of all, subjects as well as rulers, to use their influence against it: And where the subjects have no constitutional right to do any thing to prevent or, remove such an evil, they are already slaves, and it may be tho't improper to talk of their defending their liberty, though they ought, doubtless, to endeavor to recover it. However, I say, it is highly necessary that this freedom from unreasonable restraints be preserved, in order to a people's retaining a spirit of liberty, and being in a capacity to defend themselves against a common enemy. It is justly observed by that great statesman, Lord Verulam, that "the blessing of Judah and Issachar will never meet, that the same people or nation should be both the lion's whelp, and the ass between two burdens: neither will it be, that a people overlaid with taxes, should ever become valiant and martial."[13] The laying unreasonable burdens and restraints upon a people, will, if they are submitted to, debase their minds, break their spirits, enervate their courage, and sink them into cowards: if they are not

---

[12] Bp. Hoadly.

[13] Bacon's Essays, p. 113

submitted to, the consequence will be internal tumult, disorder, strife and contempt of government; and in either case, the defensive power of the state is greatly diminished. Behold, then the policy, or rather the madness and folly of oppressive rulers: if they are successful in their injurious measures, they are exposing themselves and their subjects as helpless prey to the ravages of some ambitious neighbour: if they are not; they are raising up enemies against themselves at home, and, as it were, setting fire to their own habitations.

4. A people who would stand fast in their liberty, should furnish themselves with weapons proper for their defence, and learn the use of them.

It is indeed a hard case, that those who are happy in the blessings of providence, and disposed to live peaceably with all men, should be obliged to keep up the idea of blood and slaughter, and expend their time and treasure to acquire the arts and instruments of death. But this is a necessity which the depravity of human nature has laid upon every state. Nor was there ever a people that continued, for any considerable time, in the enjoyment of liberty, who were not in a capacity to defend themselves against invaders, unless they were too poor and inconsiderable to tempt an enemy.

So much depends upon the military art, in the present day, that no people can reasonably expect to defend themselves successfully without it. However numerous they may be, if they are unskilled in arms, their number will tend little more to their security, than that of a flock of sheep does to preserve them from the depredations of the world: accordingly it is looked upon as a point of wisdom, in every state, to be furnished with this skill, though it is not to be obtained without great labor and expence.

In some nations the method has been to trust for defence and security to what is called a STANDING ARMY; a number of men paid by the public, to devote themselves wholly to the military profession; while the body of the people followed their peaceable employments, without paying any attention to the art of war.

But this has ever been thought, by the wise and prudent, a precarious defence.

Such armies are, as to the greater part of them, generally composed of men who have no real estate in the dominions which they are to defend; their pay is their living, and the main thing that attaches them to their employers, their manner of life tends to corrupt their morals, and, though they are naturally of the same temper with other men, they seldom continue long in this profession, before they become distinguished by their vices: So that neither their temporal interest, nor their regard to virtue can be supposed to attach them so strongly to the country that employs them, but that there will always be danger of their being tempted by the promise of larger pay to betray their trust, and turn their arms against it. No people therefore, can with safety trust entirely to a standing army, even for defence against foreign enemies.

But without any such enemy, a standing army may be fatal to the happiness and liberty of a community. *They* generally propagate corruption and vice where they reside, they frequently insult and abuse the unarmed and defenseless people:

When there is any difference between rulers and subjects, they will generally be on the side of the former, and ready to assist them in oppressing and enslaving the latter. For though they are really servants of the people, and paid by them; yet this is not commonly done in their name; but in the name of the supreme magistrate.[14] THE KING'S BREAD, and the KING'S SERVICE, are familiar expressions among soldiers, and tend to make them consider him as their only master, and prefer his personal interest to that of the people. So that an army may be the means, in the hands of a wicked and oppressive sovereign, of overturning the constitution of a country, and establishing the most intolerable despotism. It would be easy to shew from history, that this measure has been fatal to the liberties of many nations. And indeed, it has seldom been approved by the body of a people.

But rulers of an arbitrary disposition, have ever endeavored to have a standing army at their command, under a pretence indeed, of being for the safety of the state, though really with a view of giving efficacy to their orders. It has sometime been pretended, that this is necessary to aid and support civil government. But whoever considers, that the design of government is the good of the people, and the great improbability there is, that a people, in general, should be against measures calculated for their good, and that such measures only ought to be enforced, will look upon this as the idlest pretence. For rulers to use a military power, to enforce measures of a contrary tendency, is one of the wickedest and most unjustifiable kinds of offensive war; a violation not only of the common laws of justice and humanity, but of their own sacred engagements to promote the public good. The keeping up troops sufficient to guard exposed frontier posts, may be proper; but to have an army continually stationed in the midst of a people, in time of peace, is a precarious and dangerous method of security.

A safer way, and which has always been esteemed the wisest and best, by impartial men, is to have the power of defence in the body of the people, to have a well-regulated and well-disciplined militia.[15] This is placing the sword in hands that will not be likely to betray their trust, and who will have the strongest motives to act their part well, in defence of their country, whenever they shall be called for. An army composed of men of property, who have been all their days inured to labour, will generally equal the best veteran troops, in point of strength of body and firmness of mind, and when fighting in defence of their religion, their estates, their liberty, and families, will have stronger motives to exert themselves, and may, if they have been properly disciplined, be not much inferior to them in the skill of arms.

---

[14] "What are we to expect, if in a future age an ambitious Prince should arise, with a dissolute and debauched army, a flattering Clergy, a prostitute Ministry, a bankrupt house of L—d's, a pensioned house of C—ns, and a slavish and corrupted nation?'" Trenchard's history of standing armies in England.

[15] Our trained bands are the trustiest and most proper strength of a free nation. MILTON'S *Eikon.*

It was by a militia, by an army composed of men of property and worth of their own nation, that ancient Rome rose to be mistress of the world. The battles of *Agincourt, Poitiers* and *Cressy* are memorable proofs of the martial prowess of the ancient militia of England. Our own country will also furnish us with many instances of the bravery of a militia, both formerly and latterly.

Caution however ought to be used in constituting a militia, that it may answer the end for which it is designed, and not be liable to be made an instrument of tyranny and oppression. It should be subject to discipline and order, and somewhere in the state should be lodged a power of calling it forth to action, whenever the safety of the people required it. But this power should be so limited and restrained, as that it cannot call it unnecessarily, or oblige it to commit violence or oppression upon any of the subjects.[16]

5. Once more, it is necessary for a people who would preserve their liberty, to maintain the general practice of religion and virtue. This will tend to make them courageous: The truest fortitude is ever to be found where the passions and affections are in subjection to the laws of God. Religion conciliates the favor of God, upon whom success in war essentially depends, and the hope of this favor will naturally inspire a brave and undaunted resolution. Not to mention that the unity, riches, and bodily strength of a people are greatly favored by virtue. On the other hand, vice naturally makes men timerous, and Bacon on government, lib. 2 chap. 22 fills the breast with baseness and cowardise. What is here said is agreeable to the observation of that wise King and inspired writer, who tells us, "the wicked flee, when no man pursueth, but the righteous are bold as a lion."

III. Let me now offer a few considerations to shew the obligations men are under to defend that liberty which providence has conferred upon them.

This is a trust committed to us by heaven: we are accountable for the use we make of it, and ought therefore, to the best of our power to defend it. The servant, who hid his talent in a napkin, is condemned in our Lord's parable, and he who through inattention, indolence or cowardice, suffers it to be wrested from him, is little less criminal. Should a person, for instance, whose ability and circumstances enable him to do good in the world, to relieve his distressed brethren, and be an example of charity and other virtues, tamely yield up all his interest and become an absolute slave to some unjust and wicked oppressor, when he might by a manly resistance have secured his liberty, would he not be guilty of great unfaithfulness to God, and justly liable to his condemnation? This would in its consequences be really worse than hiding his talent in a napkin; it

---

[16] That wise men have thought a people might be in danger from their own militia, unless great caution was used in the direction of it, appears from the following quotation: "Take away from the king the absolute power to compel men to take up arms, otherwise than in case of foreign invasion; power to compel men to go out of their counties to war, to charge men for the maintenance of wars, power to make them find arms at his pleasure, and lastly power to break the peace, or do aught that may tend thereto; certainly the power of the militia that remaineth, though never so surely settled in the king's hand, can never bite this nation."

would be not only not improving it for the glory of the giver, but conveying it into hands which will, in all probability, employ it greatly to his dishonor. This reasoning is as applicable to a community as to an individual. A kingdom or commonwealth, as such, is accountable for the improvement it makes of its advantages: It is bound to preserve them, and employ them for the honor of God, so far as it can, to be an example of virtue to neighboring communities, and afford them relief when they are in distress: but by yielding up their possessions and liberties to an encroaching oppressive power, they become, in a great measure, incapable of these duties, and are liable to be made the ministers of sin through the compulsion of their masters. Out of faithfulness then, to God, and in order to escape the doom of slothful servants, we should endeavor to defend our rights and liberties.

Men are bound to preserve their own lives, as long as they can, consistently with their duty in other respects. Would not he, who should lose his life by neglecting to resist a wild beast, be criminal in the sight of God? And can he be innocent who loses it by neglecting to oppose the violent attacks of wicked men, oftentimes as fierce and cruel as the most savage beast? Men are also bound, individuals and societies, to take care of their temporal happiness, and do all they lawfully can, to promote it. But what can be more inconsistent with this duty, than submitting to great encroachments upon our liberty? Such submission tends to slavery; and compleat slavery implies every evil that the malice of man and devils can inflict. Again,

The regard which we owe to the happiness of others makes this a duty.

Every man is bound both by the law of nature and revelation, to provide in the best manner he can, for the temporal happiness of his family, and he that neglects this, has, according to the declaration of an inspired apostle, *denied the faith, and is worse than an infidel.* But in what way can a man be more justly chargeable with this neglect, than by suffering himself to be deprived of his life, liberty or property, when he might lawfully have preserved them?

Reason, humanity and religion, all conspire to teach us, that we ought in the best manner we can, to provide for the happiness of posterity. We are allied to them by the common tie of nature: They are not here to act their part: A concern for them is a debt which we owe for the care which our progenitors took for us: Heaven has made us their guardians, and intrusted to our care their liberty, honor, and happiness: For when they come upon the state, they will be deeply affected by the transactions of their fathers, especially by their public transactions. If the present inhabitants of a country submit to slavery, slavery is the inheritance which they will leave their children. And who that has the bowels of a father, or even the common feelings of humanity, can think without horror, of being the means of subjecting unborn millions to the iron scepter of tyranny?

But further; a regard to the happiness of mankind in general, makes it a duty to resist great injuries. Yielding to the unjust demands of bad men, not only lessens our power of doing good, but encourages them to repeat their injuries, and strengthens their hands to do mischief: It enables them to give fuller scope to their lusts, and more effectually to spread corruption, distress and misery. It is therefore an act of benevolence to oppose and destroy that power which is employed in injuring others, and as much, when it is that of a tyrant, as of a wild beast.

Once more, from a regard to religion men are obliged to defend their liberty against encroachments, though the attack should not immediately affect religion. Slavery exposes to many temptations to vice, and by debasing and weakening the mind, destroying its fortitude and magnanimity renders it less capable of resisting them, and creates a dependence upon, and subjection to wicked men, highly prejudicial to virtue. Hence it has been often observed, and is confirmed by experience that the loss of liberty is soon followed by the loss of all virtue and religion.[17]

Besides; the destruction of civil liberty is generally fatal to *religions*. The latter has seldom existed long in any place without the former. Nor is it to be expected that those who are wicked enough to deprive a people of *that*, should, when they have got them under their power, suffer them long to enjoy *this*; especially as tyranny has generally made these two evils subservient to each other.

But I may not enlarge: The considerations which have been suggested shew, if I mistake not, that it is not only the right but the duty of men to defend that liberty, with which providence has made them free: And a duty of high obligation, as the neglect of it may be attended with consequences, the most prejudicial to human virtue and happiness, and greatly dishonorary to God.

All that now remains is to offer some reflections, and apply the subject to the present occasion.

1. What has been said may serve to caution all against invading the liberty of others;—Whoever does this, obliges others to resist him: he puts himself into a state of war with them, and is justly liable to all the evil which their necessary self-defence may bring upon him. And though he may think that his power is so great, and theirs so little, that he can be in no danger from their resentment, the event may convince him of his mistake. Men, who have a just sense and value of liberty, will sometimes do wonders in its defence.

> —— "They have great odds
> Against the astonished sons of violence,
> Who fight with awful justice on their side."[18]

Oppressors may indeed for a time, be successful and overcome all opposition; yet it seldom happens that they persevere in their injurious practice, without meeting with such resistance as causes their mischief to return upon their own heads, and their violent dealings to come down upon their own pates: It is an old observation, that few tyrants descend in peace to the grave. If therefore,

---

[17] "The conquer'd also, and inslav'd by war shall with their freedom lost all virtue lose and fear of God." *Paradise Lost*

[18] Thompson.

the laws of God will not, a regard to their own safety should restrain men from invading the rights of the innocent.

2. If it be so important a duty for men to resist encroachments upon their liberty; then it cannot be improper for the Christian minister, to inculcate this upon his hearers; to exhort them to be watchful over it, and ready to oppose all attempts against it. This is so far from being improper, that it is, I humbly conceive, his indispensible duty. Nor can I see how he could answer it to God, or his own conscience, if, when he thought his country was in danger of being enslaved, for want of a proper sense of, and opposition to, the approaches of tyranny, he should neglect to point out the danger and with

— "honest zeal
To rouse the watchmen of the public weal."[19]

It is readily owned, that *designedly* to spread false alarms, to fill the minds of people with groundless prejudices against their rulers, or a neighboring state, to stir up faction and encourage opposition to *good* government, are things highly criminal, and whoever does thus, whatever character he may wear among men, is in reality a minister, not of Christ, but of the devil, the father of falsehood, confusion and rebellion. But to shew people their real danger, point out the source of it, and exhort them to such exertions as are necessary to avoid it, are acts of benevolence becoming every disciple, and especially every professed minister of Christ.

3. Since the preservation of public liberty depends so much upon a people's being possessed of the art of war; those who exert themselves to encourage and promote this art, act a laudable part, and are intitled to the thanks of their brethren. Upon this account, the company, which is the occasion of this solemnity, deserves to be esteemed *honorable* though its institution were much less *ancient* than it is. And as this society has in former days furnished many brave men, who died worthily in defence of our country, so, from the spirit which at present prevails among the gentlemen who compose it, we doubt not but it will furnish others, whenever there shall be occasion for it. How far this institution, by exciting in others a spirit of imitation or emulation, has been the occasion of the present general attention to the military art among us, I pretend not to say: But whatever be the cause, it must give pleasure to every friend of public liberty, to see this people so generally engaged in military exercises. This argues a manly spirit, a sense of liberty, a just apprehension of its danger, a resolution to stand fast in it, and, as far as any thing in our power can do it, promises freedom to our country.

We are not, I hope, insensible that peace is a great blessing, and, in itself, ever to be prefered to war; nor unthankful to Him who ruleth among the nations, the God of peace, for the enjoyment we have had of this blessing for a number of years past. But we have little reason to expect, however ardently we may wish, that this country will always be the habitation of peace. Ambition, avarice, and

---

[19] Pope.

other unruly passions have a great hand in directing the conduct of most of the kingdoms of this world. British America is already become considerable among the European nations for its numbers, and their easiness of living; and is continually rising into greater importance. I will not undertake to decypher the *signs of the times*, or to say from what quarter we are most likely to be molested. But from the course of human affairs, we have the utmost reason to expect that the time will come, when we must either submit to *slavery*, or defend our liberties by our own sword. And this perhaps may be the case sooner than some imagine. No one can doubt but there are powers on the continent of Europe, that would be glad to add North America to their dominions, and who, if they thought the thing practicable, would soon find a pretence for attempting it. The naval power of Great Britain has been hitherto our chief security against invasions from that continent. But every thing belonging to the present state, is uncertain and fluctuating. Things may soon be in such a situation with Great Britain, that it will be no longer proper for us to confide in her power, for the protection of our liberty. Our greatest security, under God, will be our being in a capacity to defend ourselves. Were we, indeed, sure that Great Britain would always be both *able* and *willing* to protect us in our liberty, which, from present appearances, we have little reason to expect, it would be shameful for so numerous a people as this, and a people of so much natural strength and fortitude, to be, thro' inattention to the art of war, incapable of bearing a part in their own defence. Such weakness must render them contemptible to all the world.

British America, especially the northern part of it, is by its situation calculated to be a nursery of heroes. Nothing is wanting but our own care and application to make us, with the neighboring colonies, a formidable people. And religion, honor, patriotism, and even self-love, all unite in demanding from us this application and care. This people, it may be presumed, will never of choice, keep among them a *standing army* in time of peace: Virtue, domestic peace, the insulated walls of our State-House, and even the once crimsoned *stones of the street*, all loudly *cry out* against this measure. But every well-wisher to the public, should countenance and encourage a military spirit among our militia through the province.

Our political Fathers have it in their power to do much for this end; and we have a right to expect that, out of faithfulness to God and this people, they will not neglect it. From the countenance which his Excellency and the honorable Council shew to the military transactions of this day, we would gladly hope, that, they in conjunction with the other branch of the legislature, will, in this way, as well as others, prove themselves to be God's ministers for good to the people.

It is also in the power of persons of rank and fortune, in their private capacity, greatly to promote this cause by their example and otherwise. It is highly absurd, though not uncommon, that those who have most to lose by the destruction of a state, should be least capable of bearing a part in its defence. Riches are frequently the main temptation to war. Where a people are all poor, there is little danger of their being invaded: So that there being men of affluence among a people, is often the cause of their being obliged to defend themselves by the sword. It is therefore especially *their* duty, as well as interest, to do what they can to put the people into a capacity of defence. When *they* spend their time in idleness, effeminating pleasures, or even in accumulating riches, to the total neglect of the art of war, and every measure to promote it, they act unbecoming good members of society, and set an example highly prejudicial to the community.

Whereas when gentlemen of fortune, notwithstanding the allurements of pleasure on the one hand, and the fatiguing exercise of a soldier on the other, exert themselves to acquire and promote the military art, they are an honor to their circumstances, and a blessing to the public: Their example will have great influence upon others; and, other things being equal, such men will be most likely to fight valiantly in defence of their liberty, whenever it shall be necessary. By such a conduct, they shew their regard to their country, in a way that will probably be much more beneficial to it, than merely talking, writing, or preaching in favor of liberty. And it ought to be esteemed as no inconsiderable evidence, among many others, of a public, truly patriotic spirit in the honorable gentleman,[20] who leads his Excellency's company of Cadets, that he has so cheerfully endured the fatigue of qualifying himself to be a good officer, and, by his generous exertions in conjunction with their own, rendered his company an honor to the town, to their commanders and themselves. This company in general, is indeed an example of what I was urging; of gentlemen of easy circumstances giving proper attention to the art of war, and is on that account the more respectable and important.

But we have other laudable examples of attention to arms. The Train of Artillery[21] has for a number of years past been honorably distinguished, by their military address. And the respectable appearance which the whole militia of the town made a few days ago, when called together in honor of his Majesty's birthday, and the dexterity with which they went through their exercises, must convince all who had the satisfaction of seeing them, that they are no strangers to a military spirit, and lead us to hope that by perseverance, the whole body will soon equal those, who at present excel most. May this spirit still revive and prevail through the province, till this whole people become as considerable for their skill in arms, as they are for their natural strength and courage.

The gentlemen who are engaged in acquiring this art will remember that the true end of it is only defence; that it is to be employed, not to destroy, but to protect and secure the liberty and happiness of mankind; not to infringe the rights of others, but to defend their own. While, therefore, they endeavor to resemble such men as *Alexander* and *Ceasar* in military skill and valour, they will detest the principles from which they acted, in invading and distressing inoffensive people. For though they have been honored with the name of heroes, they were, in reality, public robbers and murderers.

---

[20] The Hon. John Hancock, Esq.
[21] A Company commanded by Major Paddock.

They will also remember that the most desirable liberty, and which we should be ready to defend, is that of a well governed society, which is as essentially different from the licentiousness, which is without law or government, as it is from an absolute subjection to the arbitrary will of another. This is the liberty wherewith Christ has made us free; to which he has given us a right. While, therefore, these gentlemen will be always ready to stand forth in defence of true civil liberty, whenever they shall see her assaulted and be properly called upon; they will never on any consideration be prevailed with, to employ their arms for the destruction of good government by aiding either tyranny on the one hand, or licentiousness on the other.

But above all they will remember, that religion is the main concern of man, and a necessary qualification for a good soldier. This, beyond any thing else, inspires with the love of liberty, with fortitude and magnanimity; and this alone can enable them to meet death with a rational composure and tranquility of mind, which is an enemy before which the bravest soldier must fall at last.

To conclude: This whole assembly will bear in mind, that there is another and more valuable kind of liberty, than that to which the foregoing discourse more immediately relates, and which, at this day, so generally employs our attention and conversation; a liberty, which consists in being free from the power and dominion of sin, through the assistance of the divine spirit, concurring with our own pious, rational and persevering endeavors. Whatever our outward circumstances may be, if we are destitute of this spiritual liberty, we are in reality slaves, how much soever we may hate the name; if we possess it we are *free indeed*: And our being free in this sense, will give us the best grounds to hope for temporal freedom, through the favor of heaven; and, at length, gain us admission into the regions of perfect and uninterrupted liberty, peace and happiness.

9

The Declaration of Independence

In Congress, July 4, 1776

*The Unanimous Declaration of
the Thirteen United States of America*

When in the Course of human events, it becomes necessary for one people to dissolve the political bands which have connected them with another, and to assume among the Powers of the earth, the separate and equal station to which the Laws of Nature and of Nature's God entitle them, a decent respect of the opinions of mankind requires that they should declare the causes which impel them to the separation.

We hold these truths to be self-evident: that all men are created equal, that they are endowed by their Creator with certain unalienable Rights, that among these are Life, Liberty and the pursuit of Happiness. That to secure these rights, Governments are instituted among Men, deriving their just powers from the consent of the governed, that whenever any Form of Government becomes destructive of these ends, it is the Right of the People to alter or to abolish it, and to institute new Government, laying its foundation on such principles and organizing its powers in such form, as to them shall seem most likely to effect their Safety and Happiness. Prudence, indeed, will dictate that Governments long established should not be changed for light and transient causes; and accordingly all experience hath shown, that mankind are more disposed to suffer, while evils are sufferable, than to right themselves by abolishing the forms to which they are accustomed. But when a long train of abuses and usurpations, pursuing invariably the same Object evinces a design to reduce them under absolute Despotism, it is their right, it is their duty, to throw off such Government, and to provide new Guards for their future security.— Such has been the patient sufferance of these Colonies; and such is now the necessity which constrains them to alter their former Systems of Government. The history of the present King of Great Britain is a history of repeated injuries and usurpations, all having in direct object the establishment of an absolute Tyranny over these States. To prove this, let Facts be submitted to a candid world.

He has refused his Assent to Laws, the most wholesome and necessary for the public good.

He has forbidden his Governors to pass Laws of immediate and pressing importance, unless suspended in their operation till his Assent should be obtained; and when so suspended, he has utterly neglected to attend to them.

He has refused to pass other Laws for the accommodation of large districts of people, unless those people would relinquish the right of Representation in the Legislature, a right inestimable to them and formidable to tyrants only.

He has called together legislative bodies at places unusual, uncomfortable, and distant from the depository of their Public Records, for the sole purpose of fatiguing them into compliance with his measures.

He has dissolved Representative Houses repeatedly, for opposing with manly firmness his invasions on the rights of the people.

He has refused for a long time, after such dissolutions, to cause others to be elected; whereby the Legislative Powers, incapable of Annihilation, have returned to the People at large for their exercise; the State remaining in the mean time exposed to all the dangers of invasion from without, and convulsions within.

He has endeavoured to prevent the population of these States; for that purpose obstructing the Laws for Naturalization of Foreigners; refusing to pass others to encourage their migration hither, and raising the conditions of new Appropriations of Lands.

He has obstructed the Administration of Justice, by refusing his Assent to Laws for establishing Judiciary Powers.

He has made Judges dependent on his Will alone, for the tenure of their offices, and the amount and payment of their salaries.

He has erected a multitude of New Offices, and sent hither swarms of Officers to harrass our People, and eat out their substance.

He has kept among us, in times of peace, Standing Armies without the Consent of our legislatures.

He has affected to render the Military independent of and superior to the Civil Power.

He has combined with others to subject us to a jurisdiction foreign to our constitution, and unacknowledged by our laws; giving his Assent to their acts of pretended legislation:

For quartering large bodies of armed troops among us:

For protecting them, by a mock Trial, from Punishment for any Murders which they should commit on the Inhabitants of these States:

For cutting off our Trade with all parts of the world:

For imposing taxes on us without our Consent:

For depriving us in many cases, of the benefits of Trial by Jury:

For transporting us beyond Seas to be tried for pretended offences:

For abolishing the free System of English Laws in a neighbouring Province, establishing therein an Arbitrary government, and enlarging its Boundaries so as to render it at once an example and fit instrument for introducing the same absolute rule into these Colonies:

For taking away our Charters, abolishing our most valuable Laws, and altering fundamentally the Forms of our Governments:

For suspending our own Legislatures, and declaring themselves invested with Power to legislate for us in all cases whatsoever.

He had abdicated Government here, by declaring us out of his Protection and waging War against us.

He has plundered our seas, ravaged our Coasts, burnt our towns, and destroyed the lives of our people.

He is at this time transporting large armies of foreign mercenaries to compleat the works of death, desolation and tyranny, already begun with circumstances of Cruelty & perfidy scarcely paralleled in the most barbarous ages, and totally unworthy Head of a civilized nation.

He has constrained our fellow Citizens taken Captive on the high Seas to bear Arms against their Country, to become the executioners of their friends and Brethren, or to fall themselves by their Hands.

He has excited domestic insurrections amongst us, and has endeavoured to bring on the inhabitants of our frontiers, the merciless Indian Savages, whose known rule of warfare, is an undistinguished destruction of all ages, sexes and conditions.

In every stage of these oppressions We have Petitioned for Redress in the most humble terms: Our repeated Petitions have been answered only by repeated injury. A Prince, whose character is thus marked by every act which may defined a Tyrant, is unfit to be the ruler of a free People.

Nor have We been wanting in attention to our British brethren. We have warned them from time to time of attempts by their legislature to extend an unwarrantable jurisdiction over us. We have reminded them of the circumstances of our emigration and settlement here. We have appealed to their native justice and magnanimity, and we have conjured them by the ties of our common kindred to disavow these usurpations, which, would inevitably interrupt our connections and correspondence. They too have been deaf to the voice of justice and of consanguinity. We must, therefore, acquiesce in the necessity, which denounces our Separation, and hold them, as we hold the rest of mankind, Enemies in War, in Peace Friends.

We, therefore, the Representatives of the United States of America, in General Congress, Assembled, appealing to the Supreme Judge of the world for the rectitude of our intentions, do, in the Name, and by Authority of the good People of these Colonies, solemnly publish and declare, That these United Colonies are, and of Right ought to be Free and Independent States; they are Absolved from all Allegiance to the British Crown, and that all political connection between them and the State of Great Britain, is and ought to be totally dissolved; and that as Free and Independent States, they have full Power to levy War, conclude Peace, contract Alliances, establish Commerce, and to do all other Acts and Things which Independent States may of right do. And for the support of this Declaration, with a firm reliance on the Protection of Divine Providence, we mutually pledge to each other our Lives, and Fortunes and our sacred Honor.

10

"On the Right to Rebel against Governors"

Samuel West

One of the most influential citizens in Massachusetts during the founding era, Congregationalist minister Samuel West delivered this sermon before the Massachusetts Council and House of Representatives in Boston, 1776.

PUT THEM IN MIND TO BE SUBJECT TO PRINCIPALITIES AND POWERS, TO OBEY MAGISTRATES, TO BE READY TO EVERY GOOD WORK.—Titus iii. 1.

The great Creator, having designed the human race for society, has made us dependent on one another for happiness. He has so constituted us that it becomes both our duty and interest to seek the public good; and that we may be the more firmly engaged to promote each other's welfare, the Deity has endowed us with tender and social affections, with generous and benevolent principles: hence the pain that we feel in seeing an object of distress; hence the satisfaction that arises in relieving the afflictions, and the superior pleasure which we experience in communicating happiness to the miserable. The Deity has also invested us with moral powers and faculties, by which we are enabled to discern the difference between right and wrong, truth and falsehood, good and evil; hence the approbation of mind that arises upon doing a good action, and the remorse of conscience which we experience when we counteract the moral sense and do that which is evil. This proves that, in what is commonly called a state of nature, we are the subjects of the divine law and government; that the Deity is our supreme magistrate, who has written his law in our hearts, and will reward or punish us according as we obey or disobey his commands. Had the human race uniformly persevered in a state of moral rectitude, there would have been little or no need of any other law besides that which is written in the heart,—for every one in such a state would be a law unto himself. There could be no occasion for enacting or enforcing of penal laws; for such are "not made for the righteous man, but for the lawless and disobedient, for the ungodly, and for sinners, for the unholy and profane, for murderers of fathers and murderers of mothers, for manslayers, for whoremongers, for them that defile themselves with mankind, for men-stealers, for liars, for perjured persons, and if there be any other thing that is contrary to" moral rectitude and the happiness of mankind. The necessity of forming ourselves into politic bodies, and granting to our rulers a power to enact laws for the public safety, and to enforce them by proper penalties, arises from our being in a fallen and degenerate state. The slightest view of the present state and condition of the human race is abundantly sufficient to convince any person of common sense and common honesty that civil government is absolutely necessary for the peace and safety of mankind; and, consequently, that all good magistrates, while they faithfully discharge the trust reposed in them, ought to be religiously and conscientiously obeyed. An enemy to good government is an enemy not only to his country, but to all mankind; for he plainly shows himself to be divested of those tender and social sentiments which are characteristic of a human temper, even of that generous and benevolent disposition which is the peculiar glory of a rational creature. An enemy to good government has degraded himself below the rank and dignity of a man, and deserves to be classed with the lower creation. Hence we find that wise and good men, of all nations and religions, have ever inculcated subjection to good government, and have borne their testimony against the licentious disturbers of the public peace.

Nor has Christianity been deficient in this capital point. We find our blessed Saviour directing the Jews to render to Caesar the things that were Caesar's; and the apostles and first preachers of the gospel not only exhibited a good example of subjection to the magistrate, in all things that were just and lawful, but they have also, in several places in the New Testament, strongly enjoined upon Christians the duty of submission to that government under which Providence had placed them. Hence we find that those who despise government, and are not afraid to speak evil of dignities, are, by the apostles Peter and Jude, classed among those presumptuous, self-willed sinners that are reserved to the judgment of the great day. And the apostle Paul judged submission to civil government to be a matter of such great importance, that he thought it worth his while to charge Titus to put his hearers in mind to be submissive to principalities and powers, to obey magistrates, to be ready to every good work; as much as to say, none can be ready to every good work, or be properly disposed to perform those actions that tend to promote the public good, who do not obey magistrates, and who do not become good subjects of civil government. If, then, obedience to the civil magistrates is so essential to the character of a Christian, that without it he cannot be disposed to perform those good works that are necessary for the welfare of mankind,—if the despisers of governments are those presumptuous, self-willed sinners who are reserved to the judgment of the great day,—it is certainly a matter of the utmost importance to us all to be thoroughly acquainted with the nature and extent of our duty, that we may yield the obedience required; for it is impossible that we should properly discharge a duty when we are strangers to the nature and extent of it.

In order, therefore, that we may form a right judgment of the duty enjoined in our text, I shall consider the nature and design of civil government, and shall show that the same principles which oblige us to submit to government do equally oblige us to resist tyranny; or that tyranny and magistracy are so opposed to each other that where the one begins the other ends. I shall then apply the present discourse to the grand controversy that at this day subsists between Great Britain and the American colonies.

That we may understand the nature and design of civil government, and discover the foundation of the magistrate's authority to command, and the duty of subjects to obey, it is necessary to derive civil government from its original, in order to which we must consider what "state all men are naturally in, and that is (as Mr. Locke observes) a state of perfect freedom to order all their actions, and dispose of their possessions and persons as they think fit, within the bounds of the law of nature, without asking leave or depending upon the will of any man." It is a state wherein all are equal,—no one having a right to control another, or oppose him in what he does, unless it be in his own defence, or in the defence of those that, being injured, stand in need of his assistance.

Had men persevered in a state of moral rectitude, every one would have been disposed to follow the law of nature, and pursue the general good. In such a state, the wisest and most experienced would undoubtedly be chosen to guide and direct those of less wisdom and experience than themselves,—there being nothing else that could afford the least show or appearance of any one's having the superiority or precedency over another; for the dictates of conscience and the precepts of natural law being uniformly and regularly obeyed, men would only need to be informed what things were most fit and prudent to be done in those cases where their inexperience or want of acquaintance left their minds in doubt what was the wisest and most regular method for them to pursue. In such cases it would be necessary for them to advise with those who were wiser and more experienced than themselves. But these advisers could claim no authority to compel or to use any forcible measures to oblige any one to comply with their direction or advice. There could be no occasion for the exertion of such a power; for every man, being under the government of right reason, would immediately feel himself constrained to comply with everything that appeared reasonable or fit to be done, or that would any way tend to promote the general good. This would have been the happy state of mankind had they closely adhered to the law of nature, and persevered in their primitive state.

Thus we see that a state of nature, though it be a state of perfect freedom, yet is very far from a state of licentiousness. The law of nature gives men no right to do anything that is immoral, or contrary to the will of God, and injurious to their fellow-creatures; for a state of nature is properly a state of law and government, even a government founded upon the unchangeable nature of the Deity, and a law resulting from the eternal fitness of things. Sooner shall heaven and earth pass away, and the whole frame of nature be dissolved, than any part even the smallest iota, of this law shall ever be abrogated; it is unchangeable as the Deity himself, being a transcript of his moral perfections. A revelation, pretending to be from God, that contradicts any part of natural law, ought immediately to be rejected as an imposture; for the Deity cannot make a law contrary to the law of nature without acting contrary to himself,—a thing in the strictest sense impossible, for that which implies contradiction is not an object of the divine power. Had this subject been properly attended to and understood, the world had remained free from a multitude of absurd and pernicious principles, which have been industriously propagated by artful and designing men, both in politics and divinity. The doctrine of nonresistance and unlimited passive obedience to the worst of tyrants could never have found credit among mankind had the voice of reason been hearkened to for a guide, because such a doctrine would immediately have been discerned to be contrary to natural law.

In a state of nature we have a right to make the persons that have injured us repair the damages that they have done us; and it is just in us to inflict such punishment upon them as is necessary to restrain them from doing the like for the future,—the whole end and design of punishing being either to reclaim the individual punished, or to deter others from being guilty of similar crimes. Whenever punishment exceeds these bounds it becomes cruelty and revenge, and directly contrary to the law of nature. Our wants and necessities being such as to render it impossible in most cases to enjoy life in any tolerable degree without entering into society, and there being innumerable cases wherein we need the assistance of others, which if not afforded we should very soon perish; hence the law of nature requires that we should endeavor to help one another to the utmost of our power in all cases where our assistance is necessary. It is our duty to endeavor always to promote the general good; to do to all as we would be willing to be done by were we in their circumstances; to do justly, to love mercy, and to walk humbly before God. These are some of the laws of nature which every man in the world is bound to observe, and which whoever violates exposes himself to the resentment of mankind, the lashes of his own conscience, and the judgment of Heaven. This plainly shows that the highest state of liberty subjects us to the law of nature and the government of God. The most perfect freedom consists in obeying the dictates of right reason, and submitting to natural law. When a man goes beyond or contrary to the law of nature and reason, he becomes the slave of base passions and vile lusts; he introduces confusion and disorder into society, and brings misery and destruction upon himself. This, therefore, cannot be called a state of freedom, but a state of the vilest slavery and the most dreadful bondage. The servants of sin and corruption are subjected to the worst kind of tyranny in the universe. Hence we conclude that where licentiousness begins, liberty ends.

The law of nature is a perfect standard and measure of action for beings that persevere in a state of moral rectitude; but the case is far different with us, who are in a fallen and degenerate estate. We have a law in our members which is continually warring against the law of the mind, by which we often become enslaved to the basest lusts, and are brought into bondage to the vilest passions. The strong propensities of our animal nature often overcome the sober dictates of reason and conscience, and betray us into actions injurious to the public and destructive of the safety and happiness of society. Men of unbridled lusts, were they not restrained by the power of the civil magistrate, would spread horror and desolation all around them. This makes it absolutely necessary that societies should form themselves into politic bodies, that they may enact laws for the public safety, and appoint particular penalties for the violation of their laws, and invest a suitable number of persons with authority to put in execution and enforce the laws of the state, in order that wicked men may be restrained from doing mischief to their fellow-creatures, that the injured may have their rights restored to them, that the virtuous may be encouraged in doing good, and that every member of society may be protected and secured in the peaceable, quiet possession and enjoyment of all those liberties and privileges which the Deity has bestowed upon him; i.e., that he may safely enjoy and pursue whatever he chooses, that is consistent with the public good. This shows that the end and design of civil government cannot be to deprive men of their liberty or take away their freedom; but, on the contrary, the true design of civil government is to protect men in the enjoyment of liberty.

From hence it follows that tyranny and arbitrary power are utterly inconsistent with and subversive of the very end and design of civil government, and directly contrary to natural law, which is the true foundation of civil government and all politic law. Consequently, the authority of a tyrant is of itself null and void; for as no man can have a right to act contrary to the law of nature, it is impossible that any individual, or even the greatest number of men, can confer a right upon another of which they themselves are not possessed; i.e., no body of men can justly and lawfully authorize any person to tyrannize over and enslave his fellow-creatures, or do anything contrary to equity and goodness. As magistrates have no authority but what they derive from the people, whenever they act contrary to the public good, and pursue measures destructive of the peace and safety of the community, they forfeit their right to govern the people. Civil rulers and magistrates are properly of human creation; they are set up by the people to be the guardians of their rights, and to secure their persons from being injured or oppressed,—the safety of the public being the supreme law of the state, by which the magistrates are to be governed, and which they are to consult upon all occasions. The modes of administration may be very different, and the forms of government may vary from each other in different ages and nations; but, under every form, the end of civil government is the same, and cannot vary: It is like the laws of the Medes and Persians—it altereth not.

Though magistrates are to consider themselves as the servants of the people, seeing from them it is that they derive their power and authority, yet they may also be considered as the ministers of God ordained by him for the good of mankind; for, under him, as the Supreme Magistrate of the universe, they are to act: and it is God who has not only declared in his word what are the necessary qualifications of a ruler, but who also raises up and qualifies men for such an important station. The magistrate may also, in a more strict and proper sense, be said to be ordained of God, because reason, which is the voice of God, plainly requires such an order of men to be appointed for the public good. Now, whatever right reason requires as necessary to be done is as much the will and law of God as though it were enjoined us by an immediate revelation from heaven, or commanded in the sacred Scriptures.

From this account of the origin, nature, and design of civil government, we may be very easily led into a thorough knowledge of our duty; we may see the reason why we are bound to obey magistrates, viz., because they are the ministers of God for good unto the people. While, therefore, they rule in the fear of God, and while they promote the welfare of the state,— i.e., while they act in the character of magistrates,—it is the indispensable duty of all to submit to them, and to oppose a turbulent, factious, and libertine spirit, whenever and wherever it discovers itself. When a people have by their free consent conferred upon a number of men a power to rule and govern them, they are bound to obey them. Hence disobedience becomes a breach of faith; it is violating a constitution of their own appointing, and breaking a compact for which they ought to have the most sacred regard. Such a conduct discovers so base and disingenuous a temper of mind, that it must expose them to contempt in the judgment of all the sober, thinking part of mankind. Subjects are bound to obey lawful magistrates by every tender tie of human nature, which disposes us to consult the public good, and to seek the good of our brethren, our wives, our children, our friends and acquaintance; for he that opposes lawful authority does really oppose the safety and happiness of his fellow-creatures. A factious, seditious person, that opposes good government, is a monster in nature; for he is an enemy to his own species, and destitute of the sentiments of humanity.

Subjects are also bound to obey magistrates, for conscience' sake, out of regard to the divine authority, and out of obedience to the will of God; for if magistrates are the ministers of God, we cannot disobey them without being disobedient to the law of God; and this extends to all men in authority, from the highest ruler to the lowest officer in the state. To oppose them when in the exercise of lawful authority is an act of disobedience to the Deity, and, as such, will be punished by him. It will, doubtless, be readily granted by every honest man that we ought cheerfully to obey the magistrate, and submit to all such regulations of government as tend to promote the public good; but as this general definition may be liable to be misconstrued, and every man may think himself at liberty to disregard any laws that do not suit his interest, humor, or fancy, I would observe that, in a multitude of cases, many of us, for want of being properly acquainted with affairs of state, may be very improper judges of particular laws, whether they are just or not. In such cases it becomes us, as good members of society, peaceably and conscientiously to submit, though we cannot see the reasonableness of every law to which we submit, and that for this plain reason: if any number of men should take it upon themselves to oppose authority for acts, which may be really necessary for the public safety, only because they do not see the reasonableness of them, the direct consequence will be introducing confusion and anarchy into the state.

It is also necessary that the minor part should submit to the major; e.g., when legislators have enacted a set of laws which are highly approved by a large majority of the community as tending to promote the public good, in this case, if a small number of persons are so unhappy as to view the matter in a very different point of light from the public, though they have an undoubted right to show the reasons of their dissent from the judgment of the public, and may lawfully use all proper arguments to convince the public of what they judge to be an error, yet, if they fail in their attempt, and the majority still continue to approve of the laws that are enacted, it is the duty of those few that dissent peaceably and for conscience' sake to submit to the public judgment, unless something is required of them which they judge would be sinful for them to comply with; for in that case they ought to obey the dictates of their own consciences rather than any human authority whatever. Perhaps, also, some cases of intolerable oppression, where compliance would bring on inevitable ruin and destruction, may justly warrant the few to refuse submission to what they judge inconsistent with their peace and safety; for the law of self-preservation will always justify opposing a cruel and tyrannical imposition, except where opposition is attended with greater evils than submission, which is frequently the case where a few are oppressed by a large and powerful majority.[1] Except the above-named cases, the minor ought always to submit to the major; otherwise, there can be no peace nor harmony in society. And, besides, it is the major part of a community that have the sole right of establishing a constitution and authorizing magistrates; and consequently it is only the major part of the community that can claim the right of altering the constitution, and displacing the magistrates; for certainly common sense will tell us that it requires as great an authority to set aside a constitution as there was at first to establish it. The collective body, not a few individuals, ought to constitute the supreme authority of the state.

The only difficulty remaining is to determine when a people may claim a right of forming themselves into a body politic, and assume the powers of legislation. In order to determine this point, we are to remember that all men being by nature equal, all the members of a community have a natural right to assemble themselves together, and act and vote for such regulations as they judge are necessary for the good of the whole. But when a community is become very numerous, it is very difficult, and in many cases impossible, for all to meet together to regulate the affairs of the state; hence comes the necessity of appointing delegates to represent the people in a general assembly. And this ought to be looked upon as a sacred and inalienable right, of which a people cannot justly divest themselves, and which no human authority can in equity ever take from them, viz., that no one be obliged to submit to any law except such as are made either by himself or by his representative.

If representation and legislation are inseparably connected, it follows, that when great numbers have emigrated into a foreign land, and are so far removed from the parent state that they neither are or can be properly represented by the government from which they have emigrated, that then nature itself points out

---

[1] This shows the reason why the primitive Christians did not oppose the cruel persecutions that were inflicted upon them by the heathen magistrates. They were few compared with the heathen world, and for them to have attempted to resist their enemies by force would have been like a small parcel of sheep endeavoring to oppose a large number of ravening wolves and savage beasts of prey. It would, without a miracle, have brought upon them inevitable ruin and destruction. Hence the wise and prudent advice of our Saviour to them is, "When they persecute you in this city, flee ye to another."

the necessity of their assuming to themselves the powers of legislation; and they have a right to consider themselves as a separate state from the other, and, as such, to form themselves into a body politic.

In the next place, when a people find themselves cruelly oppressed by the parent state, they have an undoubted right to throw off the yoke, and to assert their liberty, if they find good reason to judge that they have sufficient power and strength to maintain their ground in defending their just rights against their oppressors; for, in this case, by the law of self-preservation, which is the first law of nature, they have not only an undoubted right, but it is their indispensable duty, if they cannot be redressed any other way, to renounce all submission to the government that has oppressed them, and set up an independent state of their own, even though they may be vastly inferior in numbers to the state that has oppressed them. When either of the aforesaid cases takes place, and more especially when both concur, no rational man, I imagine, can have any doubt in his own mind whether such a people have a right to form themselves into a body politic, and assume to themselves all the powers of a free state. For, can it be rational to suppose that a people should be subjected to the tyranny of a set of men who are perfect strangers to them, and cannot be supposed to have that fellow-feeling for them that we generally have for those with whom we are connected and acquainted; and, besides, through their unacquaintedness with the circumstances of the people over whom they claim the right of jurisdiction, are utterly unable to judge, in a multitude of cases, which is best for them?

It becomes me not to say what particular form of government is best for a community,—whether a pure democracy, aristocracy, monarchy, or a mixture of all the three simple forms. They have all their advantages and disadvantages, and when they are properly administered may, any of them, answer the design of civil government tolerably. Permit me, however, to say, that an unlimited, absolute monarchy, and an aristocracy not subject to the control of the people, are two of the most exceptionable forms of government: firstly, because in neither of them is there a proper representation of the people; and, secondly, because each of them being entirely independent of the people, they are very apt to degenerate into tyranny. However, in this imperfect state, we cannot expect to have government formed upon such a basis but that it may be perverted by bad men to evil purposes. A wise and good man would be very loth to undermine a constitution that was once fixed and established, although he might discover many imperfections in it; and nothing short of the most urgent necessity would ever induce him to consent to it; because the unhinging a people from a form of government to which they had been long accustomed might throw them into such a state of anarchy and confusion as might terminate in their destruction, or perhaps, in the end, subject them to the worst kind of tyranny.

Having thus shown the nature, end, and design of civil government, and pointed out the reasons why subjects are bound to obey magistrates,—viz., because in so doing they both consult their own happiness as individuals, and also promote the public good and the safety of the state,—I proceed, in the next place, to show that the same principles that oblige us to submit to civil government do also equally oblige us, where we have power and ability, to resist and oppose tyranny; and that where tyranny begins government ends. For, if magistrates have no authority but what they derive from the people; if they are properly of human creation; if the whole end and design of their institution is to promote the general good, and to secure to men their just rights,—it will follow, that when they act contrary to the end and design of their creation they cease being magistrates, and the people which gave them their authority have the right to take it from them again. This is a very plain dictate of common sense, which universally obtains in all similar cases; for who is there that, having employed a number of men to do a particular piece of work for him, but what would judge that he had a right to dismiss them from his service when he found that they went directly contrary to his orders, and that, instead of accomplishing the business he had set them about, they would infallibly ruin and destroy it? If, then, men, in the common affairs of life, always judge that they have a right to dismiss from their service such persons as counteract their plans and designs, though the damage will affect only a few individuals, much more must the body politic have a right to depose any persons, though appointed to the highest place of power and authority, when they find that they are unfaithful to the trust reposed in them, and that, instead of consulting the general good, they are disturbing the peace of society by making laws cruel and oppressive, and by depriving the subjects of their just rights and privileges. Whoever pretends to deny this proposition must give up all pretence of being master of that common sense and reason by which the Deity has distinguished us from the brutal herd.

As our duty of obedience to the magistrate is founded upon our obligation to promote the general good, our readiness to obey lawful authority will always arise in proportion to the love and regard that we have for the welfare of the public; and the same love and regard for the public will inspire us with as strong a zeal to oppose tyranny as we have to obey magistracy. Our obligation to promote the public good extends as much to the opposing every exertion of arbitrary power that is injurious to the state as it does to the submitting to good and wholesome laws. No man, therefore, can be a good member of the community that is not as zealous to oppose tyranny as he is ready to obey magistracy. A slavish submission to tyranny is a proof of a very sordid and base mind. Such a person cannot be under the influence of any generous human sentiments, nor have a tender regard for mankind.

Further: if magistrates are no farther ministers of God than they promote the good of the community, then obedience to them neither is nor can be unlimited; for it would imply a gross absurdity to assert that, when magistrates are ordained by the people solely for the purpose of being beneficial to the state, they must be obeyed when they are seeking to ruin and destroy it. This would imply that men were bound to act against the great law of self-preservation, and to contribute their assistance to their own ruin and destruction, in order that they may please and gratify the greatest monsters in nature, who are violating the laws of God and destroying the rights of mankind. Unlimited submission and obedience is due to none but God alone. He has an absolute right to command; he alone has an uncontrollable sovereignty over us, because he alone is unchangeably good; he never will nor can require of us, consistent with his nature and attributes, anything that is not fit and reasonable; his commands are all just and good; and to suppose that he has given to any particular set of men a power to require obedience to that which is unreasonable, cruel, and unjust, is robbing the Deity of his justice and goodness, in which consists the peculiar glory of the divine character, and it is representing him under the horrid character of a tyrant.

If magistrates are ministers of God only because the law of God and reason points out the necessity of such an institution for the good of mankind, it follows, that whenever they pursue measures directly destructive of the public good they cease being God's ministers, they forfeit their right to obedience from the subject, they become the pests of society, and the community is under the strongest obligation of duty, both to God and to its own members, to resist and oppose them, which will be so far from resisting the ordinance of God that it will be strictly obeying his commands. To suppose otherwise will imply that the Deity requires of us an obedience that is self-contradictory and absurd, and that one part of his law is directly contrary to the other; i.e., while he commands us to pursue virtue and the general good, he does at the same time require us to persecute virtue, and betray the general good, by enjoining us obedience to the wicked commands of tyrannical oppressors. Can any one not lost to the principles of humanity undertake to defend such absurd sentiments as these? As the public safety is the first and grand law of society, so no community can have a right to invest the magistrate with any power or authority that will enable him to act against the welfare of the state and the good of the whole. If men have at any time wickedly and foolishly given up their just rights into the hands of the magistrate, such acts are null and void, of course; to suppose otherwise will imply that we have a right to invest the magistrate with a power to act contrary to the law of God,—which is as much as to say that we are not the subjects of divine law and government. What has been said is, I apprehend, abundantly sufficient to show that tyrants are no magistrates, or that whenever magistrates abuse their power and authority to the subverting the public happiness, their authority immediately ceases, and that it not only becomes lawful, but an indispensable duty to oppose them; that the principle of self-preservation, the affection and duty that we owe to our country, and the obedience we owe the Deity, do all require us to oppose tyranny.

If it be asked, Who are the proper judges to determine when rulers are guilty of tyranny and oppression? I answer, the public. Not a few disaffected individuals, but the collective body of the state, must decide this question; for, as it is the collective body that invests rulers with their power and authority, so it is the collective body that has the sole right of judging whether rulers act up to the end of their institution or not. Great regard ought always to be paid to the judgment of the public. It is true the public may be imposed upon by a misrepresentation of facts; but this may be said of the public, which cannot always be said of individuals, viz., that the public is always willing to be rightly informed, and when it has proper matter of conviction laid before it its judgment is always right.

This account of the nature and design of civil government, which is so clearly suggested to us by the plain principles of common sense and reason, is abundantly confirmed by the sacred Scriptures, even by those very texts which have been brought by men of slavish principles to establish the absurd doctrine of unlimited passive obedience and nonresistance, as will abundantly appear by examining the two most noted texts that are commonly brought to support the strange doctrine of passive obedience. The first that I shall cite is in 1 Peter ii. 13, 14: "submit yourselves to every ordinance of man,"—or, rather, as the words ought to be rendered from the Greek, submit yourselves to every human creation, or human constitution,—"for the Lord's sake, whether it be to the king as supreme, or unto governors, as unto them that are sent by him for the punishment of evil-doers, and for the praise of them that do well." Here we see that the apostle asserts that magistracy is of human creation or appointment; that is, that magistrates have no power or authority but what they derive from the people; that this power they are to exert for the punishment of evil-doers, and for the praise of them that do well; i.e., the end and design of the appointment of magistrates is to restrain wicked men, by proper penalties, from injuring society, and to encourage and honor the virtuous and obedient. Upon this account Christians are to submit to them for the Lord's sake; which is as if he had said, Though magistrates are of mere human appointment, and can claim no power or authority but what they derive from the people, yet, as they are ordained by men to promote the general good by punishing evil-doers and by rewarding and encouraging the virtuous and obedient, you ought to submit to them out of a sacred regard to the divine authority; for as they, in the faithful discharge of their office, do fulfill the will of God, so ye, by submitting to them, do fulfill the divine command. If the only reason assigned by the apostle why magistrates should be obeyed out of a regard to the divine authority is because they punish the wicked and encourage the good, it follows, that when they punish the virtuous and encourage the vicious we have a right to refuse yielding any submission or obedience to them; i. e., whenever they act contrary to the end and design of their institution, they forfeit their authority to govern the people, and the reason for submitting to them, out of regard to the divine authority, immediately ceases; and they being only of human appointment, the authority which the people gave them the public have a right to take from them, and to confer it upon those who are more worthy. So far is this text from favoring arbitrary principles, that there is nothing in it but what is consistent with and favorable to the highest liberty that any man can wish to enjoy; for this text requires us to submit to the magistrate no further than he is the encourager and protector of virtue and the punisher of vice; and this is consistent with all that liberty which the Deity has bestowed upon us.

The other text which I shall mention, and which has been made use of by the favorers of arbitrary government as their great sheet anchor and main support, is in Rom. xiii., the first six verses: "Let every soul be subject to the higher powers;

for there is no power but of God. The powers that be are ordained of God. Whosoever therefore resisteth the power, resisteth the ordinance of God; and they that resist shall receive to themselves damnation; for rulers are not a terror to good works, but to the evil. Wilt thou then not be afraid of the power? Do that which is good, and thou shalt have praise of the same: for he is the minister of God to thee for good. But if thou do that which is evil, be afraid; for he beareth not the sword in vain: for he is the minister of God, a revenger to execute wrath upon him that doth evil. Wherefore ye must needs be subject not only for wrath, but also for conscience' sake. For, for this cause pay you tribute also; for they are God's ministers, attending continually upon this very thing." A very little attention, I apprehend, will be sufficient to show that this text is so far from favoring arbitrary government, that, on the contrary, it strongly holds forth the principles of true liberty. Subjection to the higher powers is enjoined by the apostle because there is no power but of God; the powers that be are ordained of God; consequently, to resist the power is to resist the ordinance of God: and he repeatedly declares that the ruler is the minister of God. Now, before we can say whether this text makes for or against the doctrine of unlimited passive obedience, we must find out in what sense the apostle affirms that magistracy is the ordinance of God, and what he intends when he calls the ruler the minister of God.

I can think but of three possible senses in which magistracy can with any propriety be called God's ordinance, or in which rulers can be said to be ordained of God as his ministers. The first is a plain declaration from the word of God that such a one and his descendants are, and shall be, the only true and lawful magistrates: thus we find in Scripture the kingdom of Judah to be settled by divine appointment in the family of David. Or,

Secondly, By an immediate commission from God, ordering and appointing such a one by name to be the ruler over the people: thus Saul and David were immediately appointed by God to be kings over Israel. Or,

Thirdly, Magistracy may be called the ordinance of God, and rulers may be called the ministers of God, because the nature and reason of things, which is the law of God, requires such an institution for the preservation and safety of civil society. In the two first senses the apostle cannot be supposed to affirm that magistracy is God's ordinance, for neither he nor any of the sacred writers have entailed the magistracy to any one particular family under the gospel dispensation. Neither does he nor any of the inspired writers give us the least hint that any person should ever be immediately commissioned from God to bear rule over the people. The third sense, then, is the only sense in which the apostle can be supposed to affirm that the magistrate is the minister of God, and that magistracy is the ordinance of God; viz., that the nature and reason of things require such an institution for the preservation and safety of mankind. Now, if this be the only sense in which the apostle affirms that magistrates are ordained of God as his ministers, resistance must be criminal only so far forth as they are the ministers of God, i.e., while they act up to the end of their institution, and ceases being criminal when they cease being the ministers of God, i.e., when they act contrary to the general good, and seek to destroy the liberties of the people.

That we have gotten the apostle's sense of magistracy being the ordinance of God, will plainly appear from the text itself for, after having asserted that to resist the power is to resist the ordinance of God, and they that resist shall receive to themselves damnation, he immediately adds as the reason of this assertion, "For rulers are not a terror to good works, but to the evil. Wilt thou then not be afraid of the power? Do that which is good, and thou shalt have praise of the same: for he is the minister of God to thee for good. But if thou do that which is evil, be afraid; for he beareth not the sword in vain: for he is the minister of God, a revenger to execute wrath upon him that doth evil." Here is a plain declaration of the sense in which he asserts that the authority of the magistrate is ordained of God, viz., because rulers are not a terror to good works, but to the evil; therefore we ought to dread offending them, for we cannot offend them but by doing evil; and if we do evil we have just reason to fear their power; for they bear not the sword in vain, but in this case the magistrate is a revenger to execute wrath upon him that doeth evil: but if we are found doers of that which is good, we have no reason to fear the authority of the magistrate; for in this case, instead of being punished, we shall be protected and encouraged. The reason why the magistrate is called the minister of God is because he is to protect, encourage, and honor them that do well, and to punish them that do evil; therefore it is our duty to submit to them, not merely for fear of being punished by them, but out of regard to the divine authority, under which they are deputed to execute judgment and to do justice. For this reason, according to the apostle, tribute is to be paid them, because, as the ministers of God, their whole business is to protect every man in the enjoyment of his just rights and privileges, and to punish every evil-doer.

If the apostle, then, asserts that rulers are ordained of God only because they are a terror to evil works and a praise to them that do well; if they are ministers of God only because they encourage virtue and punish vice; if for this reason only they are to be obeyed for conscience' sake; if the sole reason why they have a right to tribute is because they devote themselves wholly to the business of securing to men their just rights, and to the punishing of evil-doers,—it follows, by undeniable consequence, that when they become the pests of human society, when they promote and encourage evil-doers, and become a terror to good works, they then cease being the ordinance of God; they are no longer rulers nor ministers of God; they are so far from being the powers that are ordained of God that they become the ministers of the powers of darkness, and it is so far from being a crime to resist them, that in many cases it may be highly criminal in the sight of Heaven to refuse resisting and opposing them to the utmost of our power; or, in other words, that the same reasons that require us to obey the ordinance of God, do equally oblige us, when we have power and opportunity, to oppose and resist the ordinance of Satan.

Hence we see that the apostle Paul, instead of being a friend to tyranny and arbitrary government, turns out to be a strong advocate for the just rights of mankind, and is for our enjoying all that liberty with which God has invested us; for no power (according to the apostle) is ordained of God but what is an encourage of every good and virtuous action,— "Do that which is good, and thou shalt have praise of the same." No man need to be afraid of this power which is ordained of God who does nothing but what is agreeable to the law of God; for this power will not restrain us from exercising any liberty which the Deity has granted us; for the minister of God is to restrain US from nothing but the doing of that which is evil, and to this we have no right. To practise evil is not liberty, but licentiousness. Can we conceive of a more perfect, equitable, and generous plan of government than this which the apostle has laid down, viz., to have rulers appointed over us to encourage us to every good and virtuous action, to defend and protect us in our just rights and privileges, and to grant us everything that can tend to promote our true interest and happiness; to restrain every licentious action, and to punish everyone that would injure or harm us; to become a terror of evil-doers; to make and execute such just and righteous laws as shall effectually deter and hinder men from the commission of evil, and to attend continually upon this very thing; to make it their constant care and study, day and night, to promote the good and welfare of the community, and to oppose all evil practices? Deservedly may such rulers be called the ministers of God for good. They carry on the same benevolent design towards the community which the great Governor of the universe does towards his whole creation. 'Tis the indispensable duty of a people to pay tribute, and to afford an easy and comfortable subsistence to such rulers, because they are the ministers of God, who are continually laboring and employing their time for the good of the community. He that resists such magistrates does, in a very emphatical sense, resist the ordinance of God; he is an enemy to mankind, odious to God, and justly incurs the sentence of condemnation from the great Judge of quick and dead. Obedience to such magistrates is yielding obedience to the will of God, and, therefore, ought to be performed from a sacred regard to the divine authority.

For any one from hence to infer that the apostle enjoins in this text unlimited obedience to the worst of tyrants, and that he pronounces damnation upon those that resist the arbitrary measures of such pests of society, is just as good sense as if one should affirm, that because the Scripture enjoins us obedience to the laws of God, therefore we may not oppose the power of darkness; or because we are commanded to submit to the ordinance of God, therefore we may not resist the ministers of Satan. Such wild work must be made with the apostle before he can be brought to speak the language of oppression! It is as plain, I think, as words can make it, that, according to this text, no tyrant can be a ruler; for the apostle's definition of a ruler is, that he is not a terror to good works, but to the evil; and that he is one who is to praise and encourage those that do well. Whenever, then, the ruler encourages them that do evil, and is a terror to those that do well,—i.e., as soon as he becomes a tyrant,—he forfeits his authority to govern, and becomes the minister of Satan, and, as such, ought to be opposed.

I know it is said that the magistrates were, at the time when the apostle wrote, heathens, and that Nero, that monster of tyranny, was then Emperor of Rome; that therefore the apostle, by enjoining submission to the powers that then were, does require unlimited obedience to be yielded to the worst of tyrants. Now, not to insist upon what has been often observed, viz., that this epistle was written most probably about the beginning of Nero's reign, at which time he was a very humane and merciful prince, did everything that was generous and benevolent to the public, and showed every act of mercy and tenderness to particulars, and therefore might at that time justly deserve the character of the minister of God for good to the people,— I say, waiving this, we will suppose that this epistle was written after that Nero was become a monster of tyranny and wickedness; it will by no means follow from thence that the apostle meant to enjoin unlimited subjection to such an authority, or that he intended to affirm that such a cruel, despotic authority was the ordinance of God. The plain, obvious sense of his words, as we have already seen, forbids such a construction to be put upon them, for they plainly imply a strong abhorrence and disapprobation of such a character, and clearly prove that Nero, so far forth as he was a tyrant, could not be the minister of God, nor have a right to claim submission from the people; so that this ought, perhaps, rather to be viewed as a severe satire upon Nero, than as enjoining any submission to him.

It is also worthy to be observed that the apostle prudently waived mentioning any particular persons that were then in power, as it might have been construed in an invidious light, and exposed the primitive Christians to the severe resentments of the men that were then in power. He only in general requires submission to the higher powers, because the powers that be are ordained of God. Now, though the emperor might at that time be such a tyrant that he could with no propriety be said to be ordained of God, yet it would be somewhat strange if there were no men in power among the Romans that acted up to the character of good magistrates, and that deserved to be esteemed as the ministers of God for good unto the people. If there were any such, notwithstanding the tyranny of Nero, the apostle might with great propriety enjoin submission to those powers that were ordained of God, and by so particularly pointing out the end and design of magistrates, and giving his definition of a ruler, he might design to show that neither Nero, nor any other tyrant, ought to be esteemed as the minister of God. Or, rather, —which appears to me to be the true sense,—the apostle meant to speak of magistracy in general, without any reference to the emperor, or any other person in power, that was then at Rome; and the meaning of this passage is as if he had said, It is the duty of every Christian to be a good subject of civil government, for the power and authority of the civil magistrate are from God; for the powers that be are ordained of God; i.e., the authority of the magistrates that are now either at Rome or elsewhere is ordained of the Deity. Wherever you find any lawful magistrates, remember, they are of divine ordination. But that you may understand what I mean when I say that magistrates are of divine ordination, I will show you how you may discern who are lawful magistrates, and ordained of

God, from those who are not. Those only are to be esteemed lawful magistrates, and ordained of God, who pursue the public good by honoring and encouraging those that do well and punishing all that do evil. Such, and such only, wherever they are to be found, are the ministers of God for good: to resist such is resisting the ordinance of God, and exposing yourselves to the divine wrath and condemnation.

In either of these senses the text cannot make anything in favor of arbitrary government. Nor could he with any propriety tell them that they need not be afraid of the power so long as they did that which was good, if he meant to recommend an unlimited submission to a tyrannical Nero; for the best characters were the likeliest to fall a sacrifice to his malice. And, besides, such an injunction would be directly contrary to his own practice, and the practice of the primitive Christians, who refused to comply with the sinful commands of men in power; their answer in such cases being this, We ought to obey God rather than men. Hence the apostle Paul himself suffered many cruel persecutions because he would not renounce Christianity, but persisted in opposing the idolatrous worship of the pagan world.

This text, being rescued from the absurd interpretations which the favorers of arbitrary government have put upon it, turns out to be a noble confirmation of that free and generous plan of government which the law of nature and reason points out to us. Nor can we desire a more equitable plan of government than what the apostle has here laid down; for, if we consult our happiness and real good, we can never wish for an unreasonable liberty, viz., a freedom to do evil, which, according to the apostle, is the only thing that the magistrate is to refrain us from. To have a liberty to do whatever is fit, reasonable, or good, is the highest degree of freedom that rational beings can possess. And how honorable a station are those men placed in, by the providence of God, whose business it is to secure to men this rational liberty, and to promote the happiness and welfare of society, by suppressing vice and immorality, and by honoring and encouraging everything that is honorable, virtuous, and praiseworthy! Such magistrates ought to be honored and obeyed as the ministers of God and the servants of the King of Heaven. Can we conceive of a larger and more generous plan of government than this of the apostle? Or can we find words more plainly expressive of a disapprobation of an arbitrary and tyrannical government? I never read this text without admiring the beauty and nervousness of it; and I can hardly conceive how he could express more ideas in so few words than he has done. We see here, in one view, the honor that belongs to the magistrate, because he is ordained of God for the public good. We have his duty pointed out, viz., to honor and encourage the virtuous, to promote the real good of the community, and to punish all wicked and injurious persons. We are taught the duty of the subject, viz., to obey the magistrate for conscience' sake, because he is ordained of God; and that rulers, being continually employed under God for our good, are to be generously maintained by the paying them tribute; and that disobedience to rulers is highly criminal, and will expose us to the divine wrath. The liberty of the subject is also clearly asserted, viz., that subjects are to be allowed to do everything that is in itself just and right, and are only to be restrained from being guilty of wrong actions. It is also strongly implied, that when rulers become oppressive to the subject and injurious to the state, their authority, their respect, their maintenance, and the duty of submitting to them, must immediately cease; they are then to be considered as the ministers of Satan, and, as such, it becomes our indispensable duty to resist and oppose them.

Thus we see that both reason and revelation perfectly agree in pointing out the nature, end, and design of government, viz., that it is to promote the welfare and happiness of the community; and that subjects have a right to do everything that is good, praiseworthy, and consistent with the good of the community, and are only to be restrained when they do evil and are injurious either to individuals or the whole community; and that they ought to submit to every law that is beneficial to the community for conscience' sake, although it may in some measure interfere with their private interest; for every good man will be ready to forgo his private interest for the sake of being beneficial to the public. Reason and revelation, we see, do both teach us that our obedience to rulers is not unlimited, but that resistance is not only allowable, but an indispensable duty in the case of intolerable tyranny and oppression. From both reason and revelation we learn that, as the public safety is the supreme law of the state,—being the true standard and measure by which we are to judge whether any law or body of laws are just or not,—so legislatures have a right to make, and require subjection to, any set of laws that have a tendency to promote the good of the community.

Our governors have a right to take every proper method to form the minds of their subjects so that they may become good members of society. The great difference that we may observe among the several classes of mankind arises chiefly from their education and their laws: hence men become virtuous or vicious, good commonwealthsmen or the contrary, generous, noble, and courageous, or base, mean-spirited, and cowardly, according to the impression that they have received from the government that they are under, together with their education and the methods that have been practised by their leaders to form their minds in early life. Hence the necessity of good laws to encourage every noble and virtuous sentiment, to suppress vice and immorality, to promote industry, and to punish idleness, that parent of innumerable evils; to promote arts and sciences, and to banish ignorance from among mankind.

And as nothing tends like religion and the fear of God to make men good members of the commonwealth, it is the duty of magistrates to become the patrons and promoters of religion and piety, and to make suitable laws for the maintaining public worship, and decently supporting the teachers of religion. Such laws, I apprehend, are absolutely necessary for the well-being of civil society. Such laws may be made, consistent with all that liberty of conscience which every good member of society ought to be possessed of; for, as there are few, if any, religious societies among us but what profess to believe and practise all the great duties of religion and morality that are necessary for the well-being of society and the safety of the state, let every one be allowed to attend worship in his own society, or in that way that he judges most agreeable to the will of

God, and let him be obliged to contribute his assistance to the supporting and defraying the necessary charges of his own meeting. In this case no one can have any right to complain that he is deprived of liberty of conscience, seeing that he has a right to choose and freely attend that worship that appears to him to be most agreeable to the will of God; and it must be very unreasonable for him to object against being obliged to contribute his part towards the support of that worship which he has chosen. Whether some such method as this might not tend, in a very eminent manner, to promote the peace and welfare of society, I must leave to the wisdom of our legislators to determine; be sure it would take off some of the most popular objections against being obliged by law to support public worship while the law restricts that support only to one denomination.

But for the civil authority to pretend to establish particular modes of faith and forms of worship, and to punish all that deviate from the standard which our superiors have set up, is attended with the most pernicious consequences to society. It cramps all free and rational inquiry, fills the world with hypocrits and superstition bigots—nay, with infidels and skeptics; it exposes men of religion and conscience to the rage and malice of fiery, blind zealots, and dissolves every tender tie of human nature; in short, it introduces confusion and every evil work. And I cannot but look upon it as a peculiar blessing of Heaven that we live in a land where every one can freely deliver his sentiments upon religious subjects, and have the privilege of worshipping God according to the dictates of his own conscience without any molestation or disturbance,—a privilege which I hope we shall ever keep up and strenuously maintain. No principles ought ever to be discountenanced by civil authority but such as tend to the subversion of the state. So long as a man is a good member of society, he is accountable to God alone for his religious sentiments; but when men are found disturbers of the public peace, stirring up sedition, or practicing against the state, no pretence of religion or conscience ought to screen them from being brought to condign punishment. But then, as the end and design of punishment is either to make restitution to the injured or to restrain men from committing the like crimes for the future, so, when these important ends are answered, the punishment ought to cease; for whatever is inflicted upon a man under the notion of punishment after these important ends are answered, is not a just and lawful punishment, but is properly cruelty and base revenge.

From this account of civil government we learn that the business of magistrates is weighty and important. It requires both wisdom and integrity. When either are wanting, government will be poorly administered; more especially if our governors are men of loose morals and abandoned principles; for if a man is not faithful to God and his own soul, how can we expect that he will be faithful to the public? There was a great deal of propriety in the advice that Jethro gave to Moses to provide able men,—men of truth, that feared God, and that hated covetousness,—and to appoint them for rulers over the people. For it certainly implies a very gross absurdity to suppose that those who are ordained of God for the public good should have no regard to the laws of God, or that the ministers of God should be despisers of the divine commands. David, the man after God's own heart, makes piety a necessary qualification in a ruler: "He that ruleth over men (says he) must be just, ruling in the fear of God." It is necessary it should be so, for the welfare and happiness of the state; for, to say nothing of the venality and corruption, of the tyranny and oppression, that will take place under unjust rulers, barely their vicious and irregular lives will have a most pernicious effect upon the lives and manners of their subjects: their authority becomes despicable in the opinion of discerning men. And, besides, with what face can they make or execute laws against vices which they practise with greediness? A people that have a right of choosing their magistrates are criminally guilty in the sight of Heaven when they are governed by caprice and humor, or are influenced by bribery to choose magistrates that are irreligious men, who are devoid of sentiment, and of bad morals and base lives. Men cannot be sufficiently sensible what a curse they may bring upon themselves and their posterity by foolishly and wickedly choosing men of abandoned characters and profligate lives for their magistrates and rulers.

We have already seen that magistrates who rule in the fear of God ought not only to be obeyed as the ministers of God, but that they ought also to be handsomely supported, that they may cheerfully and freely attend upon the duties of their station; for it is a great shame and disgrace to society to see men that serve the public laboring under indigent and needy circumstances; and, besides, it is a maxim of eternal truth that the laborer is worthy of his reward.

It is also a great duty incumbent on people to treat those in authority with all becoming honor and respect,—to be very careful of casting any aspersion upon their characters. To despise government, and to speak evil of dignities, is represented in Scripture as one of the worst of characters; and it was an injunction of Moses, "Thou shalt not speak evil of the ruler of thy people." Great mischief may ensue upon reviling the character of good rulers; for the unthinking herd of mankind are very apt to give ear to scandal, and when it falls upon men in power, it brings their authority into contempt, lessens their influence, and disheartens them from doing that service to the community of which they are capable; whereas, when they are properly honored, and treated with that respect which is due to their station, it inspires them with courage and a noble ardor to serve the public: their influence among the people is strengthened, and their authority becomes firmly established. We ought to remember that they are men like to ourselves, liable to the same imperfections and infirmities with the rest of us, and therefore, so long as they aim at the public good, their mistakes, misapprehensions, and infirmities, ought to be treated with the utmost humanity and tenderness.

But though I would recommend to all Christians, as a part of the duty that they owe to magistrates, to treat them with proper honor and respect, none can reasonably suppose that I mean that they ought to be flattered in their vices, or honored and caressed while they are seeking to undermine and ruin the state; for this would be wickedly betraying our just rights, and we should be guilty of our own destruction. We ought ever to persevere with firmness and fortitude in maintaining and contending for all that liberty that the Deity has granted us. It is our duty to be ever watchful over our just rights, and not suffer them to be wrested out of our hands by any of the artifices of tyrannical oppressors. But there is a wide difference between being jealous of our rights, when we have the strongest reason to conclude that they are invaded by our rulers, and being unreasonably suspicious of men that are zealously endeavoring to support the constitution, only because we do not thoroughly comprehend all their designs. The first argues a noble and generous mind; the other, a low and base spirit.

Thus have I considered the nature of the duty enjoined in the text, and have endeavored to show that the same principles that require obedience to lawful magistrates do also require us to resist tyrants; this I have confirmed from reason and Scripture.

It was with a particular view to the present unhappy controversy that subsists between us and Great Britain that I chose to discourse upon the nature and design of government, and the rights and duties both of governors and governed, that so, justly understanding our rights and privileges, we may stand firm in our opposition to ministerial tyranny, while at the same time we pay all proper obedience and submission to our lawful magistrates; and that, while we are contending for liberty, we may avoid running into licentiousness; and that we may preserve the due medium between submitting to tyranny and running into anarchy. I acknowledge that I have undertaken a difficult task; but, as it appeared to me, the present state of affairs loudly called for such a discourse; and, therefore, I hope the wise, the generous, and the good, will candidly receive my good intentions to serve the public. I shall now apply this discourse to the grand controversy that at this day subsists between Great Britain and the American colonies.

And here, in the first place, I cannot but take notice how wonderfully Providence has smiled upon us by causing the several colonies to unite so firmly together against the tyranny of Great Britain, though differing from each other in their particular interest, forms of government, modes of worship, and particular customs and manners, besides several animosities that had subsisted among them. That, under these circumstances, such a union should take place as we now behold, was a thing that might rather have been wished than hoped for.

And, in the next place, who could have thought that, when our charter was vacated, when we became destitute of any legislative authority, and when our courts of justice in many parts of the country were stopped, so that we could neither make nor execute laws upon offenders,—who, I say, would have thought, that in such a situation the people should behave so peaceably, and maintain such good order and harmony among themselves? This is a plain proof that they, having not the civil law to regulate themselves by, became a law unto themselves; and by their conduct they have shown that they were regulated by the law of God written in their hearts. This is the Lord's doing, and it ought to be marvelous in our eyes.

From what has been said in this discourse, it will appear that we are in the way of our duty in opposing the tyranny of Great Britain; for, if unlimited submission is not due to any human power, if we have an undoubted right to oppose and resist a set of tyrants that are subverting our just rights and privileges, there cannot remain a doubt in any man, that will calmly attend to reason, whether we have a right to resist and oppose the arbitrary measures of the King and Parliament; for it is plain to demonstration, nay, it is in a manner self-evident, that they have been and are endeavoring to deprive us not only of the privileges of Englishmen, and our charter rights, but they have endeavored to deprive us of what is much more sacred, viz., the privileges of men and Christians;[2] i.e., they are robbing us of the inalienable rights that the God of nature has given us as men and rational beings, and has confirmed to us in his written word as Christians and disciples of that Jesus who came to redeem us from the bondage of sin and the tyranny of Satan, and to grant us the most perfect freedom, even the glorious liberty of the sons and children of God; that here they have endeavored to deprive us of the sacred charter of the King of Heaven. But we have this for our consolation: the Lord reigneth; he governs the world in righteousness, and will avenge the cause of the oppressed when they cry unto him. We have made our appeal to Heaven, and we cannot doubt but that the Judge of all the earth will do right.

Need I upon this occasion descend to particulars? Can any one be ignorant what the things are of which we complain? Does not every one know that the King and Parliament have assumed the right to tax us without our consent? And can any one be so lost to the principles of humanity and common sense as not to view their conduct in this affair as a very grievous imposition? Reason and equity require that no one be obliged to pay a tax that he has never consented to, either by himself or by his representative. But, as Divine Providence has placed us at so great a distance from Great Britain that we neither are nor can be properly represented in the British Parliament, it is a plain proof that the Deity designed that we should have the powers of legislation and taxation among ourselves; for can any suppose it to be reasonable that a set of men that are perfect strangers to us should have the uncontrollable right to lay the most heavy and grievous burdens upon us that they please, purely to gratify their unbounded avarice and luxury? Must we be obliged to perish with cold and hunger to maintain them in idleness, in all kinds of debauchery and dissipation? But if they have the right to take our property from us without our consent, we must be wholly at their mercy for our food and raiment, and we know by sad experience that their tender mercies are cruel.

But because we were not willing to submit to such an unrighteous and cruel decree,—though we modestly complained and humbly petitioned for a redress of our grievances,—instead of hearing our complaints, and granting our requests, they have gone on to add iniquity to transgression, by making several cruel and unrighteous acts. Who can forget the cruel act to block up the harbor of Boston, whereby thousands of innocent persons must have been inevitably ruined had

---

[2] The meaning is not that they have attempted to deprive us of liberty of conscience, but that they have attempted to take away those rights which God has invested us with as his creatures and confirmed in his gospel, by which believers have a covenant right to the good things of this present life and world.

they not been supported by the continent? Who can forget the act for vacating our charter, together with many other cruel acts which it is needless to mention? But, not being able to accomplish their wicked purposes by mere acts of Parliament, they have proceeded to commence open hostilities against us, and have endeavored to destroy us by fire and sword. Our towns they have burnt, our brethren they have slain, our vessels they have taken, and our goods they have spoiled. And, after all this wanton exertion of arbitrary power, is there the man that has any of the feeling of humanity left who is not fired with a noble indignation against such merciless tyrants, who have not only brought upon us all the horrors of a civil war, but have also added a piece of barbarity unknown to Turks and Mohammedan infidels, yea, such as would be abhorred and detested by the savages of the wilderness,—I mean their cruelly forcing our brethren whom they have taken prisoners, without any distinction of whig or tory, to serve on board their ships of war, thereby obliging them to take up arms against their own countrymen, and to fight against their brethren, their wives, and their children, and to assist in plundering their own estates! This, my brethren, is done by men who call themselves Christians, against their Christian brethren,—against men who till now gloried in the name of Englishmen, and who were ever ready to spend their lives and fortunes in the defence of British rights. Tell it not in Gath, publish it not in the streets of Askelon, lest it cause our enemies to rejoice and our adversaries to triumph! Such a conduct as this brings a great reproach upon the profession of Christianity; nay, it is a great scandal even to human nature itself.

It would be highly criminal not to feel a due resentment against such tyrannical monsters. It is an indispensable duty, my brethren, which we owe to God and our country, to rouse up and bestir ourselves, and, being animated with a noble zeal for the sacred cause of liberty, to defend our lives and fortunes, even to the shedding the last drop of blood. The love of our country, the tender affection that we have for our wives and children, the regard we ought to have for unborn posterity, yea, everything that is dear and sacred, do now loudly call upon us to use our best endeavors to save our country. We must beat our ploughshares into swords, and our pruning-hooks into spears, and learn the art of self-defence against our enemies. To be careless and remiss, or to neglect the cause of our country through the base motives of avarice and self-interest, will expose us not only to the resentments of our fellow-creatures, but to the displeasure of God Almighty; for to such base wretches, in such a time as this, we may apply with the utmost propriety that passage in Jeremiah xlviii. 10: "Cursed be he that doth the work of the Lord deceitfully, and cursed be he that keepeth back his sword from blood." To save our country from the hands of our oppressors ought to be dearer to us even than our own lives, and, next the eternal salvation of our own souls, is the thing of the greatest importance,—a duty so sacred that it cannot justly be dispensed with for the sake of our secular concerns. Doubtless for this reason God has been pleased to manifest his anger against those who have refused to assist their country against its cruel oppressors. Hence, in a case similar to ours, when the Israelites were struggling to deliver themselves from the tyranny of Jabin, the King of Canaan, we find a most bitter curse denounced against those who refused to grant their assistance in the common cause; see Judges v. 23: "Curse ye Meroz, said the angel of the Lord, curse ye bitterly the inhabitants thereof; because they came not to the help of the Lord, to the help of the Lord against the mighty."

Now, if such a bitter curse is denounced against those who refused to assist their country against its oppressors, what a dreadful doom are those exposed to who have not only refused to assist their country in this time of distress, but have, through motives of interest or ambition, shown themselves enemies to their country by opposing us in the measures that we have taken, and by openly favoring the British Parliament! He that is so lost to humanity as to be willing to sacrifice his country for the sake of avarice or ambition, has arrived to the highest stage of wickedness that human nature is capable of, and deserves a much worse name than I at present care to give him. But I think I may with propriety say that such a person has forfeited his right to human society, and that he ought to take up his abode, not among the savage men, but among the savage beasts of the wilderness. Nor can I wholly excuse from blame those timid persons who, through their own cowardice, have been induced to favor our enemies, and have refused to act in defence of their country; for a due sense of the ruin and destruction that our enemies are bringing upon us is enough to raise such a resentment in the human breast that would, I should think, be sufficient to banish fear from the most timid male. And, besides, to indulge cowardice in such a cause argues a want of faith in God; for can he that firmly believes and relies upon the providence of God doubt whether he will avenge the cause of the injured when they apply to him for help? For my own part, when I consider the dispensations of Providence towards this land ever since our fathers first settled in Plymouth, I find abundant reason to conclude that the great Sovereign of the universe has planted a vine in this American wilderness which he has caused to take deep root, and it has filled the land, and that he will never suffer it to be plucked up or destroyed.

Our fathers fled from the rage of prelatical tyranny and persecution, and came into this land in order to enjoy liberty of conscience, and they have increased to a great people. Many have been the interposition of Divine Providence on our behalf, both in our fathers' days and ours; and, though we are now engaged in a war with Great Britain, yet we have been prospered in a most wonderful manner. And can we think that he who has thus far helped us will give us up into the hands of our enemies? Certainly he that has begun to deliver us will continue to show his mercy towards us, in saving us from the hands of our enemies: he will not forsake us if we do not foresake him. Our cause is so just and good that nothing can prevent our success but only our sins. Could I see a spirit of repentance and reformation prevail through the land, I should not have the least apprehension or fear of being brought under the iron rod of slavery, even though all the powers of the globe were combined against us. And though I confess that the irreligion and profaneness which are so common among us gives something of a damp to my spirits, yet I cannot help hoping, and even believing, that Providence has designed this continent for to be the asylum of liberty and true religion; for can we suppose that the God who created us free agents, and designed that we should glorify and serve him in this world that we might enjoy him forever hereafter, will suffer liberty and true religion to be banished from off the face of the earth? But do we not find that both religion and liberty seem to be expiring and gasping for life in the other continent?—where, then, can they find a harbor or place of refuge but in this?

There are some who pretend that it is against their consciences to take up arms in defence of their country; but can any rational being suppose that the Deity can require us to contradict the law of nature which he has written in our hearts, a part of which I am sure is the principle of self-defence, which strongly prompts us all to oppose any power that would take away our lives, or the lives of our friends? Now, for men to take pains to destroy the tender feelings of human nature, and to eradicate the principles of self-preservation, and then to persuade themselves that in so doing they submit to and obey the will of God, is a plain proof how easily men may be led to pervert the very first and plainest principles of reason and common sense, and argues a gross corruption of the human mind. We find such persons are very inconsistent with themselves; for no men are more zealous to defend their property, and to secure their estates from the encroachments of others, while they refuse to defend their persons, their wives, their children, and their country, against the assaults of the enemy. We see to what unaccountable lengths men will run when once they leave the plain mad of common sense, and violate the law which God has written in the heart. Thus some have thought they did God service when they unmercifully butchered and destroyed the lives of the servants of God; while others, upon the contrary extreme, believe that they please God while they sit still and quietly behold their friends and brethren killed by their unmerciful enemies, without endeavoring to defend or rescue them. The one is a sin of omission, and the other is a sin of commission, and it may perhaps be difficult to say, under certain circumstances, which is the most criminal in the sight of Heaven. Of this I am sure, that they are, both of them, great violations of the law of God.

Having thus endeavored to show the lawfulness and necessity of defending ourselves against the tyranny of Great Britain, I would observe that Providence seems plainly to point to us the expediency, and even necessity, of our considering ourselves as an independent state. For, not to consider the absurdity implied in making war against a power to which we profess to owe subjection, to pass by the impracticability of our ever coming under subjection to Great Britain upon fair and equitable terms, we may observe that the British Parliament has virtually declared us an independent state by authorizing their ships of war to seize all American property, wherever they can find it, without making any distinction between the friends of administration and those that have appeared in opposition to the acts of Parliament. This is making us a distinct nation from themselves. They can have no right any longer to style us rebels; for rebellion implies a particular faction risen up in opposition to lawful authority, and, as such, the factious party ought to be punished, while those that remain loyal are to be protected. But when war is declared against a whole community without distinction, and the property of each party is declared to be seizable, this, if anything can be, is treating us as an independent state. Now, if they are pleased to consider us as in a state of independency, who can object against our considering ourselves so too?

But while we are nobly opposing with our lives and estates the tyranny of the British Parliament, let us not forget the duty which we owe to our lawful magistrates; let us never mistake licentiousness for liberty. The more we understand the principles of liberty, the more readily shall we yield obedience to lawful authority; for no man can oppose good government but he that is a stranger to true liberty.

Let us ever check and restrain the factious disturbers of the peace; whenever we meet with persons that are loth to submit to lawful authority, let us treat them with the contempt which they deserve, and even esteem them as the enemies of their country and the pests of society. It is with peculiar pleasure that I reflect upon the peaceable behavior of my countrymen at a time when the courts of justice were stopped and the execution of laws suspended. It will certainly be expected of a people that could behave so well when they had nothing to restrain them but the laws written in their hearts, that they will yield all ready and cheerful obedience to lawful authority. There is at present the utmost need of guarding ourselves against a seditious and factious temper; for when we are engaged with so powerful an enemy from without, our political salvation, under God, does, in an eminent manner, depend upon our being firmly united together in the bonds of love to one another, and of due submission to lawful authority. I hope we shall never give any just occasion to our adversaries to reproach us as being men of turbulent dispositions and licentious principles, that cannot bear to be restrained by good and wholesome laws, even though they are of our own making, nor submit to rulers of our own choosing. But I have reason to hope much better things of my countrymen, though I thus speak. However, in this time of difficulty and distress, we cannot be too much guarded against the least approaches to discord and faction. Let us, while we are jealous of our rights, take heed of unreasonable suspicions and evil surmises which have no proper foundation; let us take heed lest we hurt the cause of liberty by speaking evil of the ruler of the people.

Let us treat our rulers with all that honor and respect which the dignity of their station requires; but let it be such an honor and respect as is worthy of the sons of freedom to give. Let us ever abhor the base arts that are used by fawning parasites and cringing courtiers, who by their low artifices and base flatteries obtain offices and posts which they are unqualified to sustain, and honors of which they are unworthy, and oftentimes have a greater number of places assigned them than any one person of the greatest abilities can ever properly fill, by means of which the community becomes greatly injured, for this reason, that many an important trust remains undischarged, and many an honest and worthy member of society is deprived of those honors and privileges to which he has a just right, whilst the most despicable, worthless courtier is loaded with honorable and profitable commissions. In order to avoid this evil, I hope our legislators will always despise flattery as something below the dignity of a rational mind, and that they will ever scorn the man that will be corrupted or take a bribe. And let us all resolve with ourselves that no motives of interest, nor hopes of preferment shall ever induce us to act the part of fawning courtiers towards men in power. Let the honor and respect which we show our superiors be true and genuine, flowing from a sincere and upright heart.

The honors that have been paid to arbitrary princes have often been very hypocritical and insincere. Tyrants have been flattered in their vices, and have often had an idolatrous reverence paid them. The worst princes have been the most flattered and adored; and many such, in the pagan world, assumed the title of gods, and had divine honors paid them. This idolatrous reverence has ever been the inseparable concomitant of arbitrary power and tyrannical government; for even Christian princes, if they have not been adored under the character of gods, yet the titles given them strongly savor of blasphemy, and the reverence paid them is really idolatrous. What right has a poor sinful worm of the dust to claim the title of his most sacred Majesty? Most sacred certainly belongs only to God alone,—for there is none holy as the Lord,—yet how common is it to see this title given to kings! And how often have we been told that the king can do no wrong! Even though he should be so foolish and wicked as hardly to be capable of ever being in the right, yet still it must be asserted and maintained that it is impossible for him to do wrong!

The cruel, savage disposition of tyrants, and the idolatrous reverence that is paid them, are both most beautifully exhibited to view by the apostle John in the Revelation, thirteenth chapter, from the first to the tenth verse, where the apostle gives a description of a horrible wild beast[3] which he saw rise out of the sea,

---

[3] Wild beast. By the beast with seven heads and ten horns I understand the tyranny of arbitrary princes, viz., the emperors and kings of the Eastern and Western Roman Empire, and not the tyranny of the Pope and clergy; for the description of every part of this beast will answer better to be understood of political than of ecclesiastical tyrants. Thus the seven heads are generally interpreted to denote the several forms of Roman government; the ten horns are understood of the ten kingdoms that were set up in the Western Empire; and by the body of the beast it seems most natural to understand the Eastern, or Greek Empire, for it is said to be like a leopard. This image is taken from Daniel vii. 6, where the third beast is said to be like a leopard. Now, by the third beast in Daniel is understood, by the best interpreters, the Grecian Monarchy. It is well known that John frequently borrows his images from Daniel, and I believe it will be found, upon a critical examination of the matter, that whenever he does so he means the same thing with Daniel; if this be true (as I am fully persuaded it is), then, by the body of this beast being like a leopard in the Revelation of John, is to be understood the Eastern, or Greek Empire, which was that part of the old Roman Empire that remained whole for several ages after the Western Empire was broken into ten kingdoms. Further: after the beast was risen it is said that the dragon gave him his seat. Now, by the dragon is meant the devil, who is represented as presiding over the Roman Empire in its pagan state; but the seat of the Roman Empire in its pagan state was Rome. Here, then, is a prophecy that the emperor of the East should become possessed of Rome, which exactly agrees with what we know from history to be fact; for the Emperor Justinian's generals having expelled the

having seven heads and ten horns, and upon his heads the names of blasphemy. By heads are to be understood forms of government, and by blasphemy, idolatry; so that it seems implied that there will be a degree of idolatry in every form of tyrannical government. This beast is represented as having the body of a leopard, the feet of a bear, and the mouth of a lion; i.e., a horrible monster, possessed of the rage and fury of the lion, the fierceness of the bear, and the swiftness of the leopard to seize and devour its prey. Can words more strongly point out, or exhibit in more lively colors, the exceeding rage, fury, and impetuosity of tyrants, in their destroying and making havoc of mankind? To this beast we find the dragon gave his power, seat, and great authority; i.e., the devil constituted him to be his vicegerent on earth; this is to denote that tyrants are the ministers of Satan, ordained by him for the destruction of mankind.

Such a horrible monster, we should have thought, would have been abhorred and detested of all mankind, and that all nations would have joined their powers and forces together to oppose and utterly destroy him from off the face of the earth; but, so far are they from doing this, that, on the contrary, they are represented as worshipping him (verse 8): "And all that dwell on the earth shall worship him," viz., all those "whose names are not written in the Lamb's book of life", i.e., the wicked world shall pay him an idolatrous reverence, and worship him with a godlike adoration. What can in a more lively manner show the gross stupidity and wickedness of mankind, in thus tamely giving up their just rights into the hands of tyrannical monsters, . . . and in so readily paying them such an unlimited obedience as is due to God alone?

We may observe, further, that these men are said (verse 4) to "worship the dragon";—not that it is to be supposed that they, in direct terms, paid divine homage to Satan, but that the adoration paid to the beast, who was Satan's vicegerent, did ultimately centre in him. Hence we learn that those who pay an undue and sinful veneration to tyrants are properly the servants of the devil; they are worshipers of the prince of darkness, for in him all that undue homage and

---

Goths our of Italy, Rome was brought into subjection to the emperor of the East, and was for a long time governed by the emperor's lieutenant, who resided at Ravenna. These considerations convince me that the Greek Empire, and not the Pope and his clergy, is to be understood by the body of the beast, which was like a leopard. And what further confirms me in this belief is, that it appears to me that the Pope and the papal clergy are to be understood by the second beast which we read of in Revelation xiii. 11-17, for of him it is said that "he had two horns like a lamb." A lamb, we know, is the figure by which Jesus Christ is signified in the Revelation and many other parts of the New Testament. The Pope claims both a temporal and spiritual sovereignty, denoted by the two horns, under the character of the vicar of Jesus Christ, and yet under this high pretence of being the vicar of Jesus Christ, he speaks like a dragon; i.e., he promotes idolatry in the Christian Church, in like manner as the dragon did in the heathen world. To distinguish him from the first beast, he is called (Revelation xix.) "the false prophet that wrought miracles;" i.e., like Mahomet, he pretends to be a lawgiver, and claims infallibility, and his emissaries endeavor to confirm this doctrine by pretended miracles. How wonderfully do all these characters agree to the Pope! Wherefore I conclude that the second, and not the first beast, denotes the tyranny of the Pope and his clergy.

adoration centres that is given to his ministers. Hence that terrible denunciation of divine wrath against the worshippers of the beast and his image: "If any man worship the beast and his image, and receive his mark in his forehead, or in his hand, the same shall drink of the wine of the wrath of God which is poured out without mixture into the cup of his indignation, and he shall be tormented with fire and brimstone in the presence of the holy angels, and in the presence of the Lamb; and the smoke of their torment ascendeth for ever and ever: and they have no rest day nor night, who worship the beast and his image, and who receive the mark of his name."[4] We have here set forth in the clearest manner, by the inspired apostle, God's abhorrence of tyranny and tyrants, together with the idolatrous reverence that their wretched subjects are wont to pay them, and the awful denunciation of divine wrath against those who are guilty of this undue obedience to tyrants.

Does it not, then, highly concern us all to stand fast in the liberty wherewith Heaven hath made us free, and to strive to get the victory over the beast and his image—over every species of tyranny? Let us look upon a freedom from the power of tyrants as a blessing that cannot be purchased too dear, and let us bless God that he has so far delivered us from that idolatrous reverence which men are so very apt to pay to arbitrary tyrants; and let us pray that he would be pleased graciously to perfect the mercy he has begun to show us by confounding the devices of our enemies and bringing their counsels to nought, and by establishing our just rights and privileges upon such a firm and lasting basis that the powers of earth and hell shall not prevail against it.

Under God, every person in the community ought to contribute his assistance to the bringing about so glorious and important an event; but in a more eminent manner does this important business belong to the gentlemen that are chosen to represent the people in this General Assembly, including those that have been appointed members of the Honorable Council Board.

Honored fathers, we look up to you, in this day of calamity and distress, as the guardians of our invaded rights, and the defenders of our liberties against British tyranny. You are called, in Providence, to save your country from ruin. A trust is reposed in you of the highest importance to the community that can be conceived of, its business the most noble and grand, and a task the most arduous and difficult to accomplish that ever engaged the human mind—I mean as to things of the present life. But as you are engaged in the defence of a just and righteous cause, you may with firmness of mind commit your cause to God, and depend on his kind providence for direction and assistance. You will have the fervent wishes and prayers of all good men that God would crown all your labors with success, and direct you into such measures as shall tend to promote the welfare and happiness of the community, and afford you all that wisdom and prudence which is necessary to regulate the affairs of state at this critical period.

Honored fathers of the House of Representatives: We trust to your wisdom and goodness that you will be led to appoint such men to be in council whom you know to be men of real principle, and who are of unblemished lives; that

---

[4] Rev. xiv. 9, 10.

have shown themselves zealous and hearty friends to the liberties of America; and men that have the fear of God before their eyes; for such only are men that can be depended upon uniformly to pursue the general good.

My reverend fathers and brethren in the ministry will remember that, according to our text, it is part of the work and business of a gospel minister to teach his hearers the duty they owe to magistrates. Let us, then, endeavor to explain the nature of their duty faithfully, and show them the difference between liberty and licentiousness; and, while we are animating them to oppose tyranny and arbitrary power, let us inculcate upon them the duty of yielding due obedience to lawful authority. In order to the right and faithful discharge of this part of our ministry, it is necessary that we should thoroughly study the law of nature, the rights of mankind, and the reciprocal duties of governors and governed. By this means we shall be able to guard them against the extremes of slavish submission to tyrants on one hand, and of sedition and licentiousness on the other. We may, I apprehend, attain a thorough acquaintance with the law of nature and the rights of mankind, while we remain ignorant of many technical terms of law, and are utterly unacquainted with the obscure and barbarous Latin that was so much used in the ages of popish darkness and Superstition.

To conclude: While we are fighting for liberty, and striving against tyranny, let us remember to fight the good fight of faith, and earnestly seek to be delivered from that bondage of corruption which we are brought into by sin, and that we may be made partakers of the glorious liberty of the sons and children of God: which may the Father of Mercies grant us all, through Jesus Christ. AMEN.

11

"An Antidote against Toryism"

Nathaniel Whitaker

A native of Long Island, New York, Nathaniel Whitaker (1732-1783) served as minister to the Third Church in Salem, Massachusetts, from 1769 until shortly before his death. This sermon was delivered in Salem, was printed in 1777 as the American war effort began in earnest, and was dedicated to General George Washington.

The sum of the law of nature, as well as of the written law, is love. Love to God and man, properly exercised in tender feelings of the heart, and beneficent actions of life, constitutes perfect holiness. The gospel breathes the same spirit, and acknowledges none as the disciples of Christ but those who love not their friends only, but even their enemies. Bless and curse not, is one of the laws of his kingdom. Yet the aversion of men to this good and benevolent law prompts them to frequent violations of it, which is the source of all the evils we feel or fear. And so lost are many to all the tender feelings required in this law, as to discover their enmity to their Creator, by opposing the happiness of his creatures, and spreading misery and ruin among them.

When such characters as these present themselves to our view, if we are possessed with the spirit of love required in the law and gospel, we must feel a holy abhorrence of them. Love itself implies hatred to malevolence, and the man who feels no abhorrence of it, may be assured he is destitute of a benevolent temper, and ranks with the enemies of God and man. For, as God himself hates sin with a perfect hatred from the essential holiness of his nature, and sinners cannot stand in his sight, so the greater our conformity to him is, the greater will be our abhorrence of those persons and actions which are opposite to the divine law. David mentions this as an evidence of his love to God: *"Do not I hate them, O Lord, that hate thee? and am I not grieved with them that rise up against thee? I hate them with a perfect hatred. I count them mine enemies."*[1] True benevolence is, therefore, exercised in opposing those who seek the hurt of society, and none are to be condemned as acting against the law of love, because

---

[1] Ps. 89: 21, 22.

they hate and oppose such as are injurious to happiness.[2] But the weakness and corruption of nature, in the best, is such, that God hath not intrusted to men at large the exercise of the resentment due to such characters, nor allowed them to inflict those punishments which their crimes call for, even in this world, except in some special cases. On the contrary, he hath strictly prohibited all his subjects taking vengeance for private or personal injuries in a private and personal matter, and require, that if "one smite us on the one cheek, we turn to him the other also";[3] and, in the language of love, exhorts us: "Dearly beloved, avenge not yourselves." Yet there are cases in which he requires us, as his servants, to take vengeance on his enemies. And it deserves our particular notice, that all these cases respect crimes which tend to destroy human happiness.

Even his commands to punish blasphemy and other sins which strike more directly against himself, are not given because his own happiness is thereby diminished, but because they tend to erase from our minds that sense of his glorious majesty, authority, and government, without the belief of which, all order and peace among men would come to an end. So God requires us to execute vengeance on the murderer, the thief, the adulterer, reviler, and the like; all which sins strike at the peace and happiness of human society. God's heart is so much set upon diffusing happiness among his creatures, by which he most displays his glory, that he perfectly abhors whatever tends to frustrate this end; and has threatened the least opposition to it with everlasting death in the world to come. But some (through corruption of nature by sin) have not faith in a future state of rewards and punishments sufficient to influence them to their duty, or deter them from opposing God's gracious purpose, therefore, to strike our senses with full conviction of his anger against such as counteract his benevolent designs, he has commanded every society of men, to inflict punishment on them in this world, and has specified the crimes, the punishments, and the officers who are to inflict them.

Every punishment involves in it a curse, and presupposes some crime; and the curse or punishment is by God exactly proportioned to the nature, heinousness, and circumstances of the crime. Therefore, when a grievous punishment is inflicted, we justly infer the aggravation of the offence. To inflict punishment, is actively to curse, and when we pronounce a curse, we do, as far as we can, consign over the object to some punishment. But when God commands us to curse any person or people, we are bound by his authority actually to punish them.

These observations may lead us to some apprehension of the aggravated nature of the sin of Meroz, whom Israel are commanded to curse bitterly for their conduct in an affair of a public nature.

The text I have chosen as the theme of my discourse, is part of a song uttered by Deborah and Barak, in holy triumph and praise for a signal victory obtained over Jabin, king of Canaan, and Sisera, the captain of his host. This

---

[2] Even God's hatred of sin, and the punishment he inflicts on the wicked, arise from his happiness, from the benevolence of his nature.
[3] Matt. 5:39.

powerful prince, who had nine hundred chariots of iron, and a mighty army, had brought Israel into subjection, and grievously oppressed them for twenty years. This cruel and galling yoke awakened them to a sense of their sin against God, and to cry to him for deliverance. No sooner are they made sensible of their sin against, and dependence upon him, and to repent and seek his favor and protection, than he appears for their help, and raises up and inspires Deborah and Barak with courage, and faith in his power and grace, to oppose the tyrant, and shake off his yoke. A few men of Zebulon and Naphtali, viz., ten thousand, were designed by God to have the honor of conquering this potent king; for ten other tribes mustered and were ready for the war, yet it seems Zebulon and Naphtali only, were the people that jeoparded their lives to the death, in the high places of the field. And the little army—raised from two tribes only out of twelve—of Deborah and Barak march out and wage war against their oppressor, for the recovery of their freedom.[4]

Jabin, it seems had no knowledge or thought that Israel was arming against him. The first intelligence brought him was, that Barak was gone up to Mount Tabor, that he had already marched, and was on his way to invade the country. Some traitors, who pretended friendship to Israel, carried him the news, hoping, doubtless, to ingratiate themselves with Jabin, by giving him the earliest notice possible of this revolt.

No doubt, both Jabin and Sisera despised this small body of undisciplined, unarmed troops, and were confident they should carry all before them, and quickly reduce those rebels (as he, doubtless, termed them) to their former obedience. But God, who disposes all events, not only gave the victory to Israel, but utterly destroyed the whole host of Jabin, that not one escaped, except Sisera the captain-general, and him God delivered to be slain by the hand of a woman. Women have sometimes been the deliverers of their country, and can, when God inspires them with courage, face the proudest foe. Oh, how easy is it with God to

---

[4] Some people, not the inhabitants of Meroz, fear the event of our present struggle, (1), on account of our inability, however we may exert ourselves, to oppose the power of the tyrant; and hence, though desirous of freedom, through want of faith in the power and grace of God, dare not act, and so weaken the cause they wish might succeed. Or, (2), they despair of success, because of so many in these states who are lukewarm in the cause, and secretly or openly friends to the tyrant. And, (3), some serious people despair of success because of the abounding sins of our land. For the relief and establishment of such, I entreat them to consider that none of the twelve tribes are mentioned as entering the field but Zebulon and Naphtali; and not another as remotely favoring the cause, but Ephraim, Benjamin, Issachar, and Machir, of the family of Caleb. Their divisions then were much greater than ours. For the divisions of Reuben there were great searchings of heart. . . . As to their power, their army was but ten thousand, and these without arms; for Deborah informs us, that neither shield nor spear was seen among forty thousand in Israel. As to their sins, they had greatly revolted, and chosen them new gods, which was high treason against their king. But, notwithstanding all the discouragements, we find victory declaring for them on their repentence, and proper exertion of the little power they had. This must surely remove all our fears in our present struggle, unless impenitence and unbelief still rule in our hearts, by which we shall incur the curse of Meroz.

save from the greatest danger, and, by the weakest instruments, conquer the most powerful enemies!

Deborah and Barak, deeply impressed with a sense of God's mercy in this deliverance, sang this song as an expression of their joy and gratitude, from which, would time allow, many instructive lessons might be deduced. But the words of my text lead us more directly to consider some things most worthy our attention this day, and therefore I have chosen them as the theme of the following discourse, and in them we may observe:

I. The crime for which this bitter curse is denounced on the inhabitants of Meroz. Probably this was some town or state in Israel, who, being called to furnish their quota of men and money for the war, through fear of bad success and, in that case, of a heavier burden; or from a secret lurch to the enemy, arising from hope of court preferment, or favors already bestowed on some of their leading men; or from some other sinister motive, thought best to lie still, and not meddle in the quarrel. So much is certain, they did not go with Barak to the war. The crime they are charged with, is not their aiding, assisting, or furnishing the enemy, or holding a secret correspondence with, or taking up arms to help them; they are not charged as laying plots to circumvent the rest, or striving to discourage their neighbors from going to the war, or as terrifying others with descriptions of the irresistible power of Jabin's nine hundred chariots of iron and the like. No, the inhabitants of Meroz were innocent people compared to these; they were only negatively wicked; they only failed in their duty; they did not arm to recover their liberties when wrested from them by the hand of tyranny. This is all the fault charged on them, yet for this they incurred the fearful curse in my text. Now, if for mere negligence they deserved this curse, what must they have deserved who aided and assisted the enemy? Surely a sevenfold bitterer curse.

II. Observe the curse pronounced: "Curse ye Meroz, curse ye bitterly the inhabitants thereof." Their conduct, on that occasion, was such as deserved a severe punishment from the other states, who are commanded to separate them unto evil, as a just reward of their neglect.

III. We observe by whom this curse was to be pronounced and inflicted. Not by Deborah and Barak alone, in a fit of anger, as profane persons in a rage curse their neighbors, and undertake to punish them; such often pronounce curses without cause, but the curse causeless shall not come. This curse was to be pronounced and inflicted by all the people, who are here required to be of one heart, and engage seriously, religiously, and determinately in cursing them, and as God's ministers to execute his wrath upon them. We may not suppose that this work was left to the people at large, or to a mob; but the rulers are first to proceed against them,[5] and all the people to support and assist them in this work; and so all were to join, as one man, to curse them, and that bitterly, i.e., they were fully and without hesitation to condemn them to severe punishment, and inflict it on them. They were not to deal gingerly with them, nor palliate their offence. They are allowed to make no excuses for them, nor to plead "that they were of a different opinion; that they thought it their duty not to take up arms

---

[5] This is evident from the order of government God established in Israel.

against their king that ruled over them, but to submit to the higher powers; that liberty of conscience ought to be allowed to every one, and that it would be hard to punish them for acting their own judgments."[6] No such pleas might be made for them, nor one word spoken in their favor, their sin being against the great law of love and light of nature; but all, with full purpose of heart, were to curse those cowardly, selfish, cringing, lukewarm, half-way, two-faced people, and to treat them as outcasts, and unworthy the common protection or society of others.

IV. Observe by whose command they were required to curse Meroz. It was not by the command of Deborah and Barak, but of God himself; yea by the command of Jesus Christ, the meek and compassionate Saviour of men. Curse ye Meroz, said the angel of the Lord. This was the angel of God's presence, who then fought for Israel, and who was so offended with the people of Meroz for their selfishness and indifference in this important cause, that he not only cursed them himself, but commands all the people to curse them, and inflict his wrath on them in this world.

V. Observe the circumstances which aggravated their crime, viz.: the enemy that enslaved them was mighty. Had the foe been weak and contemptible, there had been less need of their help. But when a powerful tyrant oppressed them, and they were called upon to unite with their suffering brethren in shaking off his yoke, and all their strength little enough to oppose him, then to excuse themselves, was highly criminal, and in effect to join with the tyrant to rivet slavery and misery on the whole nation. This was highly provoking to God, whose great end is, to diffuse happiness, and not misery, among his creatures, and who never punishes but when his subjects oppose this design.

This was the crisis when their all lay at stake. They well knew that their brethren (however they themselves might be distinguished with court favors by the tyrant) were groaning under cruel bondage. But as selfishness renders people callous and unfeeling to the distresses of others, so they were easy and satisfied to see their brethren tortured by the unrelenting hand of oppression, if so be they might sleep in a whole skin. They were contented that others should go forth and endure the hardships of war, but refused to engage in the work, or bear any part of the burden with them, though all was hazarded through their neglect. How base was this conduct, while they knew the strength of the enemy? This consideration was enough to have engaged every one, not lost to the feelings of humanity, to the firmest union, and the most vigorous exertions. But these servile wretches would rather bear the yoke, and see the whole land involved in slavery, than enter the field, and share the glory of regaining their freedom from a powerful foe. They preferred their present ease, or some court favor, with chains and slavery, to the glorious freedom they were born to enjoy.

---

[6] Liberty of conscience is often pleaded in excuse for the worst of crimes. In matters of mere conscience the plea is valid, but nothing else. Those are matters of mere conscience in which none are concerned but God and the person acting; as in matters of faith and worship. But when actions respect society, and become injurious to the civil rights of men, they are proper subjects of civil laws, and may be punished, notwithstanding the plea for liberty of conscience.

From this view of the text and context, we may deduce the following doctrinal observations:

I. That the cause of liberty is the cause of God and truth.

II. That to take arms and repel force by force, when our liberties are invaded, is well pleasing to God.

III. That it is lawful to levy war against those who oppress us, even when they are not in arms against us.

IV. That indolence and backwardness in taking arms, and exerting ourselves in the service of our country, when called thereto by the public voice, in order to recover and secure our freedom, is an heinous sin in the sight of God.

V. That God requires a people, struggling for their liberties, to treat such of the community who will not join them, as open enemies, and to reject them as unworthy the privileges which others enjoy.

I. The cause of freedom is the cause of God. To open this, I will inquire:

1st. What we are to understand by liberty, or freedom? and then,

2d. Prove that this is the cause of God.

1. What is meant by liberty, or freedom?

It is sufficient to my present purpose to distinguish liberty into moral, natural and civil.[7]

Moral liberty lies in an ability, or opportunity, to act or conduct as the agent pleases.

He that is not hindered by any external force from acting as he chooses or wills to act, is perfectly free in a moral sense; and so far as he possesses this freedom, so far, and no farther, is he a moral, accountable creature, and his actions worthy of praise or blame.

By natural liberty, I mean that freedom of action and conduct which all men have a right to, antecedent to their being members of society. This Mr. Locke defines to be "that state or condition in which all men naturally are to order all their actions, and dispose of themselves and possessions as they think fit, within the bounds of the law of nature, without asking leave, or depending on the will of any man." In this state all men are equal, and no one hath a right to govern or control another. And the law of nature or the eternal reason and fitness of things, is to be the only rule of his conduct; of the meaning of which every one is to be his own judge.

But since the corruption of nature by sin, the lusts and passions of men so blind their minds, and harden their hearts, that this perfect law of love is little

---

[7] I purposely omit what Dr. Price, in his excellent Observations on Civil Liberty, p. 2, calls physical liberty; which, I venture to say, with deference to this great man, is not to be found, as he defines it, in any intelligent agent in the universe. For, that actions may be "properly ours," he makes them the effects of self-determination only, "without the operation of any foreign cause." This, at one blow, demolishes all the power and value of motives which are always foreign to the actions they produce, as the cause is to the effect. And thus the issue is, that we must act without any reason, motive, aim, or end of our actions, in order that they may be properly our own. But this reduces us to mere machines.

considered, and less practised; so that a state of nature, which would have been a state of perfect freedom and happiness had man continued in his first rectitude, is a state of war, rapine and murder. Hence arises an absoluted necessity that societies should form themselves into politics bodies, in order to enact laws for the public safety, and appoint some to put them in execution, that the good may be encouraged, and the vicious deterred from evil practices; and these laws should always be founded on the law of nature.[8]

Hence it appears, that perfect civil liberty differs from natural only in this, that in a natural state our actions, persons and possessions, are under the direction, judgment and control of none but ourselves; but in a civil state, under the direction of others, according to the laws of that state in which we live; which, by the supposition, are perfectly agreeable to the law of nature. In the first case, private judgment; in the second, the public judgment of the sense of the law of nature, is to be the rule of conduct. When this is the case, civil liberty is perfect, and every one enjoys all that freedom which God designed for his rational creatures in a social state. All liberty beyond this is mere licentiousness—a liberty to sin, which is the worst of slavery. But when any laws are enacted which cross the law of nature, there civil liberty is invaded, and God and man justly offended. Therefore, when those appointed to enact and execute laws, invade this liberty, they violate their trust, and oppress their subjects, and their constituents may lawfully depose them by force of arms, if they refuse to reform.

Now, if it be unlawful for magistrates in a state, to bind their subjects by laws contrary to the law of nature, and if in this case it is lawful for their subjects to depose them, it follows, *a fortiori*, that should the rulers of one state assume a power to bind the people of another state who never intrusted them with a legislative power, by such unrighteous laws, those oppressed people would be under no kind of obligation to submit to them, but ought, if in their power, to oppose them and recover their liberty. Therefore the freedom of a society or state consists in acting according to their own choice, within the bounds of the law of nature, in governing themselves independent of all other states. This is the liberty wherewith God hath made every state free, and which no power on earth may lawfully abridge, but by their own consent; nor can they lawfully consent to have it abridged, but where it appears for the greater good of society in general: and when this end cannot be attained, they have a right to resume their former freedom, if in their power.

2. I proceed to prove that the cause of civil liberty is the cause of God. This follows from what hath now been said. For if the law of nature is the law of God, and if God hath given every society or state liberty independent of all other states, to act according to their own choice in governing themselves within the bounds of the law of nature, then it follows that this freedom is of God, and he

---

[8] Civil liberty is the freedom of bodies politic, or states. This is well defined by Dr. Price, p. 2, to be "the power of a civil society or state to govern itself by its own discretion, or by laws of its own making, without being subject to any foreign direction or the impositions of any extraneous power."

that is an advocate for it espouses the cause of God, and he that opposes it opposes God himself. This liberty hath God not only given, but entailed on all men, so that they cannot resign it to any creature without sin. Therefore, should any state, through fear, resign this freedom to any other power, it would be offensive to God. Thus, had America submitted to, and acquiesced in the declaration of the British Parliament, "That they have a right to bind us in all cases whatsoever," we should have greatly provoked God by granting that prerogative to men, which belongs to God only; nor could we have reason to hope for pardon and the divine favor on our land, without unfeigned repentence; but, as repentence implies a change of conduct as well as of mind, so we must have exerted ourselves to undo what we had done, and by every method in our power to cast off the chains and resume our liberty. But, to leave the dim light of reason, let us hear what divine revelation says in my text and context.

Israel were a free, independent commonwealth, planted by God in Canaan, in much the same manner that he planted us in America. The nations around always viewed them with an envious and jealous eye, as well they might, since they drove out seven nations more powerful than themselves, and possessed their land. But when, by their grievous sins they provoked God, he often permitted those neighboring nations to invade their rights, that they might be brought to a sense of their sin and duty.

Jabin, the king of Canaan, one of those states, was God's rod to humble them. He invaded Israel, robbed them of their rights, and held them in slavery twenty years; in all which he acted the part of a cruel tyrant, and provoked God, to his own destruction. Jabin had long ruled over Israel; but this gave him no right. His dominion was still mere usurpation, as he robbed them of the liberty God had given them; and with a single view to recover this and punish the invader, God commanded them to wage war on the tyrant, and shake off his yoke. They obey the divine mandate, assemble their forces, call on the various states to join them in the glorious conflict; and God himself curses those who would not assist to punish this oppressor.

No doubt, Jabin called this rebellion, and made proclamation that all who were found in arms, or any way aiding the revolt, should be deemed and treated as rebels, and their estates confiscated; but that all who would make their submissions, should enjoy all their privileges, as before, at his sovereign disposal. A glorious offer! How worthy the joyful and thoughtful acceptance of men born to freedom! Rather where's the wretch so sordid as not to feel this as an insult to human nature: or where's the Christian that does not view it as a reproach of his God? and who will not, with good Hezekiah, spread before the Lord, in humble prayer, the words of this Rabshekah, published to reproach our God, as unable to defend us, though engaged in his cause? Or where is the man, so lost to all noble and generous feelings, that would not choose to die in the field of martial glory, rather than accept such insulting terms of peace, or rather of misery; to live and see himself, his friends, his wife, children and country, subjugated to the arbitrary will and disposal of a merciless tyrant?

But doubtless these inviting, gracious terms of peace, had great influence on some. The inhabitants of Meroz seem to have been such dastardly, low-spirited, court sycophants; and also many in the tribe of Reuben, for whose divisions there were great searchings of heart. These probably trembled at the power of Jabin, and thought him invincible, though opposing God himself, whose cause they were called to espouse. Some might call the war rebellion, and others, by open or secret practices, discourage and weaken the cause.

This is very applicable to our present case. We are declared rebels by the king of England. His servants offer pardon to all those who will lay themselves at his feet to dispose of as he shall see fit, and "to bind them, their children and estates, at his pleasure, in all cases whatsoever." What gracious terms of peace! Must not this yoke sit with peculiar ease and pleasure on the necks of freeborn Americans! Yet, with horror be it spoken, there are freeborn sons of America so lost to all sense of honor, liberty, and every noble feeling, as to join the cry, and press for submission. O tell it not in Gath, publish it not in the streets of Ashkelon. We have some, but blessed be God, that we have no more of the inhabitants of Meroz scattered among us; some whose endeavors to divide us, cause great searchings of heart. But be it known to them, and to all men, that they, as Meroz, are fighting against God. This assertion is confirmed by the curse denounced on Meroz by God's command; for had they not opposed him, he would not have cursed them. They, then, were the rebels, in the judgment of God, and not those who took up arms to recover their liberties; rebels against the God of Heaven; and therefore fell under his and his people's curse; as well as those shall, who oppose or neglect to promote the like glorious cause.

From what hath been said, the truth of the second observation appears, viz.:

II. That to take arms, and repel force by force, when our liberties are invaded, is well pleasing to God.

This is a natural consequence from what is said above, and from the text itself. Deborah and Barak, in taking arms against Jabin, acted agreeably to the law of nature, which is the law of love; were also particularly excited, directed, and commanded thereto by God himself.[9] They did not, by this war, aim at dominion over others, nor seek to deprive any of their natural rights; but only to recover and secure the liberties and rights which had been wrested from them, that they might thereby spread peace and happiness through all the tribes of Israel; while the real happiness of others would not thereby be diminished. This, by the law of nature, was sufficient to justify them. If, then, they conformed to the law of love in taking up arms, and if God required them to make war on Jabin, then it was undeniably pleasing to him. But, if God approved their conduct in this case, he certainly will approve the like conduct in all similar cases. Therefore, when one country or state invades the liberties of another, it is lawful, and well pleasing to God, for the oppressed to defend their rights by force of arms. Yea, to neglect this, when there is a rational prospect of success, is a sin—a sin against God, and discovers a want of that benevolence, and desire of happiness of our fellow-creatures, which is the highest glory of saints.

I need not spend time to prove that our struggle with Great Britain is very similar to that of Israel and Jabin. As they had, so have we been long oppressed

---

[9] Judg., 4:6,7.

by a power that never had any equitable right to our land, or to rule over us, but by our own consent, and agreeably to a solemn compact. When they violated this, all their right ceased, and they could have no better claim to dominion than Jabin had over Israel. A power, indeed, has been usurped by Great Britain, "to bind us in all cases whatsoever"; which claim hath already produced many most unrighteous and oppressive laws, which they have attempted to enforce by their fleets and armies; in all which they can be no more justified than Jabin in his tyranny over Israel. Therefore, if it was their duty to fight for the recovery of their freedom, it must likewise be ours. And to neglect this, when called to it by the public voice, will expose us to the curse of Meroz. Yea,

III. It is lawful, yea duty, to levy war against those who oppress us, even when they are not in arms against us, if there be a rational probability of success.

I say, if there be a rational probability of success. For the law of love or nature will not justify opposition to the greatest oppression, when such opposition must be attended with greater evils than submission. Therefore, the primitive Christians, and many of later ages, did not opposed their cruel persecutors; as it would, without a miracle, have brought on them inevitable destruction. But where there is a rational probability of success, any people may lawfully, and it is their duty to, levy war on those who rob them of their rights, whether they be rulers in the state they live in, or any more distant powers, even before war is waged against them.

The truth of this appears from the instance before us. Jabin at this time was not at war with Israel; no, they had been conquered and under his government twenty years; and nothing was heard, but the groans and cries of the oppressed. How then, it may be asked, can they be justified in commencing a war? Doubtless they had often petitioned for redress of grievances, as we have done, and to as little purpose. What more could they do in a peaceable way? They were reduced to the dreadful alternative, either tamely to submit themselves and children after them, to the galling yoke of merciless tyranny, or wage war on the tyrant. The last was the measure God approved, and therefore, by a special command, enjoined it on them. This we are sure he would not have done, had it been offensive to him. He did not require Israel to wait till Jabin had invaded their country and struck the first blow (as we did in respect to our British oppressors), but while all the peace in his kingdom, for aught we find, God commands Israel to raise an army, and invade the tyrant's dominions.

The moral reason of this is obvious. For usurpation or oppression, is offensive war, already levied. Any state which usurps a power over another state, or rulers who, by a wanton use of their power, oppress their subjects, do thereby break the peace, and commence an offensive war. In such a case opposition is mere self-defence, and is no more criminal, yea, as really our duty as to defend ourselves against a murderer, or highway robber. Self-preservation is an instinct God implanted in our nature. Therefore we sin against God and nature, when we tamely resign our rights to tyrants, or quietly submit to public oppressors, if it be in our power to defend ourselves.

A rebel, indeed, is a monster in nature, an enemy not only to his country, but to all mankind; he is destitute of that benevolence which is the highest honor and glory of the rational nature. But what is a rebel?—what those actions, for which a man or people deserve this opprobrious charge? Those only are rebels who are enemies to good government, and oppose such as duly execute it. A state of nature is a state of war. Civil government, which is founded in the consent of society to be governed by certain laws framed for the general good, and duly executed by some appointed thereto, puts an end to this sate, and secures peace and safety. He, therefore, who transgresses this compact, even he opposes good government, and is a rebel, *rebellat*—he raises war again.

In this, it matters not whether the person be a king or a subject; he is the rebel that breaks the compact, he renews the war, and is the aggressor; and every member of the body politic is bound, by the eternal law of benevolence, to set himself against him, and, if he persists, the whole must unite to root him from the earth, whether he be high or low, rich or poor, a king or a subject. The latter, indeed, less deserves it, by how much less mischief he is capable of doing. But when a king or ruler turns rebel (which is vastly more frequent, in proportion to their numbers), being armed with power, he ever spreads desolation and misery around his dominions before he can be regularly and properly punished, and therefore is proportionably higher in guilt. Witness Pharaoh, Saul, Manasseh, Antiochus, Julian, Charles I, of blessed memory, and George III, who vies with the chief in this black catalogue, in spreading misery and ruin round the world.

The ruler who invades the civil or religious rights of his subjects, levies war on them, puts them out of his protection, and dissolves all their allegiance to him; for allegiance and protection are reciprocal, and where one is denied the other must cease.

If these observations are true (and they cannot be denied with modesty), then it is as lawful, and as strongly our duty, to prosecute a war against the king of England for invading our rights and liberties as to bring an obstinate rebel to justice, or take arms against some foreign power that might invade us. Oppression alone, if persisted in, justifies the oppressed in making war on the oppressors; whether they be rulers or private persons, in our own or a foreign state. The reason is, because oppressors are enemies to the great law of nature, and to the happiness of mankind. For this, God commanded Israel to commence a war against Jabin, that, being free from his power, happiness and peace might be restored.

In our contest with the tyrant of Great Britain, we did not, indeed, commence the war. No. But though under a load of almost insupportable insult, abuse and reproach, we raised our humble and earnest petitions, and prayed only for peace, liberty and safety, the natural rights of all men. But, be astonished, O heavens! and tremble, O England! while our dutiful supplications ascended before the throne, the monster was meditating the blow; and ere we rose from our knees, he fixed his dagger in our heart! If this is to be a father, where can be the monster? If this be the exercise of lenity and mercy, as he vainly boasts,[10] what must be his acts of justice? O, merciful God, look down and behold our distress, and avenge us of our cruel foe. Can we reflect on those scenes of

---

[10] See Gen. Howe's proclamation of November 30th, 1776.

slaughter and desolation which he hath spread before our eyes, and doubt of our duty? Is it any longer a scruple whether God calls us to war? If such insults and abuse will not justify us, no abuses ever can. Yea, had George withheld his hand from shedding our blood, the grievous oppressions we groaned under before, and the contempt and insult with which he treated our petitions, were fully sufficient to justify us in the sight of God, and all wise men, had we begun the war, and expelled his troops from our country by fire and sword. Is it possible that Jabin could treat Israel with greater insult or more unjustly invade their rights? But for this, God commanded Israel to make war on him, and pronounces a heavy curse on those who refused to join in carrying it on.

This leads me to show,

IV. That those who are indolent, and backward to take up arms and exert themselves in the service of their country, in order to recover and secure their freedom, when called thereto by the public voice, are highly criminal in the sight of God and man.

This doctrine is wrapt up in the very bowels of my text. "Curse ye Meroz, said the angel of the Lord, curse ye bitterly the inhabitants thereof, because they came not to the help of the Lord, to the help of the Lord against the mighty." The curse of God falls on none but for sin; for he delights in blessing, not in cursing. And he never permits any of his subjects to execute his curses on their fellow-subjects, but where the crime is highly aggravated; much less does he allow them to curse them bitterly, unless their guilt is exceeding great. Now, since God commands Israel to curse Meroz bitterly, we fairly infer, that their sin was of a crimson dye, and most provoking to him and his people. And whoever is guilty of the like conduct in our contest with Great Britain, incurs the like guilt.

This needs no further proof; for if it be allowed that the state of the case between Great Britain and America, is, in its main parts, parallel with that between Jabin and Israel, as hath been shown, then the crime of negligence is as heinous in this struggle as in that. And as Israel were required to curse bitterly those cowardly, selfish, half-way people, so are we to curse the like characters at this day. And as those people, for their neglect, exposed themselves to the loss of all the privileges and blessings of a free state in this world, and to the eternal vengeance of God in the next; so it highly concerns all to take heed that they do not fall under the same condemnation. That we may avoid the rock on which they were lost, I will,

1. Give their character.

2. Mention some aggravations of their sin.

3. I will hint at some things which discover people to be like the inhabitants of Meroz.

Few, I fear, are perfectly clear in this matter. Alas, there is too great negligence among people in general. Private interests and selfish considerations, engross the thoughts and cares of many, who wish well the cause of liberty, and divert their attention and exertions from the main thing which calls for our first and chief regard, viz., the defence of our country from tyranny, and securing our civil and religious freedom. It is mournful to see most men eagerly pursuing worldly gain, and heaping up unrighteous mammon by cruel oppression and grinding the faces of the poor, while our country lies bleeding of her wounds, and so few engaged to bind them up. Let such consider that they are guilty of the sin of Meroz, and, though they may not feel the curse of men in this world, they shall not, without sincere repentence, escape the wrath and curse of God in the world to come. Every one is called, at this day, to come to the help of the Lord against the mighty; either to go out to war, or in some way vigorously exert himself for the public good. There are various things necessary for the defence of our country besides bearing arms, though this is the chief; and all may, one way or other, put to a helping hand. There are various arts and manufactures essential to the support of the inhabitants and army, without which we must soon be overcome. In one or other of these, men and women, youth, and even children, may be employed, and as essentially help in the deliverance of their country as those who go out to war. All are now called to have more than ordinary frugality and diligence in their respective callings;[11] and those of ability should be liberal and forward to encourage manufactures for the public good.[12] But alas, that so few make the interest and welfare of the public the main object of their pursuit. Yet there are some, and I hope many, who with the truth can say, they have done their best, according to their circumstances, for the defence and safety of their country. Such, however the contest may arise, will enjoy the approbation of God, their own consciences, and of all the friends of mankind.

But not to make our case appear better than it really is, I fear there are many among us, in one disguise or other, who, when stript of their vizards, will appear to be of the inhabitants of Meroz; and who, if their characters were justly drawn, would secretly, if not openly, say, as the Pharisees in another case, In saying this, thou reproachest us also. But as birds which are hit, show it by their fluttering, and it may serve to bring such contemptible characters to view, and expose them to the curse they deserve, and on the other hand, may convince some real friends to freedom of their sinful negligence in the common cause; I will venture to point out a few.

Among these characters I do not include such as aid, or in words or actions defend, or openly declare for the enemy, and plead the right of Great Britain "to bind us in all things whatsoever." Of such there are not many among us, owing, probably, to their fear of a vast majority, which is on the side of freedom; and therefore they put on the guise of friendship, while they endeavor secretly to work destruction to the cause. These may be known by the following marks:

---

[11] Suppose every fifth man to be employed in the army, and the number of dependents to be as great as before, then every man must labor one-fifth more than formerly, in order to support those in the army and their dependents, allowing them to live as cheap in the army as at home, which is not the case.

[12] There hath been a laudable spirit, especially in some towns, to encourage manufactures. I have been informed that Newbury, by a town vote, encouraged erecting works, and carrying on the making of saltpetre. And in Salem, where the first was made in this state, several gentlemen gererously subscribed to assist me in making experiments, and erecting the works. And this winter they have subscribed above £500 to enable me to erect large salt-works—a manufacture most necessary for the good of the state.

1. Observe the man who will neither go himself, nor contribute of his substance (if able) to encourage others to go into the war. Such do what in them lies to break up the army. These incur the curse of Meroz.

2. Others will express wishes for our success, but will be sure to back them with doubts of the event, and fears of a heavier yoke. You may hear them frequently magnifying the power of the enemy, and telling of the nine hundred chariots of iron, the dreadful train of artillery, and the good discipline of the British troops, of the intolerable hardships the soldiers undergo, and of the starving condition of their families at home; and by a thousand such arts endeavoring to discourage the people from the war.

3. There are other pretended friends whose countenance betrays them. When things go ill with our army, they appear with a cheerful countenance, and assume airs of importance, and you'll see them holding conferences in one corner or another. The joy of their hearts, on such occasions, will break through all disguises, and discover their real sentiments; while grief and long faces in a reverse of fortune, are a plain index pointing to the end at which they really aim.

4. Others, who talk much of liberty, you will find ever opposing the measures of defence proposed; making objections to them, and showing their inconsistency, while they offer none in their stead, or only such as tend to embarrass the main design. They are so prudent that they will waste away the days, yea months, to consider; and are ever full of their wise cautions, but never zealous to execute any important project. When such men get into public stations—especially if they fill a seat in our public councils—they greatly endanger the state. They protract business, and often defeat the best councils. Prudence and moderation are amiable virtues; and modest mind feels pain in being suspected as sanguine, rash, and imprudent. This gives the overprudent great advantage to obstruct every vigorous measure, which they brand with the name of rashness; and every friend to vigorous action feels the reflection—who, without great fortitude, sits down abashed, and with grief sees his counsels defeated. But, if the measure be adopted, the next motion of the prudent man is to delay the execution, that the happy moment, on which all depends, may be lost.[13] These over and over prudent men ought to be suspected, and viewed with

---

[13] We have a remarkable instance of this nature in 2 Samuel, xvii. 1-14. David had just retreated from Jerusalem, with only six hundred men, when Absalom entered the city, and night came on. Ahithophel counselled for an immediate pursuit. This was wise and good counsel in the case, but Hushai, a friend in heart to David, and firm to Absalom in appearance, disapproved the counsel of Ahithophel as rash and imprudent at that time, and advised to more moderate and cautious measures. And, to carry his point, he magnifies the generalship of David, and the valor of his troops. He hints the great danger there was that his own troops, so near in opposition to their king, would be thrown into confusion, and melt away through fear of the valor of David and his men, and probably desert and join him on a mere report that there was a slaughter among Absalom's army; and that a defeat would be utter ruin. He therefore moves that all Israel be gathered together, as the sand of the sea, that so they might swallow up David in a moment. But mark his design! Was it to gain advantage of David? No; but to give him an opportunity to retreat, collect a larger force, and dispose his army for battle. Happy should we be if all

a watchful eye. And the discerning mind will soon be able to discover whether such counsels spring from true wisdom, or from a design to ensnare us.

5. Some are discovered by the company they keep. You may find them often with those who have given too much reason to suspect their enmity to our cause, and rarely with the zealous friends of liberty, except by accident; and then they speak and act like creatures out of their element, and soon leave the company, or grow mute, when liberty is the subject of discourse.

6. There are others who in heart wish well to our cause; but, through fear of the power of our enemies, they are backward to join vigorously to support it. They really wish we might succeed; but they dread the hardships of a campaign, and choose so to conduct, that, on whatever side victory may declare, they may be safe.

7. Others wish well to the public cause, but have a much greater value for their own private views; and, even then, they boast in her name, while, like George III, they stab her to the heart, by refusing submission to those regulations which are essential to her preservation.

All these, and many others of a like kind, might doubtless have been found in Meroz, and yet the best of them all fell under this bitter curse. For whatever were their private sentiments, they tended to the issue, viz.: to keep them back from those vigorous efforts that the cause of liberty then required, and for want of which, it was greatly hazarded. And whatever motives influence men at this day, whether a desire of ease, hope of power, honor, or wealth; if they do any thing against, or neglect to assist all in their power, this glorious cause of freedom, now in our hands, they, in a greater or less degree, incur the curse of Meroz. Now, if ever, is that text to be applied to such, *"Cursed be he that doeth the work of the Lord deceitfully; and cursed be he that holdeth back his sword from blood"*[14] This leads me

II. To mention some aggravations of this sin.

1. This conduct is a violation of the law of nature, which requires all to exert themselves to promote happiness among mankind. Love is the fulfilling of the law, but this implies a benevolent frame of heart, exercised in beneficent actions toward all men, as we have opportunity. When therefore we see our fellow-creatures, especially our friends and brethren, whose happiness is more immediately our care, reduced to a state of misery, robbed of their most dear and unalienable rights, and borne down with a heavy load of oppression and abuse by the hands of tyrants; this law requires us to stand forth in their defense, even though we are not involved with them in the same evils, and how much more, when our own happiness is equally concerned. Moses, though enjoying all the honors and pleasures of a court, from the pure benevolence of his heart, interposed and smote an Egyptian whom he saw cruelly oppressing one of his

---

Hushais were banished from our councils, or their stratagems discovered and defeated. Prudence and caution are highly necessary. But to be always deliberating, and opposing vigorous measures, and slow in executing, at such a crisis as this, is strongly characteristic of an inhabitant of Meroz.

[14] Jeremiah 48:10.

brethren. This conduct is spoken of with approbation, and was no mark of his want of meekness, in which he excelled all men on the face of the earth. How opposite to this is the character of many great pretenders to meekness in our day, who can tamely see their brethren abused and plundered, and are so meek, or rather selfish, as to pay their courts to the oppressors. One would think, that like some heathens they worship the devil to keep him in a good mood, that he may not hurt them. The man who can stand by, an idle spectator, when a murderer or robber assaults his brother, and not exert himself in his defence, is deservedly accounted as criminal, in law and reason, as the murderer or robber himself, and is exposed to the same punishment. Inactivity, in such a case, is justly esteemed an approbation of the crime. But as freedom is an inheritance entailed on all men, so whosoever invades it, robs mankind of their rights, endeavors to spread misery among God's creatures, and violates the law of nature, and all who refuse to oppose him, when in their power, are to be considered and treated as confederates and abettors of his conduct, and partakers in his crimes.

2. This sin is against posterity; our children after us must reap the fruit of our present conduct. If we nobly resist the oppressor, we shall, under God, deliver them from his galling yoke; at least shall avoid the guilt of riveting it on them. But if we bow tamely to have it fastened on our necks, unborn generations, through unknown centuries may never be able to shake it off; but must waste away a wretched existence in this world, without any other claim to the fruit of their labors, or even to the dear pledges of conjugal love, the fruit of their own bodies, than such as depends on the uncontrolled will of a haughty tyrant.

3. Let us, for a moment, glance an eye on the next and succeeding generations. What a scene opens to view! Behold these delightful and stately mansions for which we labored, possessed by the minions of power; see yonder spacious fields, subdued to fruitfulness by the sweat and toil of our fathers or ourselves, yielding their increase to clothe, pamper, and enrich the tyrant's favorites, who are base enough to assist him in his cursed plots to enslave us. Does this rouse your resentment? Stop a moment, and I will show you a spectacle more shocking than this. What meagre visages do I see in yonder field, toiling and covered with sweat, to cultivate the soil? who are those in rags, bearing burdens and drawing water for those haughty lords, and cringing to them for a morsel of bread? They are—O gracious God, support my spirits—they are my sons and daughters, the pledges of conjugal love, for whose comfort I thought myself happy to spend my days in labor, my nights in care! Thus are my hopes blasted. Oh that they had never been born, rather than to see them loaded with irons, and dragging after them wherever they go, the heavy, galling, ignominious chains of slavery. But may we not hope for an end of these miseries? Alas, what hope! Slavery debases the human faculties, and spreads a torpor and stupidity over the whole frame! They sink in despair under their load; they see no way, they feel no power to recover themselves from this pit of misery; but pine away and die in it, and leave to their children the same wretched inheritance. What then does he deserve? or rather, what curse is too heavy for the wretch that can tamely see our country enslaved?

4. This is a sin against our forefathers. They left us a fair inheritance; they forsook their native land, the land of tyranny and the furnace of iron; and, by their blood, treasure, and toil, procured this sweet, this peaceful retreat, subdued the soil when covered with eternal woods, raised for us the stately domes which afford us shelter from the storms, and safe repose, and were exceedingly careful to instruct us in the things which concern our temporal and eternal liberty and peace. And shall we resign this patrimony, so dearly bought by them, and entailed to us by their will, living and dying? Shall we, I say, resign it all to that tyrant power which drove them from their native land to this then howling wilderness? Shall we bow our necks to the yoke which they, though few in number, nobly cast off? Should our fathers rise from their graves they would disown such children, and repent their care and toil for such degenerate sons.

5. This is a sin against contemporaries. How provoking in the sight of God and man is it to see some, quite unconcerned for the good of the public, rolling in ease, amassing wealth to themselves, and slyly plotting to assist our enemies in their murderous designs, while others endure the fatigues of war, and hazard all that's dear to secure the peace, liberty, and safety of the whole! Surely, every benevolent heart must rise with indignation, and curse these enemies to God and nature.

6. This is a sin against the express command of God. He commands us to stand fast in the liberty wherewith he hath made us free, and not to bow to any tyrant on earth, when it is in our power to oppress him.

V. I proceed to show that God requires a people, struggling for their liberties, to treat such of the community who will not join them as open enemies, and to reject them as unworthy the privileges of society. The single crime of Meroz is said to be this. When they were called to arm, in order to shake off the yoke of tyranny, they did not join in the glorious cause. For this, and only this, they fell under the curse of God and man. Not only eternal wrath in the world to come was the just reward of this sin, but so highly was God provoked thereby, as to command his people to inflict his vengeance on them in this world, that, being held up as the monuments of his wrath, others might hear and fear, and do no more so wickedly.

A curse is something more than wishing ill to a person. It implies a separating him to some evil, or punishment. The command in my text therefore required Israel to separate the inhabitants of Meroz from some temporal good the rest of Israel enjoyed, and inflict on them some severe punishment; for they were to curse them bitterly.

And why may we not suppose that this curse consisted in these things:

1. That they should be deprived of that delightful freedom and liberty Israel had regained from the tyranny of Jabin. As these wretches discovered their servile temper in refusing to exert themselves for the recovery of liberty, why should they not be condemned to the slavery they chose? Jabin (like George) probably claimed a right to lay any taxes on them he pleased, and "to blind them in all cases whatsoever"; and they, rather than jeopard their lives in defence of their rights, tamely submitted to his demands. Well, since this was their choices, why should it now be denied them? Let them be taxed at the sovereign will of the

other states, without allowing them any representation, Since they loved, and sought to involve all Israel with themselves in slavery, they should have it from the rest, and receive but the just reward of their conduct. With what face could they complain of such treatment, since they chose to submit to the same from Jabin? The change of masters made no change in the task; and if they preferred slavery then, rather than fight for their liberties, let them have it now, since they would do nothing to regain them.

How absurd is their conduct who prefer, to our glorious struggle for liberty, a tame submission to the claims of the British Parliament! If we submit, we must be slaves; for to be governed and guided by the will of another, and not our own, is perfect servitude. If we fight and are conquered, we can but be slaves. If we conquer, we gain our freedom, On one hand, the event is certain, the chains are riveted. On the other, there is a possibility, and a probability, too, of a glorious deliverance; yea, were all united, there would be a moral certainty of success. On those, therefore, who, like Meroz, refuse to come to the help of the Lord in the present war, will be the sin of involving millions, besides themselves, in the most abject misery and cruel slavery. Consider this, ye inhabitants of Meroz; remember, that there is a God that judgeth in the earth, and tremble at your fearful doom. If murdering one man deserves death, what does the murder of a thousand deserve? If God made the enslaving one of his people a capital crime, to be punished with death (Exodus, xxiv. 7), what does your crime deserve, who are endeavoring to enslave a whole nation? If you choose slavery for yourselves, don't force it on others who abhor it, you may enjoy it, though others are free. It is your due. And the curse in my text, when inflicted on you aright, will give it you in full tale.

2. Why may we not suppose that they were deprived of their estates, and reduced at least to a state of tenantage at will? They had implicitly joined with the enemy, by which they put to hazard every dear and valuable enjoyment of the whole nation. Through their neglect all might have been lost. And their fault was not the less because victory declared for Israel; and all their possessions could never countervail the damage their conduct had exposed the nation to.

The application of this to our times is easy. The present war, 'tis probable, had never been commenced had none of the inhabitants of Meroz been in our land; or, if begun, could not have been carried on to this day. On them, therefore, as the confederates, abettors and supporters of the tyrants, lies the guilt of this war. And as they are partners with him in the sin, so they ought to be involved in the punishment he deserves. If it is lawful to deprive the inhabitants of Great Britain of their property, when in our power, and convert it to our use; if this be a just retaliation for the injury they have done us, and all too little to countervail the damage; much more the interest of those who live among us, and yet assist the enemy in their cruel designs, ought to be confiscated for the service of the public, by how much more mischief they have done, and are capable of doing these states, and by how much greater their sin:

I cannot but think it would have been happy for these states, had our rules, long ere now, declared all who should be found any way aiding and assisting the enemy, or holding correspondence with them, should be deemed enemies to these states and forfeit all their estates at least. Yea,

3. As the curse of Meroz, no doubt, extended to a depriving the inhabitants of a capacity to enjoy any place of honor in the government, and the ordinary privileges of freemen; and also inflicted some corporal punishment at least on their principal leaders; so the like characters among us, ought to share the same punishment. And I am persuaded, these states will still be unsafe, and all our efforts for deliverance from tyranny attended with great hazard and uncertainty, till there shall be some more effectual and vigorous means adopted by our rulers, to distinguish friends from foes, and expose the latter to some exemplary punishment. . . . The law of retaliation is sometimes just and necessary, even when the persons offending are not made the subjects of it; how much more when the transgressors themselves are in our power.[15] Nor can we do justice to

---

[15] It was a righteous act in Tamerlane the Great, to carry Bajazet, the grand Turk, in an iron cage, round the world in triumph. The magnanimous, the benevolent Tamerlane marches with a great army to repel Bajazet, who was made prisoner. "Being brought into his presence, Tamerlane asked him why he endeavored to bring the Greek emperor into his subjection? He answered, 'Even the same cause which moved thee to invade me, namely, the desire of glory and sovereignty,' 'Wherefore, then,' said Tamerlane, 'dost thou use such cruelty toward them thou overcomest, without respect to age or sex?' 'That I did,' said he, 'to strike the greater terror into mine enemies.' Then Tamerlane asked him if he had ever given thanks to God for making him so great an emperor?' 'No,' said he; 'I never so much as thought of any such thing.' 'Then,' said Tamerlane, 'it is no wonder so ungrateful a man should be made a spectacle of misery; for you,' said he, 'being blind in one eye, and I lame of a leg, was there any worth in us, that God should set us over two such great empires, to command so many men far more worthy than ourselves? But,' continued he, 'what wouldest thou have done with me, if it had been my lot to have fallen into thine hands, as thou art now in mine?' 'I would,' said Bajazet, 'have enclosed thee in a cage of iron, and carried thee in triumph up and down my kingdom.' 'Even so,' said Tamerlane, 'shalt thou be served.' And causing him to be taken out of his presence, and turning to his followers, he said: 'Behold a proud and cruel man, who deserves to be chastised accordingly, and to be made an example to all the proud and cruel of the world, of just wrath of God against them.' (See Clarke's life of Tamerlane the Great, pages 37, 38.)

But it too rarely happens, that the perpetrators of these crimes fall in the way of justice; in which case it is sometimes lawful, yea, duty, to retaliate on some of their connections. For instance, the commanders of the British troops and their master are the cruel monsters who treat such as fall into their hands with unexampled barbarity, confining them in prisons and vessels, in the extreme cold, without fire or food sufficient to preserve life; by which hundreds, yea, thousands of our dear friends have suffered the most cruel and painful deaths, and others lost their limbs by the frost. The real criminals are out of our reach. What, then, can be done? Nothing, but to inflict a like punishment on a like number of their prisoners in our hands. Accordingly, the honorable Congress, long ago, assured the public that they would retaliate all abuses offered to prisoners taken from us. Depending on this promise as the means to secure good treatment, should they fall into the enemy's hand, many who cheerfully offered themselves for the war have been made prisoners, and froze or starved to death, and no retaliation that I have heard hath yet been made—I hope for wise reasons. Hence the enemy exercise their more than brutal cruelty without fear, and many, dreading the like usage, are disinclined to the war.

ourselves or the public, or to our brethren now suffering in hard and cruel durance among the enemy; nor to our posterity; nor lastly, to the manes of murdered friends who have fallen in the field, or expired in the loathsome prisons with cold and hunger; till we inflict some just and exemplary punishment on those who have brought these calamities on us.

This discourse shows us, how defensive war is consistent with true benevolence, and a sincere desire of the happiness of mankind; and how it is consistent for the soldier to love and pray for the happiness of those he opposes and endeavors to root from the earth.

Every soldier should enter the field with benevolent, tender, compassionate sentiments, which is the temper of Jesus Christ. A morose, cruel, revengeful, unmerciful temper, is no more consistent with the character of a Christian soldier, than with that of a minister of the gospel of peace; nor can it be justified even in the height of the fiercest battle. He should ever be possessed with a

---

If something be not speedily done to convince our foes that we are not afraid to retaliate, the consequence, I fear, will be fatal to our cause. Lenity and mercy are due prisioners; and nothing can justify acts of severity, but where cruel usage makes them necessary, and then acts of severity become acts of mercy. I cannot persuade myself to put an end to this note, already too long, without transcribing a passage from the aforesaid life of Tamerlane, which at once represents the true cause of making war, and also that noble, benevolent spirit which should inspire every soldier to enter the field; both of which are exemplified in this heathen warrior, in whose presence most Christian princes have reason to blush.

After the battle before mentioned, the emperor of Constantinople sent ambassadors to Tamerlane offering him his empire, and his person as his most faithful subject, in gratitude and as a reward for the deliverance he had obtained for him from the most cruel tyrant. But Tamerlane, with a mild countenance, beheld them and said, "That he had not come so far, nor taken such pains to enlarge his dominions, big enough already (too base a thing to put himself into so great danger and hazard for), but rather to win honor, and make his name famous to future posterity; and that he would make it appear to the world that he came to assist their master, as his friend and ally, at his request; and that his upright intentions therein, he believed, were the cause that God from above had favored him and made him instrumental to bruise the head of the greatest and fiercest enemy of mankind under heaven; and therefore, to get him an immortal name, his purpose was, to make free so great and flourishing a city as Constaninople. That he always joined faith to his courage, which should never suffer him to make such a breach in his reputation as to have it reported of him that, in the color of a friend, he should come to invade the dominions of his ally. That he desired no more, but that the service he had done for the Greek emperor might remain forever engraven in the memory of his posterity, that they might ever wish well to him and his successors, by remembering the good he had done for them" (page 41).

This was truly noble ambition, to seek an immortal name and honor, not by actions which the ambitious call great, but by those which God pronounces good. The battle being ended, Tamerlane said: "This day hath God delivered into my hand a great enemy, to whom, therefore we must give thanks," which was publicly done. Excellent example!

disposition to pray for those he endeavors to destroy, and to wish their best, their eternal good. These are no more inconsistent in a soldier, engaging in battle and doing his best to kill his enemies, than they are in a judge and executioner, who take away a murderer from the earth. For, as the judge and executioner are God's ministers to execute vengeance on the wicked who endeavor to destroy the happiness of society; so the soldier, engaged in a just defensive war, is the minister of God to render vengeance to the invaders of others' right: and as the executioner may and ought to pray for the suffering criminal, so should the soldier for his foe; as benevolence is the source of vindictive laws in the states, so it should ever be of defensive war; and they both tend to the same end, the happiness of mankind. How absurd then is the pretence that the gospel of Jesus Christ forbids us to take up arms to defend ourselves! and that defensive war is inconsistent with the patient, meek long-suffering temper it requires! It may with as much reason be said, that to punish a murderer or robber is forbidden by the gospel; which is in effect to say, that the gospel of peace forbids the exercise of love and benevolence in acts absolutely necessary, in this sinful world, for the peace and happiness of society and individuals.

From what has been said, we may clearly infer, that to levy offensive war is murder, and all who engage in it are murderers in God's sight. They are guilty, not only of the murder of those they kill in battle, or who otherwise perish in the war, but they are self-murderers—they put themselves to death—their blood is on their own heads. Well, then, might Solomon say: *"With good advice make war."*

The characters, therefore, of two states or armies at war, are as opposite as their actions. The aggressor is a murderer and robber, and all who assist him are involved in his guilt. Every soldier who fights for him is a murderer too. But we know that no murderer hath eternal life. How should this make those shudder who engage on the side of the aggressor! If they fall in battle, what hope can they have of God's approbation, since they die murdering others and themselves too? But such who oppose them in defence of their own and country's peace, liberty and safety, are God's ministers, commissioned and ordered by him to punish his and his people's enemies. They, therefore, may draw their swords with a quiet, approving conscience, and with pity view the wretches slain by their hands as self-murderers; or, if they fall, they can die, in regard to the war, free of the blood of all men, and in peace resign their spirits into the hand of their Redeemer.

This consideration surely must animate every man, inspired with the benevolent temper of the gospel—which disposes to the greatest advancement of human happiness, and to relieve the miserable and oppressed—to vigorous exertions in defence of our bleeding land; bleeding under the hand of oppression, rapine and murder. Would you, my friends, count it an honor to be employed by God to restore peace and happiness to the oppressed and miserable? do you wish to perform acts of love and kindness to mankind, and therein be like your Creator and Redeemer? Do you fear the wrath and curse of God pronounced on all who spread misery among his creatures, and on all that aid or assist them, or so much as connive at, or neglect to oppose them? Do you desire to be workers together with God in restoring peace and felicity to your groaning country, and to be owned of him as his servants when you die? Are these the objects of your desire and pursuit? I know they are if the love of God and your neighbor rules your hearts. Well, then, here is an opportunity presented to you, to manifest your love, by coming to the help of the Lord against the mighty. The cause we are engaged in is the cause of God; and you may hope for his blessing and fight under his banner. In supporting and defending this cause, you may, you ought to seek for glory and honor; even that glory and honor which come from God and man for acts of benevolence, goodness and mercy, for the performance of which the fairest opportunity now offers.

But what shall I say of those whose religious principles forbid the performance of any such labors of love, and necessarily involve them in the curse of Meroz? If their religion be right, love itself must be wrong. But arguments are vain. May God in his mercy show them their error, give them repentence, and inspire them with the love which the law and gospel require, before they fall under the wrath and curse of God, for neglecting to come to his help against the mighty.

This discourse also shows us how we ought to treat those who do not join in the cause of freedom we have espoused.

1. As they are accursed of God, and we are commanded to curse them, we ought, at least, to shun their company. What a shame is it, to see those born to freedom and professing zeal for her cause, associating themselves with the willing slaves of an abandoned tyrant and murderer? Oh, how do such debase themselves, and give occasion to suspect them as belonging to the same herd. But it may be asked, how shall they be distinguished from friends? Attend to the characters already given, and you may see enough to justify you in avoiding intimacy with them; though they may so disguise that no evidence appears to condemn them to open and condign punishment. Happy would it be should our civil fathers draw some determinate line of distinction between freemen and these slaves of power.[16] For want of this we have suffered greatly already, and if this be not speedily done, the consequences, I fear, will be fatal.

2. As soon as they are discovered, we ought to disarm them; for, as they will not assist us, we should put it out of their power to hurt us or our families, when we at any time shall be called to action. Yea,

3. As such forfeit all the privileges of freemen, their estates should be forfeited and applied to support the war; and themselves banished from these states. The curse we are commanded to inflict on the inhabitants of Meroz, must imply as much as this; and benevolence to millions demands this of us; not out of hatred to their persons, but their crimes, which strike at the life and happiness of these states. This punishment must be inflicted, not by the people at large, but by our rulers, with whom, under God, we have intrusted our safety; and in whose

---

[16] Since the above was copied for the press, a proclamation by his excellency General Washington has been published, and also two acts to punish treason and other crimes of less enormity against this state; by which this line of distinction is, in a good measure drawn, which is cause of joy to all the friends of liberty.

wisdom we confide, to take proper vengeance on them in due time. But should this be delayed, without proper reasons assigned, we shall have no cause to wonder, though there should be great thoughts of heart among a people, beholding their friends and brethren barbarously murdered, or wandering forlorn, destitute of food or shelter; while the detested authors of these unparalleled distresses smile unnoticed and unpunished, at these dire calamities, and triumph in our distress. But should such delay happen, we must look on it as another instance of divine displeasure, which speaks to all, to search after, and, by sincere repentence and thorough reformation, remove, the moral cause of God's controversy with us.

When this shall take place, we shall then see our councils filled with men inspired with wisdom to know what Israel ought to do; our arms victorious and triumphant; the inhabitants of Meroz justly punished; peace, liberty and safety restored; the rod of tyranny broken; pure and undefiled religion prevailing, and the voice of joy and gladness echoing round our land. May God hasten the happy, happy day! And let all the people say, Amen, and Amen. Hallelujah!

12

Virginia Statute of Religious Liberty
(1786)

An Act for Establishing Religious Freedom

I. Whereas Almighty God hath created the mind free; that all attempts to influence it by temporal punishments or burthens, or by civil incapacitations, tend only to beget habits of hypocrisy and meanness, and are a departure from the plan of the Holy author of our religion, who being Lord both of body and mind, yet chose not to propagate it by coercions on either, as was in his Almighty power to do; that the impious presumption of legislators and rulers, civil as well as ecclesiastical, who being themselves but fallible and uninspired men, have assumed dominion over the faith of others, setting up their own opinions and modes of thinking as the only true and infallible, and as such endeavouring to impose them on others, hath established and maintained false religions over the greatest part of the world, and through all time; that to compel a man to furnish contributions of money for the propagation of opinions which he disbelieves, is sinful and tyrannical; that even the forcing him to support this or that teacher of his own religious persuasion, is depriving him of the comfortable liberty of giving his contributions to the particular pastor whose morals he would make his pattern, and whose powers he feels most persuasive to righteousness, and is withdrawing from the ministry those temporary rewards, which proceeding from an approbation of their personal conduct, are an additional incitement to earnest and unremitting labours for the instruction of mankind; that our civil rights have no dependence on our religious opinions, any more than our opinions in physics or geometry; that therefore the proscribing any citizen as unworthy the public confidence by laying upon him an incapacity of being called to offices of trust and emolument, unless he profess or renounce this or that religious opinion, is depriving him injuriously of those privileges and advantages to which in common with his fellow-citizens he has a natural right, that it tends only to corrupt the principles of that religion it is meant to encourage, by bribing with a monopoly of worldly honours and emoluments, those who will externally profess and conform to it; that though indeed these are criminal who do not withstand such temptation, yet neither are those innocent who lay the bait in their way; that to suffer the civil magistrate to intrude his powers into the field of opinion, and to restrain the profession or propagation of principles on supposition of their ill tendency, is a dangerous fallacy, which at once destroys all religious liberty, because he being of course judge of that tendency will make his opinions the rule of judgment, and approve or condemn the sentiments of others only as they shall square with or differ from his own; that it is time enough for the rightful purposes of civil government, for its officers to interfere when principles break out into overt acts against peace and good order; and finally, that truth is great and will prevail if left to herself, that she is the proper and sufficient antagonist to error, and has nothing to fear from the conflict, unless by human interposition disarmed of her natural weapons, free argument and debate, errors ceasing to be dangerous when it is permitted freely to contradict them.

II. Be it enacted by the General Assembly, that no man shall be compelled to frequent or support any religious worship, place or ministry whatsoever, nor shall be enforced, restrained, molested, or burthened in his body or good, nor shall otherwise suffer on account of his religious opinions or belief; but that all men shall be free to profess, and by argument to maintain, their opinion in matters of religion, and that the same shall in no wise diminish, enlarge or affect their civil capacities.

III. And though we well know that this assembly, elected by the people for the ordinary purposes of legislation only, have no power to restrain the acts of succeeding assemblies, constituted with powers equal to our own, and that therefore to declare this act to be irrevocable would be of no effect in law; yet as we are free to declare, and do declare, that the rights hereby asserted are of the natural rights of mankind, and that if any act shall hereafter be passed to repeal the present, or to narrow its operation, such act will be an infringement of natural right.

13

The Northwest Ordinance
July 13, 1787

The Northwest Ordinance, written the same summer as the Constitutional Convention in Philadelphia, established the principles by which new states were to be added to the Union. The following excerpts from the document speak to the founders' high regard for religious faith, and their expectations about its relation to civil affairs.

An Ordinance for the government of the Territory of the United States northwest of the River Ohio.

Be it ordained by the United States in Congress assembled,

. . . . [that] for extending the fundamental principles of civil and religious liberty, which form the basis whereon these republics, their laws and constitutions are erected; to fix and establish those principles as the basis of all laws, constitutions, and governments, which forever hereafter shall be formed in the said territory: to provide also for the establishment of States, and permanent government therein, and for their admission to a share in the federal councils on an equal footing with the original States, at as early periods as may be consistent with the general interest:

. . . . It is hereby ordained and declared by the authority aforesaid, That the following articles shall be considered as articles of compact between the original States and the people and States in the said territory and forever remain unalterable, unless by common consent, to wit:

Art. 1. No person, demeaning himself in a peaceable and orderly manner, shall ever be molested on account of his mode of worship or religious sentiments, in the said territory.

Art. 2. The inhabitants of the said territory shall always be entitled to the benefits of the writ of *habeas corpus*, and of the trial by jury; of a proportionate representation of the people in the legislature; and of judicial proceedings according to the course of the common law. All persons shall be bailable, unless for capital offenses, where the proof shall be evident or the presumption great. All fines shall be moderate; and no cruel or unusual punishments shall be inflicted. No man shall be deprived of his liberty or property, but by the judgment of his peers or the law of the land; and, should the public exigencies make it necessary, for the common preservation, to take any person's property, or to demand his particular services, full compensation shall be made for the same. And, in the just preservation of rights and property, it is understood and declared, that no law ought ever to be made, or have force in the said territory, that shall, in any manner whatever, interfere with or affect private contracts or engagements, bona fide, and without fraud, previously formed.

Art. 3. Religion, morality, and knowledge, being necessary to good government and the happiness of mankind, schools and the means of education shall forever be encouraged. The utmost good faith shall always be observed towards the Indians; their lands and property shall never be taken from them without their consent; and, in their property, rights, and liberty, they shall never be invaded or disturbed, unless in just and lawful wars authorized by Congress; but laws founded in justice and humanity, shall from time to time be made for preventing wrongs being done to them, and for preserving peace and friendship with them.

14

Selected Addresses and Letters of George Washington

First Inaugural Address

President Washington's first inaugural address was delivered at New York City, Thursday, April 30, 1789.

Fellow-Citizens of the Senate and of the House of Representatives:

Among the vicissitudes incident to life no event could have filled me with greater anxieties than that of which the notification was transmitted by your order, and received on the 14th day of the present month. On the one hand, I was summoned by my country, whose voice I can never hear but with veneration and love, from a retreat which I had chosen with the fondest predilection, and, in my flattering hopes, with an immutable decision, as the asylum of my declining years—a retreat which was rendered every day more necessary as well as more dear to me by the addition of habit to inclination, and of frequent interruptions in my health to the gradual waste committed on it by time. On the other hand, the magnitude and difficulty of the trust to which the voice of my country called me, being sufficient to awaken in the wisest and most experienced of her citizens a distrustful scrutiny into his qualifications, could not but overwhelm with despondence one who (inheriting inferior endowments from nature and unpracticed in the duties of civil administration) ought to be peculiarly conscious of his own deficiencies. In this conflict of emotions all I dare aver is that it has been my faithful study to collect my duty from a just appreciation of every circumstance by which it might be affected. All I dare hope is that if, in executing this task, I have been too much swayed by a grateful remembrance of former instances, or by an affectionate sensibility to this transcendent proof of the confidence of my fellow-citizens, and have thence too little consulted my incapacity as well as disinclination for the weighty and untried cares before me, my error will be palliated by the motives which mislead me, and its consequences be judged by my country with some share of the partiality in which they originated.

Such being the impressions under which I have, in obedience to the public summons, repaired to the present station, it would be peculiarly improper to omit in this first official act my fervent supplications to that Almighty Being who rules over the universe, who presides in the councils of nations, and whose providential aids can supply every human defect, that His benediction may consecrate to the liberties and happiness of the people of the United States a Government instituted by themselves for these essential purposes, and may enable every instrument employed in its administration to execute with success the functions allotted to his charge. In tendering this homage to the Great Author of every public and private good, I assure myself that it expresses your sentiments not less than my own, nor those of my fellow-citizens at large less than either. No people can be bound to acknowledge and adore the Invisible Hand which conducts the affairs of men more than those of the United States. Every step by which they have advanced to the character of an independent nation seems to have been distinguished by some token of providential agency; and in the important revolution just accomplished in the system of their united government the tranquil deliberations and voluntary consent of so many distinct communities from which the event has resulted cannot be compared with the means by which most governments have been established without some return of pious gratitude, along with an humble anticipation of the future blessings which the past seem to presage. These reflections, arising out of the present crisis, have forced themselves too strongly on my mind to be suppressed. You will join with me, I trust, in thinking that there are none under the influence of which the proceedings of a new and free government can more auspiciously commence.

By the article establishing the executive department it is made the duty of the President "to recommend to your consideration such measures as he shall judge necessary and expedient." The circumstances under which I now meet you will acquit me from entering into that subject further than to refer to the great constitutional charter under which you are assembled, and which, in defining your powers, designates the objects to which your attention is to be given. It will be more consistent with those circumstances, and far more congenial with the feelings which actuate me, to substitute, in place of a recommendation of particular measures, the tribute that is due to the talents, the rectitude, and the patriotism which adorn the characters selected to devise and adopt them. In these honorable qualifications I behold the surest pledges that as on one side no local prejudices or attachments, no separate views nor party animosities, will misdirect the comprehensive and equal eye which ought to watch over this great assemblage of communities and interests, so, on another, that the foundation of our national policy will be laid in the pure and immutable principles of private morality, and the preeminence of free government be exemplified by all the attributes which can win the affections of its citizens and command the respect of the world. I dwell on this prospect with every satisfaction which an ardent love for my country can inspire, since there is no truth more thoroughly established than that there exists in the economy and course of nature an indissoluble union between virtue and happiness; between duty and advantage; between the genuine maxims of an honest and magnanimous policy and the solid rewards of public prosperity and felicity; since we ought to be no less persuaded that the propitious smiles of Heaven can never be expected on a nation that disregards the eternal rules of order and right which Heaven itself has ordained; and since the preservation of the sacred fire of liberty and the destiny of the republican model of government are justly considered, perhaps, as "deeply," as "finally," staked on the experiment entrusted to the hands of the American people.

Besides the ordinary objects submitted to your care, it will remain with your judgment to decide how far an exercise of the occasional power delegated by the fifth article of the Constitution is rendered expedient at the present juncture by the nature of objections which have been urged against the system, or by the degree of inquietude which has given birth to them. Instead of undertaking particular recommendations on this subject, in which I could be guided by no lights derived from official opportunities, I shall again give way to my entire confidence in your discernment and pursuit of the public good; for I assure myself that whilst you carefully avoid every alteration which might endanger the benefits of an united and effective government, or which ought to await the future lessons of experience, a reverence for the characteristic rights of freemen and a regard for the public harmony will sufficiently influence your deliberations on the question how far the former can be impregnably fortified or the latter be safely and advantageously promoted.

To the foregoing observations I have one to add, which will be most properly addressed to the House of Representatives. It concerns myself, and will therefore be as brief as possible. When I was first honored with a call into the service of my country, then on the eve of an arduous struggle for its liberties, the light in which I contemplated my duty required that I should renounce every pecuniary compensation. From this resolution I have in no instance departed; and being still under the impressions which produced it, I must decline as inapplicable to myself any share in the personal emoluments which may be indispensably included in a permanent provision for the executive department, and must accordingly pray that the pecuniary estimates for the station in which I am placed may during my continuance in it be limited to such actual expenditures as the public good may be thought to require.

Having thus imparted to you my sentiments as they have been awakened by the occasion which brings us together, I shall take my present leave; but not without resorting once more to the benign Parent of the Human Race in humble supplication that, since He has been pleased to favor the American people with opportunities for deliberating in perfect tranquillity, and dispositions for deciding with unparalleled unanimity on a form of government for the security of their union and the advancement of their happiness, so His divine blessing may be equally "conspicuous" in the enlarged views, the temperate consultations, and the wise measures on which the success of this Government must depend.

A Proclamation of National Thanksgiving

City of New York, October 3, 1789

Whereas it is the duty of all Nations to acknowledge the providence of Almighty God, to obey his will, to be grateful for his benefits, and humbly to implore his protection and favor, and Whereas both Houses of Congress have by their joint Committee requested me "to recommend to the People of the United States a day of public thanks-giving and prayer to be observed by acknowledging with grateful hearts the many signal favors of Almighty God, especially by affording them an opportunity peaceably to establish a form of government for their safety and happiness."

Now therefore I do recommend and assign Thursday the 26th day of November next to be devoted by the People of these States to the service of that great and glorious Being, who is the beneficent Author of all the good that was, that is, or that will be. That we may then all unite in rendering unto him our sincere and humble thanks, for his kind care and protection of the People of this country previous to their becoming a Nation, for the signal and manifold mercies, and the favorable interpositions of his providence, which we experienced in the course and conclusion of the late war, for the great degree of tranquillity, union, and plenty, which we have since enjoyed, for the peaceable and rational manner in which we have been enabled to establish constitutions of government for our safety and happiness, and particularly the national One now lately instituted, for the civil and religious liberty with which we are blessed, and the means we have of acquiring and diffusing useful knowledge and in general for all the great and various favors which he hath been pleased to confer upon us.

And also that we may then unite in most humbly offering our prayers and supplications to the great Lord and Ruler of Nations and beseech him to pardon our national and other transgressions, to enable us all, whether in public or private stations, to perform our several and relative duties properly and punctually, to render our national government a blessing to all the People, by constantly being a government of wise, just and constitutional laws, discreetly and faithfully executed and obeyed, to protect and guide all Sovereigns and Nations (especially such as have shown kindness unto us) and to bless them with good government, peace, and concord. To promote the knowledge and practice of true religion and virtue, and the encrease of science among them and Us, and generally to grant unto all Mankind such a degree of temporal prosperity as he alone knows to be best.

Letter to the Hebrew Congregation of Newport, Rhode Island

August 17, 1790

Gentlemen:

While I received with much satisfaction your address replete with expressions of esteem, I rejoice in the opportunity of assuring you that I shall always retain grateful remembrance of the cordial welcome I experienced on my visit to Newport from all classes of citizens.

The reflection on the days of difficulty and danger which are past is rendered the more sweet from a consciousness that they are succeeded by days of uncommon prosperity and security

If we have wisdom to make the best use of the advantages with which we are now favored, we cannot fail, under the just administration of a good government, to become a great and happy people.

The citizens of the United States of America have a right to applaud themselves for having given to mankind examples of an enlarged and liberal policy—a policy worthy of imitation. All possess alike liberty of conscience and immunities of citizenship.

It is now no more that toleration is spoken of, as if it were by the indulgence of one class of people, that another enjoyed the exercise of their inherent natural rights, for happily the government of the United States, which gives to bigotry no sanction, to persecution no assistance, requires only that those who live under its protection should demean themselves as good citizens, in giving it on all occasions their effectual support.

It would be inconsistent with the frankness of my character not to avow that I am pleased with your favorable opinion of my administration and fervent wishes for my felicity.

May the children of the Stock of Abraham, who dwell in this land, continue to merit and enjoy the good will of the other inhabitants, while every one shall sit in safety under his own vine and fig tree, and there shall be none to make him afraid.

May the father of all mercies scatter light, and not darkness, upon our paths, and make us all in our several vocations useful here, and in His own due time and way everlastingly happy.

Farewell Address[*]

September 19, 1796

Friends and Fellow Citizens:

The period for a new election of a Citizen, to Administer the Executive Government of the United States, being not far distant, and the time actually arrived, when your thoughts must be employed in designating the person who is to be clothed with that important trust, it appears to me proper, especially as it may conduce to a more distinct expression of the public voice, that I should now apprise you of the resolution I have formed to decline being considered among the number of those out of whom a choice is to be made.

I beg you, at the same time, to do me the justice to be assured, that this resolution has not been taken, without a strict regard to all the considerations appertaining to the relation, which binds a dutiful citizen to his country, and that, in withdrawing the tender of service which silence in my situation might imply, I am influenced by no diminution of zeal for your future interest, no deficiency of grateful respect for your past kindness; but am supported by a full conviction that the step is compatible with both.

The acceptance of, and continuance hitherto in, the office to which your Suffrages have twice called me, have been a uniform sacrifice of inclination to the opinion of duty, and to a deference for what appeared to be your desire. I constantly hoped, that it would have been much earlier in my power, consistently with motives, which I was not at liberty to disregard, to return to that retirement, from which I had been reluctantly drawn. The strength of my inclination to do this, previous to the last Election, had even led to the preparation of an address to declare it to you; but mature reflection on the then perplexed and critical posture of our Affairs with foreign Nations, and the unanimous advice of persons entitled to my confidence, impelled me to abandon the idea.

I rejoice, that the state of your concerns, external as well as internal, no longer renders the pursuit of inclination incompatible with the sentiment of duty or propriety; and am persuaded, whatever partiality may be retained for my services, that, in the present circumstances of our country, you will not disapprove my determination to retire.

The impressions, with which I first undertook the arduous trust, were explained on the proper occasion. In the discharge of this trust, I will only say, that I have, with good intentions, contributed toward the Organization and

---

[*] For a thoroughgoing discussion of the Farewell Address, see Matthew Spalding and Patrick J. Garrity, *A Sacred Union of Citizens: George Washington's Farewell Address and the American Character* (Lanham, Md.: Rowman & Littlefield, 1996) —*Ed.*

Administration of the Government, the best exertions of which a very fallible judgment was capable. Not unconscious, in the outset, of the inferiority of my qualifications, experience in my own eyes, perhaps still more in the eyes of others, has strengthened the motives to diffidence of myself; and every day the increasing weight of years admonishes me more and more, that the shade of retirement is as necessary to me as it will be welcome. Satisfied that if any circumstances have given peculiar value to my services, they were temporary, I have the consolation to believe, that while choice and prudence invite me to quit the political scene, patriotism does not forbid it.

In looking forward to the moment, which is intended to terminate the career of my public life, my feelings do not permit me to suspend the deep acknowledgment of that debt of gratitude wch. I owe to my beloved country, for the many honors it has conferred upon me; still more for the steadfast confidence with which it has supported me; and for the opportunities I have thence enjoyed of manifesting my inviolable attachment, by services faithful and persevering, though in usefulness unequal to my zeal. If benefits have resulted to our country from these services, let it always be remembered to your praise, and as an instructive example in our annals, that, under circumstances in which the Passions agitated in every direction were liable to mislead, amidst appearances sometimes dubious, vicissitudes of fortune often discouraging, in situations in which not unfrequently want of Success has countenanced the spirit of criticism, the constancy of your support was the essential prop of the efforts, and a guarantee of the plans by which they were effected. Profoundly penetrated with this idea, I shall carry it with me to my grave, as a strong incitement to unceasing vows that Heaven may continue to you the choicest tokens of its beneficence; that your Union and brotherly affection may be perpetual; that the free constitution, which is the work of your hands, may be sacredly maintained; that its Administration in every department may be stamped with wisdom and Virtue; that, in fine, the happiness of the people of these States, under the auspices of liberty, may be made complete, by so careful a preservation and so prudent a use of this blessing as will acquire a preservation and so prudent a use of this blessing as will acquire to them the glory of recommending it to the applause, the affection, and adoption of every nation which is yet a stranger to it.

Here, perhaps, I ought to stop. But a solicitude for your welfare, which cannot end but with my life, and the apprehension of danger, natural to that solicitude urge me on an occasion like the present, to offer to your solemn contemplation, and to recommend to your frequent review, some sentiments; which are the result of much reflection, of no inconsiderable observation, and which appear to me all important to the permanency of your felicity as a People. These will be offered to you with the more freedom, as you can only see in them the disinterested warnings of a parting friend, who can possibly have no personal motive to bias his counsel. Nor can I forget, as an encouragement to it, your endulgent reception of my sentiments on a former and not dissimilar occasion.

Interwoven as is the love of liberty with every ligament of your hearts, no recommendation of mine is necessary to fortify or confirm the attachment.

The Unity of Government which constitutes you one people is also now dear to you. It is justly so; for it is a main Pillar in the Edifice of your real independence, the support of your tranquility at home; your peace abroad; of your safety; of your prosperity; of that very Liberty which you so highly prize. But as it is easy to foresee, that from different causes and from different quarters, much pains will be taken, many artifices employed, to weaken in your minds the conviction of this truth; as this is the point in your political fortress against which the batteries of internal and external enemies will be most constantly and actively (though often covertly and insidiously) directed, it is of infinite moment, that you should properly estimate the immense value of your national Union to your collective and individual happiness; that you should cherish a cordial, habitual and immoveable attachment to it; accustoming yourselves to think and speak of it as the Palladium of your political safety and prosperity; watching for its preservation with jealous anxiety; discountenancing whatever may suggest even a suspicion that it can in any event be abandoned, and indignantly frowning upon the first dawning of every attempt to alienate any portion of our Country from the rest, or to enfeeble the sacred ties which now link together the various parts.

For this you have every inducement of sympathy and interest. Citizens by birth or choice, of a common country, that country has a right to concentrate your affections. The name of AMERICAN, which belongs to you, in your national capacity, must always exalt the just pride of Patriotism, more than any appellation derived from local discriminations. With slight shades of difference, you have the same Religion, Manners, Habits and political Principles. You have in a common cause fought and triumphed together. The independence and liberty you possess are the work of joint councils, and joint efforts; of common dangers, sufferings and successes.

But these considerations, however powerfully they address themselves to your sensibility, are greatly outweighed by those which apply more immediately to your Interest. Here every portion of our country finds the most commanding motives for carefully guarding and preserving the Union of the whole.

The *North*, in an unrestrained intercourse with the *South*, protected by the equal laws of a common Government, finds in the production of the latter, great additional resources of Maritime and commercial enterprise and precious materials of manufacturing industry. The *South* in the same intercourse, benefiting by the Agency of the *North*, sees its agriculture grow and its commerce expand. Turning partly into its own channels the seamen of the *North*, it finds its particular navigation envigorated; and while it contributes, in different ways, to nourish and increase the general mass of the National navigation, it looks forward to the protection of a Maritime strength, to which itself is unequally adapted. The *East*, in a like intercourse with the *West*, already finds, and in the progressive improvement of interior communications, by land and water, will more and more find a valuable vent for the commodities which it brings from abroad, or manufactures at home. The *West* derives from the *East* supplies requisite to its growth and comfort, and what is perhaps of still greater consequence, it must of necessity owe the *secure* enjoyment of indispensable *outlets* for its own productions to the weight, influence, and the future Maritime strength of the Atlantic side of the Union, directed by an indissoluble community of Interest as *one Nation*. Any other tenure by which the *West* can hold this essential advantage, whether derived from its own separate strength, or from an apostate and unnatural connection with any foreign Power, must be intrinsically precarious.

While then every part of our country thus feels an immediate and particular Interest in Union, all the parts combined cannot fail to find in the united mass of means and efforts greater strength, greater resource, proportionably greater security from external danger, a less frequent interruption of their Peace by foreign Nations; and, what is of inestimable value, they must derive from union an exemption from those broils and wars between themselves, which so frequently afflict neighboring countries, not tied together by the same government; which their own rivalships alone would be sufficient to produce, but which opposite foreign alliances, attachments and intrigues would stimulate and imbitter. Hence, likewise, they will avoid the necessity of those overgrown Military establishments which, under any form of Government, are inauspicious to liberty and which are to be regarded as particularly hostile to Republican Liberty. In this sense it is that your Union ought to be considered as a main prop of your liberty, and that the love of the one ought to endear you to the preservation of the other.

These considerations speak a persuasive language to every reflecting and virtuous mind, and exhibit the continuance of the UNION as a primary object of Patriotic desire. Is there a doubt whether a common government can embrace so large a sphere? Let experience solve it. To listen to mere speculation in such a case were criminal. We are authorized to hope that a proper organization of the whole, with the auxiliary agency of governments for the respective Subdivisions, will afford a happy issue to the experiment. 'Tis well worth a fair and full experiment. With such powerful and obvious motives to Union affecting all parts of our country, while experience shall not have demonstrated its impracticability, there will always be reason to distrust the patriotism of those who in any quarter may endeavor to weaken its bands.

In contemplating the causes which may disturb our union, it occurs as a matter of serious concern, that any ground should have been furnished for characterizing parties by *Geographical* discriminations: *Northern* and *Southern*; *Atlantic* and *Western*; whence designing men may endeavor to excite a belief that there is a real difference of local interests and views. One of the expedients of party to acquire influence, within particular districts, is to misrepresent the opinions and aims of other Districts. You cannot shield yourselves too much against the jealousies and heart burnings which spring from these misrepresentations; they tend to render alien to each other those who ought to be bound together by fraternal affection. The inhabitants of our Western country have lately had a useful lesson on this head. They have seen, in the Negotiation by the Executive, and in the unanimous ratification by the Senate, of the Treaty with Spain, and in the universal satisfaction at that event, throughout the United

States, a decisive proof how unfounded were the suspicions propagated among them of a policy in the General Government and in the Atlantic States unfriendly to their Interests in regard to the MISSISSIPPI. They have been witnesses to the formation of two Treaties, that with G: Britain and that with Spain, which secure to them every thing they could desire, in respect to our Foreign relations, towards confirming their prosperity. Will it not be their wisdom to rely for the preservation of these advantages on the UNION by wch. they were procured? Will they not henceforth be deaf to those advisers, if such there are, who would sever them from their Brethren and connect them with Aliens?

To the efficacy and permanency of your union, a Government for the whole is indispensable. No Alliances however strict between the parts can be an adequate substitute. They must inevitably experience the infractions and interruptions which all Alliances in all times have experienced. Sensible of this momentous truth, you have improved upon your first essay, by the adoption of a Constitution of Government, better calculated than your former for an intimate Union, and for the efficacious management of your common concerns. This Government, the offspring of your own choice uninfluenced and unawed, adopted upon full investigation and mature deliberation, completely free in its principles, in the distribution of its powers, uniting security with energy, and containing within itself a provision for its own amendment, has a just claim to your confidence and your support. Respect for its authority, compliance with its Laws, acquiescence in its measures, are duties enjoined by the fundamental maxims of true Liberty. The basis of our political systems is the right of the people to make and to alter their Constitutions of Government. But the Constitution which at any time exists till changed by an explicit and authentic act of the whole people is sacredly obligatory upon all. The very idea of the power and the right of the People to establish Government presupposes the duty of every Individual to obey the established Government.

All obstructions to the execution of the Laws, all combinations and Associations, under whatever plausible character, with the real design to direct, controul counteract, or awe the regular deliberation and action of the Constituted authorities are distructive of this fundamental principle and of fatal tendency. They serve to organize faction, to give it an artificial and extraordinary force; to put in the place of the delegated will of the Nation, the will of a party; often a small but artful and enterprizing minority of the Community; and, according to the alternate triumphs of different parties, to make the public administration the Mirror of the ill concerted and incongruous projects of faction, rather than the organ of consistent and wholesome plans digested by common councils and modIfied by mutual interests. However combinations or Associations of the above description may now and then answer popular ends, they are likely, in the course of time and things, to become potent engines, by which cunning, ambitious and unprincipled men will be enabled to subvert the Power of the People, and to usurp for themselves the reins of Government; destroying afterwards the very engines which have lifted them to unjust dominion.

Toward the preservation of your Government and the permanency of your present happy state, it is requisite, not only that you steadily discountenance irregular oppositions to its acknowledged authority, but also that you resist with care the spirit of innovation upon its principles, however specious the pretexts. One method of assault may be to effect in the forms of the Constitution alterations which will impair the energy of the system, and thus to undermine what cannot be directly overthrown. In all the changes to which you may be invited remember that time and habit are at least as necessary to fix the true character of Governments as of other human institutions; that experience is the surest standard by which to test the real tendency of the existing Constitution of a country; that facility in changes upon the credit of mere hypothesis and opinion exposes to perpetual change, from the endless variety of hypothesis and opinion; and remember especially that for the efficient management of your common interests in a country so extensive as ours a Government of as much vigor as is consistent with the perfect security of Liberty is indispensable. Liberty itself will find in such a Government, with powers properly distributed and adjusted, its surest Guardian. It is, indeed, little else than a name where the Government is too feeble to withstand the enterprises of faction, to confine each member of the Society within the limits prescribed by the laws, and to maintain all in the secure and tranquil enjoyment of the rights of person and property.

I have already intimated to you the danger of Parties in the State, with particular reference to the founding of them on Geographical discriminations. Let me now take a more comprehensive view, and warn you in the most solemn manner against the baneful effects of the Spirit of Party generally.

This spirit, unfortunately, is inseparable from our nature, having its root in the strongest passions of the human Mind. It exists under different shapes in all Governments, more or less stifled, controlled, or repressed; but in those of the popular form it is seen in its greatest rankness and is truly their worst enemy.

The alternate domination of one faction over another, sharpened by the spirit of revenge natural to party dissention, which in different ages and countries has perpetrated the most horrid enormities, is itself a frightful despotism. But this leads at length to a more formal and permanent despotism. The disorders and miseries, which result, gradually incline the minds of men to seek security and repose in the absolute power of an Individual: and sooner or later the chief of some prevailing faction more able or more fortunate than his competitors, turns this disposition to the purposes of his own elevation, on the ruins of Public Liberty.

Without looking forward to an extremity of this kind (which nevertheless ought not to be entirely out of sight) the common and continual mischiefs of the spirit of Party are sufficient to make it the interest and duty of a wise People to discourage and restrain it.

It serves always to distract the Public Councils and enfeeble the Public administration. It agitates the Community with ill founded jealousies and false alarms; kindles the animosity of one part against another; foments occasionally riot and insurrection. It opens the door to foreign influence and corruption, which find a facilitated access to the government itself through the channels of party passion. Thus the policy and the will of one country are subjected to the policy and will of another.

There is an opinion that parties in free countries are useful checks upon the Administration of the Government, and serve to keep alive the spirit of Liberty. This within certain limits is probably true; and in governments of a Monarchial cast Patriotism may look with indulgence, if not with favor, upon the spirit of party. But in those of the popular character, in Governments purely elective, it is a spirit not to be encouraged. From their natural tendency it is certain there will always be enough of that spirit for every salutary purpose; and there being constant danger of excess, the effort ought to be by force of public opinion to mitigate and assuage it. A fire not to be quenched, it demands a uniform vigilance to prevent its bursting into a flame, lest, instead of warming, it should consume.

It is important, likewise, that the habits of thinking in a free Country should inspire caution in those intrusted with its administration to confine themselves within their respective Constitutional spheres, avoiding in the exercise of the Powers of one department to encroach upon another. The spirit of encroachment tends to consolidate the powers of all the departments in one, and thus to create, whatever the form of government, a real despotism. A just estimate of that love of power, and proneness to abuse it, which predominates in the human heart is sufficient to satisfy us of the truth of this position. The necessity of reciprocal checks in the exercise of political power; by dividing and distributing it into different depositories, and constituting each the Guardian of the Public Weal against invasion by the others, has been evinced by experiments ancient and modern; some of them in our country and under our own eyes. To preserve them must be as necessary as to institute them. If in the opinion of the People the distribution or modification of the Constitutional powers be in any particular wrong, let it be corrected by an amendment in the way which the Constitution designates. But let there be no change by usurpation; for though this in one instance may be the instrument of good, it is the customary weapon by which free governments are destroyed. The precedent must always greatly overbalance in permanent evil any partial or transient benefit which the use can at any time yield.

Of all the dispositions and habits which lead to political prosperity, Religion and morality are indispensable supports. In vain would that man claim the tribute of Patriotism, who should labor to subvert these great Pillars of human happiness, these firmest props of the duties of Men and citizens. The mere Politician, equally with the pious man, ought to respect and to cherish them. A volume could not trace all their connections with private and public felicity. Let it simply be asked, Where is the security for property, for reputation, for life, if the sense of religious obligation *desert* the oaths which are the instruments of investigation in Courts of Justice? And let us with caution indulge the supposition that morality can be maintained without religion. Whatever may be conceded to the influence of refined education on minds of peculiar structure, reason and experience both forbid us to expect that National morality can prevail in exclusion of religious principle.

'Tis substantially true that virtue or morality is a necessary spring of popular government. The rule indeed extends with more or less force to every species of free Government. Who that is a sincere friend to it can look with indifference upon attempts to shake the foundation of the fabric?

Promote, then, as an object of primary importance, Institutions for the general diffusion of knowledge. In proportion as the structure of a government gives force to public opinion, it is essential that public opinion should be enlightened.

As a very important source of strength and security, cherish public credit. One method of preserving it is to use it as sparingly as possible, avoiding occasions of expense by cultivating peace, but remembering also that timely disbursements to prepare for danger frequently prevent much greater disbursements to repel it; avoiding likewise the accumulation of debt, not only by shunning occasions of expense, but by exertions in time of Peace to discharge the Debts which unavoidable wars have occasioned, not ungenerously throwing upon posterity the burthen which we ourselves ought to bear. The execution of these maxims belongs to your Representatives, but it is necessary that public opinion should cooperate. To facilitate to them the performance of their duty, it is essential that you should practically bear in mind, that towards the payment of debts there must be Revenue; that to have Revenue there must be taxes; that no taxes can be devised which are not more or less inconvenient and unpleasant; that the intrinsic embarrassment inseparable from the selection of the proper objects (which is always a choice of difficulties) ought to be a decisive motive for a candid construction of the Conduct of the Government in making it, and for a spirit of acquiescence in the measures for obtaining Revenue which the public exigencies may at any time dictate.

Observe good faith and justice toward all Nations. Cultivate peace and harmony with all. Religion and morality enjoin this conduct. And can it be that good policy does not equally enjoin it? It will be worthy of a free, enlightened, and at no distant period a great Nation to give to mankind the magnanimous and too novel example of a People always guided by an exalted justice and benevolence. Who can doubt that in the course of time and things the fruits of such a plan would richly repay any temporary advantage which might be lost by a steady adherence to it? Can it be that Providence has not connected the permanent felicity of a Nation with its virtue? The experiment, at least, is recommended by every sentiment which ennobles human Nature. Alas! is it rendered impossible by its vices?

In the execution of such a plan nothing is more essential than that permanent, inveterate antipathies against particular Nations and passionate attachments for others should be excluded, and that in place of them just and amicable feelings toward all should be cultivated. The Nation which indulges toward another an habitual hatred or an habitual fondness is in some degree a slave. It is a slave to its animosity or to its affection, either of which is sufficient to lead it astray from its duty and its interest. Antipathy in one Nation against another disposes each more readily to offer insult and injury, to lay hold of slight causes of umbrage, and to be haughty and intractable when accidental or trifling occasions of dispute occur. Hence frequent collisions, obstinate envenomed and bloody contests. The Nation, prompted by ill will and resentment sometimes impels to War the Government, contrary to the best calculations of policy. The Government sometimes participates in the national propensity, and adopts through passion what reason would reject; at other times, it makes the animosity of the Nation subservient to projects of hostility instigated by pride, ambition and other sinister and pernicious motives. The peace often, sometimes perhaps the Liberty, of Nations has been the victim.

So likewise, a passionate attachment of one Nation for another produces a variety of evils. Sympathy for the favourite nation, facilitating the illusion of an imaginary common interest in cases where no real common interest exists, and infusing into one the enmities of the other, betrays the former into a participation in the quarrels and Wars of the latter, without adequate inducement or justification. It leads also to concessions to the favourite Nation of privileges denied to others, which is apt doubly to injure the Nation making the concessions by unnecessarily parting with what ought to have been retained, and by exciting jealousy, ill will, and a disposition to retaliate in the parties from whom equal privileges are withheld; and it gives to ambitious, corrupted, or deluded citizens (who devote themselves to the favourite Nation) facility to betray or sacrifice the interests of their own country without odium, sometimes even with popularity, gilding with the appearances of a virtuous sense of obligation, a commendable deference for public opinion, or a laudable zeal for public good the base or foolish compliances of ambition, corruption, or infatuation.

As avenues to foreign influence in innumerable ways, such attachments are particularly alarming to the truly enlightened and independent Patriot. How many opportunities do they afford to tamper with domestic factions, to practice the arts of seduction, to mislead public opinion, to influence or awe the public Councils! Such an attachment of a small or weak, towards a great and powerful Nation, dooms the former to be the satellite of the latter.

Against the insidious wiles of foreign influence (I conjure you to believe me, fellow citizens) the jealousy of a free people ought to be *constantly* awake, since history and experience prove that foreign influence is one of the most baneful foes of Republican Government. But that jealousy, to be useful, must be impartial, else it becomes the instrument of the very influence to be avoided, instead of a defense against it. Excessive partiality for one foreign nation and excessive dislike of another cause those whom they actuate to see danger only on one side, and serve to veil and even second the arts of influence on the other. Real Patriots who may resist the intrigues of the favourite are liable to become suspected and odious, while its tools and dupes usurp the applause and confidence of the people to surrender their interests.

The Great rule of conduct for us in regard to foreign Nations is in extending our commercial relations to have with them as little *political* connection as possible. So far as we have already formed engagements let them be fulfilled, with perfect good faith. Here let us stop.

Europe has a set of primary interests which to us have none or a very remote relation. Hence she must be engaged in frequent controversies, the causes of which are essentially foreign to our concerns. Hence, therefore, it must be unwise in us to implicate ourselves by artificial ties in the ordinary vicissitudes of her politics or the ordinary combinations and collisions of her friendships or enmities:

Our detached and distant situation invites and enables us to pursue a different course. If we remain one People, under an efficient government, the period is not far off when we may defy material injury from external annoyance; when we may take such an attitude as will cause the neutrality we may at any time resolve upon to be scrupulously respected; when belligerent nations, under the impossibility of making acquisitions upon us, will not lightly hazard the giving us provocation; when we may choose peace or war, as our interest, guided by our justice shall Counsel.

Why forego the advantages of so peculiar a situation? Why quit our own to stand upon foreign ground? Why, by interweaving our destiny with that of any part of Europe, entangle our peace and prosperity in the toils of European Ambition, Rivalship, Interest, Humor, or Caprice?

'Tis our true policy to steer clear of permanent Alliances with any portion of the foreign world, so far, I mean, as we are now at liberty to do it; for let me not be understood as capable of patronizing infidelity to existing engagements. (I hold the maxim no less applicable to public than to private affairs that honesty is always the best policy.) I repeat, therefore, let those engagements be observed in their genuine sense. But in my opinion it is unnecessary and would be unwise to extend them.

Taking care always to keep ourselves by suitable establishments on a respectable defensive posture, we may safely trust to temporary alliances for extraordinary emergencies.

Harmony, liberal intercourse with all Nations are recommended by policy, humanity, and interest. But even our Commercial policy should hold an equal and impartial hand, neither seeking nor granting exclusive favors or preferences; consulting the natural course of things; diffusing and diversifying by gentle means the streams of Commerce, but forcing nothing; establishing with Powers so disposed, in order to give trade a stable course, to define the rights of our Merchants, and to enable the Government to support them, conventional rules of intercourse, the best that present circumstances and mutual opinion will permit, but temporary and liable to be from time to time abandoned or varied as experience and circumstances shall dictate; constantly keeping in view that it is folly in one Nation to look for disinterested favors from another; that it must pay with a portion of its Independence for whatever it may accept under that character; that by such acceptance it may place itself in the condition of having given equivalents for nominal favors, and yet being reproached with ingratitude for not giving more. There can be no greater error than to expect or calculate upon real favors from Nation to Nation. 'Tis an illusion which experience must cure, which a just pride ought to discard.

In offering to you, my Countrymen these counsels of an old and affectionate friend, I dare not hope they will make the strong and lasting impression, I could wish; that they will controul the usual current of the passions, or prevent our Nation from running the course which has hitherto marked the Destiny of Nations: But if I may even flatter myself, that they may be productive of some partial benefit, some occasional good; that they may now and then recur to moderate the fury of party spirit, to warn against the mischiefs of foreign Intrigue, to guard against the Impostures of pretended patriotism; this hope will be a full recompense for the solicitude for your welfare, by which they have been dictated.

How far in the discharge of my Official duties, I have been guided by the principles which have been delineated, the public Records and other evidences of my conduct must Witness to You and to the world. To myself, the assurance of my own conscience is, that I have at least believed myself to be guided by them.

In relation to the still subsisting War in Europe, my Proclamation of the 22d. of April 1793 is the index to my Plan. Sanctioned by your approving voice and by that of Your Representatives in both Houses of Congress, the spirit of that measure has continually governed me; uninfluenced by any attempts to deter or divert me from it.

After deliberate examination with the aid of the best lights I could obtain I was well satisfied that our Country, under all the circumstances of the case, had a right to take, and was bound in duty and interest, to take a Neutral position. Having taken it, I determined, as far as should depend upon me, to maintain it, with moderation, perseverance and firmness.

The considerations, which respect the right to hold this conduct, it is not necessary on this occasion to detail. I will only observe, that according to my understanding of the matter, that right, so far from being denied by any of the Belligerent Powers has been virtually admitted by all.

The duty of holding a Neutral conduct may be inferred, without any thing more, from the obligation which justice and humanity impose on every Nation, in cases in which it is free to act, to maintain inviolate the relations of Peace and amity towards other Nations.

The inducements of interest for observing that conduct will best be referred to you own reflections and experience. With me, a predominant motive has been to endeavour to gain time to our country to settle and mature its yet recent institutions, and to progress without interruption, to that degree of strength and consistency, which is necessary to give it, humanly speaking, the command of its own fortunes.

Though in reviewing the incidents of my Administration, I am unconscious of intentional error, I am nevertheless too sensible of my defects not to think it probable that I may have committed many errors. Whatever they may be, I fervently beseech the Almighty to avert or mitigate the evils to which they may tend. I shall also carry with me the hope that my Country will never cease to view them with indulgence, and that, after forty-five years of my life dedicated to its Service with an upright zeal, the faults of incompetent abilities will be consigned to oblivion, as myself must soon be to the Mansions of rest.

Relying on its kindness in this as in other things, and actuated by that fervent love toward it which is so natural to a Man who views in it the native soil of himself and his progenitors for several Generations, I anticipate with pleasing expectation that retreat in which I promise myself to realize without alloy the sweet enjoyment of partaking in the midst of my fellow Citizens the benign influence of good laws under a free Government, the ever-favourite object of my heart, and the happy reward, as I trust, of our mutual cares, labors and dangers.

Geo. Washington

Index

About the Contributors

Harry V. Jaffa (Ph.D., Yale University) is Professor Emeritus of Government at Claremont McKenna College in Claremont, California, and Distinguished Fellow at the Claremont Institute. His numerous publications include *Original Intent and the Framing of the Constitution: A Disputed Question* (Regnery, 1994) and *The American Founding as the Best Regime: The Bonding of Civil and Religious Liberty* (Claremont Institute, 1990).

Daniel C. Palm (Ph.D., Claremont Graduate School) is Assistant Professor of Political Science at Azusa Pacific University in Azusa, California, and a Claremont Institute senior fellow.

James Rogers (Ph.D., University of Iowa) is Assistant Professor of Political Science at Texas A & M University. He is coeditor and publisher of *Communio: A Newsletter on Religion and Politics.*

Glen Thurow (Ph.D., Harvard University) is Provost and Academic Dean at the University of Dallas. He is the author of *Abraham Lincoln and the American Political Religion* (State University of New York Press, 1976), coauthor of *American Government: Origins, Institutions, and Public Policy* (McGraw-Hill, 1984), and coeditor of *Rhetoric and American Statesmanship* (Carolina Academic Press, 1984).

Thomas G. West (Ph.D., Claremont Graduate School) is Professor of Politics at the University of Dallas in Irving, Texas, and was a recent Ahmanson Fellow in Religion and Politics at the Claremont Institute. He is the editor of Algernon Sidney's *Discourses Concerning Government* (1698), a book much admired by the founders, and is author of *Vindicating the Founders: Race, Sex, Class and Justice in the Origins of America* (Rowman & Littlefield, 1997).